The Scots'
Crisis of Confidence

previous books by the author

*Creating Confidence: a handbook for
professionals working with young people*
(Centre for Confidence and Well-being, 2007)

The Tears that Made the Clyde (Argyll, 2010)

The Scots'
Crisis of Confidence

CAROL CRAIG

ARGYLL ✠ PUBLISHING

To my parents,
Mary and Jim Craig
with love and gratitude

First published in 2003 by
Big Thinking

This edition first published in
2011
Argyll Publishing
Glendaruel
Argyll PA22 3AE
Scotland
www.argyllpublishing.co.uk

British Library Cataloguing-in-Publication Data.

A catalogue record for this book is available from the British Library.

ISBN 978 1 906134 70 9

Printing: Martins the Printers,
Berwick on Tweed

Contents

FOREWORD TO THE FIRST EDITION

I have known Carol Craig for twenty years as a friend and colleague and as someone whose intellect I admire enormously. Each time we meet and talk, our conversation is always, as if by some invisible force, pulled towards Scotland and our complex emotions about our homeland. Scotland is infuriating, judgmental, inspiring and magnificent. We are both utterly thirled to it. Over the years I have watched Carol prepare herself to write this important book. In it she wrestles with the beliefs, attitudes and cultural preferences on which our Scottishness is based and challenges conventional cultural analysis of who we are.

Since the Scottish Parliament was set up there has been a persistent clamour for new thinking. This book provides the tools to do some of that thinking. It is very provocative. Two arguments stand out. First, Scotland does not celebrate differ-ence. Rather than our identity being too weak, Carol argues that ideas of Scottishness are too limiting and prescriptive and that the criticism of 'getting above ourselves' is not just a self-deprecating joke, but a deeply corrosive national trait. She includes a wonderful quote from the Scots poet Alexander Scott, satirising the Scots' attitude to equality:

> **Scotch Equality**
> Kaa the feet
> Frae yon big bastard

I thought that should have been the title of her book! I heard another example the other day. Several men were drinking in a Dumbarton pub and were talking about a local boy who had done well, had built his own construction business and was promoting enterprise. 'Aye,' said one of the group, 'but his uncle's an alcoholic.'

Her other main argument is that our dependence on logic and rationality, our Calvinist legacy, leads to an extraordinarily critical attitude towards others and at the same time a lack of emotional literacy. She argues that a major fault line running through Scottish society is a lack of respect for individuality, a stultifying culture of conformity.

However, this isn't a negative book. It opens the door to new ideas. By highlighting different solutions to Scottish problems, it could help make Sotland a better place. I don't agree with all she has to say, but that's the point. We are allowed to disagree!

This is an eminently readable, stimulating and enjoyable book drawing on everything from the Bible to *The Broons*.

I am very proud of Carol's achievement.

Kirsty Wark
February 2003

1. Introduction

In 2005 I gave a talk in Perth Town Hall on Scottish culture and confidence to a group of arts administrators. As I was leaving the hall a young African American woman approached me. She wore her hair in bunches but her tone was serious. 'Dr Craig, I want to thank you. I've been living here for over two years and I couldn't explain it the way you do but I recognise everything you said and it's so helpful for me to fathom it all out.' Within minutes I knew something of her story – a story which summarises in a few sentences the essence of *The Scots' Crisis of Confidence.*

The young woman explained that she had met her Scottish husband in the USA a few years before. 'Oh, he was a different man then,' she told me 'much more outgoing and confident,' adding, 'you see, it's different for him here as he's a west of Scotland, working class Catholic.' It was odd to hear an American use labels, such as social class, to describe someone but it was understandable: this young woman's husband was deliberately inducting her into his native culture. And she wasn't just picking up the lingo. 'Scotland,' she told me, 'is changing my personality.' When I asked for examples she immediately replied: 'I'm now talking quietly on buses. He doesn't like me speaking in my normal voice as he says I'm drawing attention to myself and embarrassing him.' With no additional prompting she produced another example of how Scottish culture was altering her behaviour. 'When I am in the US I just tell people I joined the arts project I work for as a temporary clerical assistant and now I'm chief executive. But I wouldn't dream of telling anyone here that in case they thought I was boasting and putting them down.'

'Don't get me wrong. I love Scotland,' she continued, 'but staying here has its price: I'm losing all sense of who I am as an individual as I've just got to fit in all the time.'

'How do you feel as a result?' I queried. She did not miss a beat – 'I'm losing my confidence and that's why your talk had such an impact on me.'

This was not the first time that a foreigner had told me such a story. Indeed I've heard lots. For example, Doug Emmons, a further education teacher, came to Scotland from the USA to work at Jordanhill College for a year. He recounts that while everyone he met was polite and kind to him, by the time he left Scotland he felt he was 'incapable of doing anything right'. He too felt that the culture, working in partnership with some of the demons from his own Lutheran childhood, undermined his personal confidence. In fact, he describes some of the organisations he dealt with in Scotland as 'killers of self-image and self-respect'.

For every story about Scotland taking the wind out of folk's sails, there are equivalent ones about Scots going elsewhere – America, Canada, Australia, England even – and feeling psychologically buoyed up by different cultural expectations. Indeed at the end of countless talks, people often tell me that they had to leave Scotland to become free of a limiting mindset which labels folk rather than encouraging their potential.

Background to *The Scots' Crisis of Confidence*

I was born and raised in Scotland and had a fairly typical 1950s childhood. My father was an engine driver and my mother worked for years in a pub. We had the good fortune to live in a new council house in a decent estate rather than in a crumbling, overcrowded tenement. I benefited from the 1960s expansion of higher education and was the first in my family to go to university. Indeed I was intrigued to learn in my first year sociology class that less than one percent of the university population comprised girls like me whose fathers came from the ranks of the semi or unskilled working class.

Postgraduate studies in a social science faculty gave me ample opportunity to consider how being a woman, and coming from a working class background, had shaped my identity and attitudes. But nothing really helped me understand how being Scottish had affected my psychological outlook. Of course, plenty of thinkers alluded to the fact that being Scottish had affected them greatly. Robert Louis Stevenson, for example, talked about a 'strong Scotch accent of the mind'.[1] In more recent times, the novelist and film-maker Alan Sharp claimed that being Scottish is a 'very specific kind of existential event.'[2] Nonetheless, no one in the modern era, had adequately analysed what this meant.

During the 1980s and 90s I was aware that if I were to write a book it would be about what it meant to be Scottish. However, I never embarked on the project as I could not devise a satisfactory way to tackle the topic. I was not a psychologist but even if I had been, psychology would have furnished few analytical tools as 'cultural psychology' is a more recent development. A study of Scottish literature would of course evince some interesting material but unless I undertook a comparative study (an imposs-ible task) how could I distinguish what was distinctly Scottish from what was also common in British, European, or indeed Western literature and culture?

In the early 1990s I started to work for myself as a trainer and for fifteen years I facilitated hundreds of training sessions with literally thousands of people in Scotland. These were training courses on assertiveness, leadership, different types of personal development, equal opportunities as well as team devel-opment sessions, so I had lots of opportunity to hear people talk about their upbringing, beliefs and behaviour. I also had the chance to observe how they acted in groups.

Many spoke about how little positive feedback they received as children from either teachers or parents. In team sessions people rarely said what they thought openly. It was only when they were chatting informally to close colleagues at tea breaks that they would begin to venture their opinions – 'I don't know why she said that' or 'that would never work', they would venture. When people did express views in formal sessions they would often do so only when they were rattled by something and so their tone would be needlessly aggressive. Indeed people from other countries working here would often take me aside and say, 'I just don't get it. Why can't people here be more open about their thoughts and feelings and why is there so little give and take?'

What struck me most over the years, and I have no reason to believe this has changed substantially, is the sheer waste of potential – how many folk, particularly women, are obsessed by what other people think of them and crippled by feelings of insecurity and under-confidence.

More generally I began to see that this reticence, and the lack of support and encouragement, was not simply undermining Scots as individuals but also Scotland as a nation. Was this not the cause of our low entrepreneurship figures and also some of our poor health statistics? In a global, competitive world were we not at risk of losing out because so many people are working far below their capabilities?

Much has changed since the early 1990s and this is not how I would frame many of my concerns today but these were the types of questions which motivated me back then. However, I was no fan of much of the personal development movement as I often thought it little more than American hype. Even a home grown version, Jack Black's 'Mindstore', was in my view too individualistic and whacky to appeal to most Scots of my generation brought up in a culture which valued logic, and encouraged healthy scepticism.

So I began to wonder if it would be possible to evoke a desire for change, and a belief this was possible, not through American-style personal development, but via an appeal to the best in Scotland's past such as the importance of logic, an emphasis on principles, equality and integrity, and a strong focus on society and the collective, not just the individual. In tune with my 1970s activism I resolved to write a pamphlet on the topic.

Within a few months of reading and research I was despondent. I had forgotten how negative many Scottish thinkers have been about Scotland over the years: how central the idea of Scots' 'schizophrenia' has been to the academic and cultural discourse and how common it has been for our cultural elite to see the country's previous religious beliefs as a 'pox on the mind'. I had no desire to reinforce such negative views of Scotland in anything I were to write. Instead I wanted to say something which was more balanced – seeing strengths and weaknesses. Of course I wanted to bring attention to problems but I wanted to replace blame and condemnation with understanding. Thus I embarked on writing the book which ultimately appeared as *The Scots' Crisis of Confidence*.

One of the words many commentators employ to describe the book is 'courageous' and I was aware that I was treading on dangerous ground. Scotland, as I knew only too well from what I was reading, has a critical and judgmental culture; going against the grain of established beliefs often results in condemnation and personal attack. Like Lady Macbeth I had to 'screw' my 'courage to the sticking place' and soldier on. Indeed even before the book's publication I experienced the anticipated acrimony. A columnist at *The Herald* newspaper, Anne Johnstone, wrote a piece about a new organisation which the broadcaster Bill Macfarlane was setting up called Confident Scotland.[3] I knew Anne and she devoted a few paragraphs to the fact that I was writing a book on the topic and that I traced the problem back to Scotland's Calvinist inheritance.

The reaction to these two paragraphs was pretty fierce. Two letters to the editor appeared in the newspaper criticising my reported views[4] and another columnist, John MacLeod, even devoted an entire article to rebuking me and putting me right.[5] 'If this was the response to a few sentences what would happen with the publication of a whole book?' I wondered. By this stage I knew how central Scotland's religious history was to my argument about contemporary Scottish attitudes and culture and clearly this was controversial ground.

My response was not to retreat but to strengthen the argument by finding someone who could advise and support me. Fortunately, an acquaintance knew the very man: Jim Greig was a retired Church of Scotland minister and a Calvin scholar. At that time he was translating one of Calvin's books into English. One of the most pleasurable parts of writing *The Scots' Crisis of Confidence* was regular visits to Mr Greig's house and, over a cup of tea, being schooled in some of the finer points of Scottish religious history and underlying beliefs. He also read everything I wrote and helped me keep my argument on firm ground.

There was another factor that galvanised me and kept me writing: the state of Scottish politics. I was acutely aware that if this book had appeared prior to 1999 and the establishment of a Scottish Parliament devolved from Westminster, it would have been dismissed out of hand. But we were now in post-devolution Scotland and things had changed.

'The Scottish cringe', the Scots' tendency to criticise Scotland and denigrate the indigenous culture was much in evidence in the previous devolution referendum campaign of 1979. Opponents of the proposed Scottish Assembly insinuated that, if it were created, it would manifest all the worst features of Scotland – insularity, parochialism and mediocrity. It would be the *Sunday Post* come to life. A glorified 'toon council'.

Of course, this view was still evident in the 1990s but it was in retreat. Scottish negativity and confidence issues were increasingly seen as a result of the country's inferior political position: once Scotland was in a position to take responsibility for her own affairs the Scottish people would mature, stop blaming the English for problems, and begin to trust themselves. Political maturity would lead to a growth in Scottish confidence. What's more, there was a growing belief that Scotland's values were inherently different from England's and would lead to a much better and more civilised political culture.

If my book had been published during the era where these ideas had great currency it would have been summarily dismissed as irrelevant – Scottish self-government, even the limited powers of devolution, was going to fix all our cultural problems.

However, within two years of the Parliament being set up things began to look different as a whole series of events conspired to sour the atmosphere surrounding it such as the spiralling costs of the Holyrood Parliament building and the loss of two First Ministers in quick succession – Donald Dewar died suddenly of a heart attack and his successor, Henry McLeish, was fatally undermined as a result of a fairly minor scandal about office expenses and had to resign. Many commentators were distinctly unimpressed by the calibre of MSPs with some critics calling the Parliament 'Monklands writ large'. However, once Jack McConnell became leader and announced a programme of fairly trivial measures, various commentators even started to complain that the Parliament was 'Monklands writ wee'. Many journalists, who had been mainly pro-devolution pre 1999, wrote extremely critical copy.

Of course, it would have been easy to minimise these difficulties or put them in perspective. For example, it was unfortunate for Scottish politics that the Parliament was established at a time when faith in politicians and the parliamentary process had dramatically declined and political parties lost much of their appeal to ordinary voters not just in the UK but in the USA and Europe. But instead of looking for extenuating circumstances, there was much personalisation of problems and blame.

Seeing all this played out in Scottish life encouraged me to keep working on the book. As I accumulated chapters I sought a publisher. A few considered it for a while before pronouncing that there wasn't a market for it. Fortunately I knew Gerry Hassan who had recently been involved in setting up a think tank called 'Big Thinking'. Gerry arranged for it to be published by them and I am eternally grateful to him for this support. This publication route meant that it came out very quickly but the book did not look as professional as it could have; it was expensive; and, as the progeny of a small publisher, never made it into some of the big bookshops.

The book was first published in February 2003. *The Herald* was keen to promote it and published two major extracts.[6] This generated a fairly predictable reaction from a few readers though some were favourable. Within a few weeks the book had also attracted a number of very supportive reviews in *The Herald, Sunday Herald, Scotsman, Times Educational Supplement Scotland* and *Holyrood Magazine*.

I received a large number of positive letters and emails from readers. I was particularly heartened by two: the historian Professor Christopher Harvie wrote to say he thought it a 'tour de force' and the renowned thinker Tom Nairn, whose theories I had questioned in the book, wrote a supportive letter saying how much he liked it and that I should 'rest assured' that I had made a 'lasting contribution' to the debate about Scotland and Scottish culture.

From the date of publication, book sales were fairly brisk. Big Thinking sold the initial two thousand copies within eighteen months and a further two thousand were printed in two separate runs. By 2009 it was out of print. For a book on Scottish cultural affairs four thousand copies is a particularly good sale. When we consider that it was expensive and difficult to find, and only available in Scotland, these figures are tremendous and contradict the publishers' views that there was not a market for it.

The Book's Popularity and Initial Impact

So how do I account for the success of *The Scots' Crisis of Confidence?*

In the concluding chapter I consider what I would change if I were to embark on this topic again. Here, I simply want to say that I have misgivings about the title. The book is not exclusively about confidence. Confidence is only one theme yet the title suggests that it is only about this and ramps up its importance by using the word 'crisis'. On the other hand, I think the title is part of its success. In his book, *The Tipping Point*, Malcolm Gladwell writes about how it is really important when trying to influence people's ideas that the message is in his terms 'sticky'.[7] I chose this title years before reading Gladwell's book but I intuitively understood that for Scots 'confidence' was the sticky word – the one that people would react to emotionally.

The Scots Crisis of Confidence is no self-help book. Indeed much of my critique is about Scottish culture and I offer nothing in the way of confidence-building tips. Nonetheless the book had a personal, and often cathartic, effect on individual readers. 'You wrote your book about me,' was the pronouncement of one young man who had come specially to hear me speak in

Ullapool. Others told me that it helped them to understand, and make peace with critical, judgmental parents. A staff member from the State Hospital in Carstairs told me recently that one of the inmates borrowed the book from the library and it helped him understand how he got there!

One of the reasons why the book is often mentioned in the media, and mentioned favourably, is that many journalists personally relate to the arguments. When I was involved in a Big Thinking conference on the book, I took part in lots of media interviews and was surprised by how many journalists – particularly young journalists – wanted to tell me their own experiences, often admitting that they found the cut and thrust of Scottish journalism difficult to take and continually doubted their own abilities.

However, while it chimed with many readers' personal experiences it was also relevant to people's jobs. When I was writing the book my target audience was not only the person brought up in Scotland who wanted to understand him/herself better but also the professional who had to fathom out the cause of the many problems they faced. I particularly thought my analysis of Scottish culture may help them understand better such disparate factors as the reticence in organisational settings, the low enterprise rates, the poor productivity or what is now called 'the Scottish effect' – the fact that, despite enhanced spending in Scotland, physical and mental health is better south of the border.

One of the first people to read the book and wonder about its relevance to Scottish policy-making was First Minister Jack McConnell. Once he had digested its contents he asked the Strategy Unit, in what was then called the Scottish Executive, to comment on whether there was any credibility in my argument.

The Strategy Unit undertook research and published a discussion paper called 'Confidence in Scotland'.[8] It suggested that there simply was not enough direct evidence to say conclusively if confidence was a problem for the Scots. However, it reported that many agreed with the analysis and went on to set out a range of problems in Scotland that may well correlate with psychological factors such as pessimism, or low self-esteem.

The book's potential relevance to policy-makers and practitioners across the public sector was given an added boost by the fact that myself and Gerry Hassan, under the banner of Big Thinking, organised a conference in Glasgow in November 2003 called 'Towards a Confident Scotland'. Over one hundred and fifty people took part. Professor Martin Seligman, a world-renowned academic psychologist and leader of the emerging 'positive psychology' movement, gave the keynote address.

The success of this event led ultimately to discussions with the McConnell administration on financial support for some kind of centre to look at confidence. I was aware that well-being was the developing international agenda and so was keen for the new centre to have a broader focus. In the final stages of negotiation Jack McConnell's advisers dragged their feet; ironic-ally they were apprehensive about the reaction of the press to the setting up of a confidence centre. I suspect the money would not have been pledged if I had sat waiting. However, I had organised a launch event for the new centre called 'Scotland's Tipping Point' with Malcolm Gladwell as the keynote speaker and had raised a considerable amount of sponsorship money from a variety of sources. The new centre's board decided that we were going ahead even without the long-term funding. In the end the Scottish Executive decided to give the Centre for Confidence and Well-being, as it was to be called, financial support. However, they changed this from core to project funding effectively ensuring that we had to gear our work for the next three years towards public sector professionals and to the confidence and well-being of young people as these were the only type of projects they would support. They were also particularly interested in positive psychology.

The New Centre for Confidence and Well-being

In the first few years the Centre ran a number of events and devised web resources to disseminate some of the ideas underlying positive psychology. I think that some of this research is interesting and useful to us in Scotland but the more I became involved with positive psychology the warier I became. However, I am indebted to Martin Seligman for one thing: during his first visit he went out of his way to alert me to the dangers of artificially attempting to boost self-esteem. I spent months reading a great deal of the growing critiques of American-style self-esteem building and the negative effects this has on academic standards, resilience and mental health.

If I had written my book in the 1970s or 80s then those of us interested in boosting confidence in Scotland could have focused on our culture and the type of actions which may make a difference. Of course, trying to influence a culture is difficult and we may not have succeeded but we would at least have known what we were dealing with. But Scots now live in a global world and consume large quantities of American media. Like it or loathe it the American obsession with self-esteem (and happiness) is now part of the way that most of us have come to see the world. All of this made me acutely aware of the potential dangers of the path we as an organisation could pursue.

So very early in the Centre's life I became aware that, unless we were careful, my book, with its emphasis on confidence, could easily encourage parents and those working with young folk down that self-esteem route. What this would mean is indulging youngsters, overprotecting them, lowering standards of achievement and playing down the importance of acquiring real skills. When I realised that the new Curriculum for Excellence in Scotland had made the creation of 'confident individuals' one of the four purposes of education I was worried. Unless the educational leaders and policy makers were aware of the dangers of this being interpreted as artificially boosting self-esteem this new educational development could have extremely negative consequences for skills, educational standards and resilience. Indeed I was so concerned that I wrote another book within a year called *Creating Confidence: A handbook for professionals working with young people* to warn people of the dangers of the self-esteem agenda (using the USA as an example) and suggesting better alternatives such as Professor Carol Dweck's work on 'growth and fixed mindsets'.[9] We sold over two and a half thousand copies of this handbook and I gave countless talks to schools and local authority staff many of whom found these arguments persuasive and refreshing.

In Search of an Integral Perspective

When I first wrote *The Scots' Crisis of Confidence* I knew very little about cognitive or social psychology: five years later I was fairly well-versed at least on the growing discipline of 'positive psychology' with its emphasis on optimism, positive emotions,

resilience and human strengths. But increasingly I felt disench-
anted. To my mind it was too limited in its focus and too eager
to see any problem as the result of individuals' faulty psychological processing and to dispense psychological remedies in
the form of interventions and programmes. In other words, it
did not seek to change external circumstances or reality, only
individuals' perceptions. I now believe that positive psychology
has a contribution to make to improving well-being and people's
lives but, despite its claims, it is most certainly not a panacea.

When I was young I was interested in politics. I have an
undergraduate and postgraduate degree in politics and taught
the subject for a short while at university before starting to work
in current affairs for the BBC. In the 1970s I was a member of
the short-lived Scottish Labour Party and was also committed
to more self-government for Scotland. Like the majority of
people in Scotland, my instinct is to believe political, economic
and social systems dominate and that real change will come
from these types of structural changes.

However, as I became more involved in personal development as a trainer I started to see that approaches which framed
everything in terms of social systems and political and economic
power were limited. Take the topic of confidence in Scotland.
Inasmuch as people recognised this is as a problem they would
relate it to the political realm: the country did not have control
over its own affairs and lived in the shadow of its more powerful
and dominant neighbour. According to such a perspective this
is why Scots feel they are second class and lack confidence.
This perspective also frames the solution in terms of political
independence or increased political powers.

Working as a trainer for over a decade and talking to

thousands of Scots about their attitudes to themselves and others I began to see the limitations of taking an exclusively structural approach. From my perspective people's individual confidence was most influenced by the attitude and behaviour of their parents, grannies, teachers, neighbours and peer groups. Yes there was a political/structural dimension but in Scotland we constantly ignored the interplay of psychological and cultural factors which were hugely influential in people's everyday lives. So in *The Scots' Crisis of Confidence* I do not seek to marginalise the importance of politics, economics or social structures: I simply attempt to add psychological, behavioural and cultural dimensions thus making for a richer and more complex picture.

In recent years the thinker who has contributed most to our understanding of the dangers of 'fragmentation' and the need for an 'integral' perspective is the American philosopher Ken Wilber.[10] From his extensive research into human knowledge he asserts that there are two important dimensions:

	INTERIOR	EXTERIOR
INDIVIDUAL	**I** Psychological Spiritual	**It** Physiological Behavioural
COLLECTIVE	**We** Rational Cultural	**Its** Structural Social

interior and exterior and individual and collective. These then combine to make four quadrants:

This is only one small aspect of Wilber's integral theory but in all facets of his work the emphasis is on taking a broad, inclusive approach. This means there is space to hear and respect the contributions of thinkers from completely different perspectives: psychologists, physicists, biologists, philosophers, religious thinkers, cultural critics, feminists, political theorists, economists, systems thinkers – Marx, Freud, Einstein, the Dalai Lama . . .

Of course, these quadrants do not exist in isolation but affect one another. Thus the political and economic systems affect culture and personal psychology and they in turn influence the other quadrants. However, thanks to a highly specialised university system, what we repeatedly see is academic experts only focusing on their often miniscule area of knowledge as if it exists in splendid isolation. The resultant knowledge and theories are incomplete yet often conveyed as 'the truth'. This is why I quickly became frustrated by positive psychology – its research has an important contribution to make to human well-being but the idea that positive psychology alone has the answer is preposterous.

Partly as a reaction to such reductionism, in my book *The Tears that Made the Clyde* I attempt to explain why Glasgow has so many health and social problems by taking a four quadrant perspective and weaving together information on aspects of the city's history (political, economic, cultural and social) with different theories and perspectives on inequality, well-being and human flourishing.[11]

Since Scotland's philosophical approach – something I touch on in this book – has historically led to a strong belief in the importance of generalism in education, not specialism, I hope that a broad, integral approach may have a particular appeal to a Scottish readership. I also hope that my work, and that of the Centre more generally, makes a small contribution to what might emerge as a Scottish integral vision or methodology.

Confidence and Politics

Despite the above comments, I often wonder if I minimised the role of politics in how the Scots feel about themselves in *The Scots' Crisis of Confidence*. I researched and wrote the book in 2001-2 during the first term of the Scottish Parliament. Labour was the biggest party and governing with the Liberal Democrats. Labour's share of the vote was 43 per cent and the SNP's 27 per cent. By the 2003 election the SNP's vote had dropped to 21 per cent as some of their support went to the minority parties of the so-called 'Rainbow Parliament'. So at the time of writing, like many commentators, I could not foresee the rise of support for the SNP and a new era in Scottish politics. As Scottish Labour did not appear to have the personnel or the ideas to refashion politics or provide compelling policy solutions, my instinctive response was to look outside of the political domain. I deliberately wanted to stress that change could happen without politicians; that our everyday lives were affected by day-to-day transactions with other people – transactions which were under our immediate control. This meant that we did not have to keep hankering after some distant election result to bring about some amount of positive change.

But then something incredible happened. The SNP secured one more seat than Labour in the 2007 election and ended up governing as a minority administration. The atmosphere in Scotland palpably changed. Even those who did not vote SNP appeared to warm to this new administration. Alex Salmond was much more popular than Jack McConnell or Henry McLeish had ever been. These new ministers appeared more professional and polished and the Scottish Parliament project started to lose 'the Monklands factor'.

Even those who dislike Alex Salmond's politics or personality cannot deny that he exudes confidence and is a skilled politician – every bit as articulate and capable as senior politicians in Westminster, Europe or the USA. Yet for all that he is most definitely one of us, Salmond has an ease in public communication, a liking for the limelight, which other senior Scottish politicians such as Donald Dewar or Gordon Brown never achieved. Salmond attributes his confidence to the fact he was a child singer. Indeed he told some school children that his experience as a youngster of 10 and 11 when he sang alone in front of thousands of folk had left him with the ability 'to be in front of audiences,' adding, 'if you could sing in front of lots of folks then speaking in the Scottish Parliament was no bother at all.'[12]

But the SNP's ability to look and then act like a credible government for Scotland involved much more than Salmond's personal confidence and facility on public platforms. It involved a conscious change in electoral strategy – a strategy which deliberately sought to breathe confidence and optimism into Scottish politics. Prior to 2007 the SNP's case for independence focused on how poorly Scotland was faring under the Union:

economic growth was lower than the rest of the UK's and the country's population falling. This was a pretty gloomy picture and not a vote-winning formula as independence was risky if Scotland was performing so badly. (Indeed it was an extremely negative message and its emotional tone was about loss, blame and victimhood.)

This was soon to change. In the period before the 2007 Scottish Parliamentary election the SNP ran workshops for all candidates and senior people with a consultant. Amongst other things, these training sessions presented them with research which showed that in the USA the presidential candidates who get elected are, almost without exception, the more optimistic of the two. These workshops also encouraged the SNP to start thinking more about voters' emotions and how they could project hope rather than negativity.

In the coming campaign, instead of exaggerating Scotland's problems the SNP talked up the country and their hopes for the future. Labour headed off in the opposite direction – now they exaggerated Scotland's dependence on England and how disastrous voting for the SNP would be for the country. In short, Labour ran a classically negative campaign. The change in strategy worked for the SNP: not only did they get one more seat than Labour but they became a credible party of government.

In the 2011 election there was a re-run of these different strategies. Labour majored on the threat of cuts and the need to protect public services and jobs. Their slogan 'Scotland deserves better,' while superficially positive, was in reality an unattractive mix of dependency and entitlement. The SNP continued with their optimistic vision for Scotland and their, albeit strangely worded, slogan 'Be part of better' at least offered voters a role in the creation of something positive. In essence, Labour's campaign was about fear and the SNP's about hope. Labour's strategy worked with its die-hard supporters (their vote hardly budged) but failed miserably in attracting floating voters and those disaffecting from the Liberal Democrats: they went in sackloads to the SNP.

The SNP's positive messages were also evident on the day after the election. Alex Salmond's speech in the grounds of Edinburgh's Prestonfield House was exquisitely crafted and delivered. He spoke of the need for Scotland ' to travel in hope and aim high'. The word 'better' was constantly repeated along with other positive phrases such as a 'heart to forgive' or words such as 'trust' and 'faith'. He ended by talking about 'Team Scotland' having won the election. Even his opponents would agree that it was an inspiring speech which eschewed triumphalism and struck the right note.

However, as I shall argue in the conclusion, one of the great dangers for this majority SNP government is that it becomes so gung-ho about being positive that anyone sounding a critical note is considered 'off-message' and rebuked or censured for being unhelpful. Rather than using optimism to deny problems and difficulties it is much better to acknowledge them while simultaneously striving to maintain the belief there must be a way to solve them.

Evidence

I now want to turn to the thorny but important topic of evidence. One of the criticisms of this book from some of the academic community is that it is little more than anecdote. In order to prove my case, they argue, I would have to come up with hard, empirical evidence from academic studies that the Scots lack confidence.[13] But this is impossible. At a personal level people understand the word 'confidence' – they know from experience what it is like to have it or not have it in specific situations. But it is a complex multi-faceted term embracing matters such as trust, optimism and self-belief. But while it is a term people intuitively understand it is not much used by psychologists as its complexity makes it difficult to measure. Psychologists use much more precise constructs such as self-efficacy or self-esteem. I am now much more aware of what these terms mean and how they differ from one another and as a Centre we have gathered considerable data from young people using some of these measures. But this was never the type of book I set out to write.

Indeed it is worth reiterating what I said in the introduction to the first edition. If you are the type of person who will only be convinced by numbers and 'hard facts' then I suggest you take the book back to the shop and get a refund. Of course, I do not simply make assertions and give different types of evidence to support my views where I can. But ultimately it is up to you as reader to decide if my arguments chime with your own experience and knowledge of the world and have credibility. Unlike many academics I trust people to be able to make this type of judgement for themselves and do not think that we should *only* rely on questionnaires and statistics for evidence.

One of the fundamental principles of Scots criminal law is corroboration. Two or more separate sources of evidence are needed for a conviction. Bearing in mind the importance of varied sources of evidence for us Scots, it was particularly gratifying for me to read a book published a year after mine

(2004) called *Watching the English* by Kate Fox, a social anthropologist. At one level there is some similarity between her book and mine in that we both attempt to understand the attitudes and behaviour of our own nationality.

In terms of methodology, Fox painstakingly creates 'a big picture' of Englishness from a thousand small observations of rules of behaviour whereas I get to a similar point with Scottishness by employing fewer personal observations and more hunches, concepts, speculations and historical insights. Fox is interested in describing what she can see; I am more interested in asking questions about how we got there and where we are now headed. The nineteenth century historian and theorist, Henry Thomas Buckle, outlined these type of differences in his history of ideas, asserting that the Scots and the English adopt different approaches.

Of even more significance is that Fox's description of the English and English culture never once mentions anything related to confidence. Certainly she believes that 'modesty' is an important English rule but she goes on to argue that this is entirely superficial: 'Our famous self-deprecation is a form of irony – saying the opposite of what we intend people to understand, or using deliberate understatement. . . English modesty is often *competitive* – 'one downmanship'.'[14]

Fox identifies 'Eeyorishness' as another major English characteristic but this refers to incessant, ineffectual moaning and whinging. Indeed she maintains that 'mock grumpiness is a form of social bonding'. Fox also argues that England's 'national catchphrase' is 'Typical!' and that this encapsulates:

our chronic pessimism, our assumption that it is in

> the nature of things to go wrong and be disappointing, but also our perverse satisfaction at seeing our gloomy predictions fulfilled – simultaneously peeved, stoically resigned and smugly omniscient.[15]

Pessimism and negativity form part of Fox's presentation on Englishness and while there is some overlap with what is typical in Scotland, these similarities are superficial and insignificant. There is nothing in Fox's descriptions of the English which equate with the blame, the self-righteousness and the fear of making mistakes and being 'found out' which permeates my analysis of Scottishness and forms the basis of Scotland's 'crisis of confidence'. I believe this is a telling point which indirectly corroborates much of my fundamental analysis not just of Scottishness but of differences between Scotland and England.

Indeed to return to the young woman who appeared in the opening paragraphs of this introduction – there is little in Fox's book on the English which would provide insight into the behaviour changes she had to make to fit into Scottish culture. I hope there is lots in this book which will help her and countless others understand Scottish culture and why it can erode personal and often collective confidence.

The Revised Edition

Argyll Publishing is producing this new, attractive edition of the book almost ten years after I started writing it. This revised edition contains the essence of the original argument and most of the original material. So what has changed? First, as the book is quite lengthy there has been some light pruning to the text throughout. In the main this has streamlined the argument and also, by eliminating contemporary examples, made the book less likely to date. However, where necessary I have updated some factual information. Secondly, in a few chapters I have replaced some of the material with new arguments and angles. This material does not substantially change the overall thesis. To make way for a new chapter with some insights from 'positive psychology' on Scottish negativity and pessimism we have removed the chapter 'The Scottish Self'. This was largely about fantasy literature and the notion of a divided self and we considered it of less interest to a general readership than this new material. The old chapter is still available online.[16] Thirdly, I have eliminated the division into sections and rearranged the chapter order as I think this may facilitate the flow of the argument. Fourthly, I have replaced the original introduction and first chapter with this new introduction and also completely rewritten the concluding chapter. Finally, I have continually resisted making such major changes that the revised edition is in fact a totally different book. The temptation to do this is not about having changed my mind: I still agree with my overall representation of Scotland and the conclusions I draw. However, I have grown intellectually in the past decade and if I were to tackle anew the subject of confidence in Scotland I would take a different route though my ultimate destination would be the same.

Given that I have resisted a major rewrite, the purpose of the book has not altered from the first edition. It aims to come up with a better way to understand Scotland and the Scots – a way which helps us to build Scottish self-confidence, reduce negativity and abject self-criticism and move on from some of the limiting beliefs of the past. In the following chapters I specifically aim to: analyse Scottish culture and the strengths and weaknesses of Scotland and the Scots; reveal some deeply held Scottish beliefs and attitudes; and understand why the Scots lack confidence in themselves and their country.

I wrote this last paragraph over a decade ago when Scotland politically was a different country and it may jar with those readers who see the election result of May 2011, when the SNP won an outright majority in the Scottish Parliament elections, as a sign of rising self-confidence. In the wake of that election many commentators argued that the SNP's momentous victory shows that a growing number of Scots have lost their fear of independence: they may still not vote for separation in a future referendum but they don't mind voting for a party committed to such an end and they are clearly not opposed to important political discussions about Scotland's future. I agree with such an analysis and think it suggests a general growth in collective confidence; whether it affects individuals' confidence in themselves is another matter.

In truth it would be foolhardy for anyone to believe that the momentum behind independence or even increased powers for the Scottish Parliament is so great that change is unstoppable. The famous Shakespearean line 'there's many a slip twixt cup and lip' reminds us of the uncertainty of life. 'The best-laid schemes o' mice an' men gang aft agley', is how our own bard Robert Burns describes the capricious nature of human life.

Little is certain but I contend that we can be sure of one thing – confidence, or the lack of it, will play an important part in the next few chapters of Scotland's story.

Notes

1 Robert Louis Stevenson 'The Foreigner at home' in *Memories and Portraits*

2 Alan Sharp, quoted in W. Gordon Smith *This is My Country: A personal blend of the purest Scotch* (Souvenir Press: London, 1976), p.33

3 Anne Johnstone 'Confident? No? Then e-mail friend' *The Herald*, 8th March 2002

4 *The Herald*, 11th March, 2002

5 John MacLeod 'Barnacled Cliché of Calvinism' *The Herald*, 11th March, 2002

6 *The Herald*, 5th and 6th February, 2003

7 Malcolm Gladwell *The Tipping Point* (Little Brown: London, 2000)

8 'Confidence in Scotland' Discussion Paper, 2005, retrieved from http://www.scotland.gov.uk/Publications/2005/03/20741/53264

9 Carol Craig *Creating Confidence: A handbook for professionals working with young people* (Centre for Confidence and Well-being: Glasgow, 2007)

10 For a summary see Ken Wilber *A Theory of Everything: An integral vision for business, politics, science and spirituality* (Shambala: Boston, 2001)

11 Carol Craig *The Tears that Made the Clyde: Well-being in Glasgow* (Argyll Publishing: Glendaruel, 2010)

12 *Daily Record*, 15th January, 2011

13 For a summary of this argument see T.M. Devine *The Scottish Nation 1700-2007*, p.643

14 14 Kate Fox *Watching the English: The hidden rules of English behaviour* (Hodder: London, 2004), p.9

15 Kate Fox *Watching the English*, pp.405-6

16 http://www.argyllpublishing.co.uk/downloads/carolcraig.pdf

2. Through a Glass Darkly

> In Scotland our cultural analysis has been obsessed
> with images of our self-hate.
>
> Cairns Craig, *Out of History*

Jekyll and Hyde

One of the strongest themes to emerge from books on Scotland
is that there is a deep division both within the Scottish psyche
and the culture Scots create. According to many writers, it is
only right and fitting that Jekyll and Hyde, the most potent
symbol of a divided self, was created by Robert Louis Stevenson
– a Scotsman.

'We are a country of paradoxes,' wrote John Grierson. 'We
have John Knox on the one side and Mary Queen of Scots on
the other. We divide our loyalties with great ease between what
is highly proper and what is thoroughly improper.'[1] Moray
McLaren, a prolific writer on Scotland, maintained the Scots
are '. . . about as confusing a collection of opposites as you are
likely to meet anywhere in the world. They have more internal
differences of character and opinion than almost any other
nation.'[2]

The novelist John Buchan wrote about 'two master elements
in the Scottish character – hard-headedness on the one hand
and romance on the other: common sense and sentiment:

practicality and poetry: business and idealism.' Buchan maintained that everybody has a little bit of both in their make-up but the 'peculiarity of the Scottish race is that it has both in a high degree.'[3]

The notion of a division within the Scots character has led a number of commentators to observe how difficult it is to say anything about the Scottish people – as soon as you make a pronouncement, you are aware of a contradiction. 'Pinning down our national character,' wrote W. Gordon Smith, 'is like trying to trap mercury with a bent fork.'[4] Given the large number of words produced on the subject, the difficulty has clearly not put such writers off.

At times writers simply attribute the split within the Scottish character to the geographical divide within Scotland. They tell us that Highlanders by nature are romantic and sentimental while Lowlanders are more rational and down to earth. Many writers also point up the division of Scotland into historical Edinburgh and industrial Glasgow. Another common contrast is between the Scottish Sabbath and the raucous Saturday night. It may seem harmless enough but in much of the literature the 'peculiar, divided Scot' is attributed to a deep split within the Scottish psyche.

The idea of a deep division within the Scot can be traced back to a book written in 1919 by the literary critic G. Gregory Smith. Smith's rather innocuous idea was that Scotland's literature is extremely varied and closer inspection shows a 'combination of opposites'. Smith famously termed these two moods 'the Caledonian antisyzygy'.[5] Smith's diagnosis was eagerly seized on by Scotland's most prominent twentieth century poet Hugh MacDiarmid who aimed to encourage a greater expression of what he termed 'Scottish psychology' in Scots literature. In the 1920s Scotland had gone through a substantial process of Anglicisation, so the problem was how to define the essence of Scottishness. Smith's thesis furnished MacDiarmid with an answer – the Scots were essentially an eccentric, contrary people. It also provided MacDiarmid with the inspiration for his great work of poetic genius – 'A Drunk Man Looks at the Thistle'.

This poem's power and energy comes from MacDiarmid's use of opposites and sudden changes in tone – the commonplace and the metaphysical, the satirical and the lyrical. Few would doubt the genius of this poem or deny it a place at the pinnacle of Scottish literature, but MacDiarmid's idea of the Scot as an extreme and divided character has provided inspiration and sustenance for some truly bizarre notions of Scotland and the Scots. Edwin Muir, another great Scots twentieth century poet and critic, also took up the idea of 'the Caledonian antisyzygy' but, unlike MacDiarmid, he argued that it is a negative, unhealthy aspect of Scotland.[6]

From MacDiarmid and Muir on, it became commonplace for writers to portray Scotland and the Scots as peculiarly and unhealthily divided. In tune with society's increasing interest in mental illness, more recent commentators have talked about Scotland's 'schizophrenia'. This is best seen in the work of Scotland's celebrated political theorist Tom Nairn. In an essay first published in 1968, 'The Three Dreams of Scottish Nationalism', Nairn wrote of 'the chronic laceration of the Scots mind' and made the customary reference to Jekyll and Hyde. The work is liberally seasoned with reference to the Scots', or particular Scottish groups' 'masochism', 'sadism', 'authoritarianism' and 'narcissism'.[7] Five years later, in an essay in *The Red Paper on Scotland* (edited by Gordon Brown), Nairn had evidently warmed to the theme. Now, alongside 'schizophrenia', Nairn diagnosed 'neurosis'.[8] He also maintained that Scotland is a country which has a deep and 'freakish' division between its sentimental Scottish heart and its rationalist British head. Two years later, by the time Nairn's highly successful book *The Break-up of Britain* had been published, the patient's condition had worsened even further: sanity has been lost and Scotland is now described as an 'asylum':

> The subjectivity of nationalism must itself be approached with the utmost effort of objectivity. It should be treated as a psychoanalyst does the outpourings of a patient. Where – as is not infrequently the case with nationalism – the patient is a roaring drunk into the bargain, even greater patience is called for.[9]

In a later book, *After Britain*, published in 2000, Nairn's Scottish patient has been 'partly lobotomised and partly placed in cold storage'.[10] But, thankfully, Nairn drops much of the medical terminology. Tom Nairn's terminology and analysis of Scotland may seem far-fetched and contrived but his work has had, and continues to have, a huge impact on Scotland's way of thinking about itself.

As devolved government was often seen as a panacea to solve Scotland's problems, the question is – has the notion of Scottish 'schizophrenia' disappeared with the advent of a Scottish Parliament and a brave new Scottish world? Unfortunately it has not. The dreaded, but ubiquitous, Jekyll and Hyde make a star appearance in a book designed to celebrate 'the new Scottish politics' exactly a year after the Parliament was set up. They are the guests of the respected political correspondent Iain Macwhirter who even names the first section of his article 'The Jekyll and Hyde Parliament'.[11] The editors also give great weight to the idea of Scotland's 'cultural schizophrenia'. The notion of splits and divisions is also rife within recent literary and journalistic analyses of Scotland.

Over the years a few Scottish commentators have deliberately avoided using the notion of a division. Douglas Dunn, for example, writes: 'a better image of Scottishness might be the kaleidoscope. . . It seems more positive and at the same time more complicated than the idea of Scottish personality as "double" or "divided".'[12] But Dunn and company have as much chance of being heard as a horse whisperer in a force ten gale, for the idea of the Scots as a peculiarly divided people could be likened, not to a wee rolling stone kicking up stoor and momentum as it travels through time, but to a huge boulder crashing its way into almost every theory on Scotland and the Scots.

Moving from the mountainside to the loch, we can also liken the 'Caledonian antisyzygy' to the fish that got away, for the idea of the 'schizophrenic' Scot has become larger and more monstrous with each retelling. If we look for real, hard evidence to support the idea of the Scot as a Jekyll and Hyde figure – a sick, pathological and divided character – we shall be disappointed. But this lack of evidence has not prevented our analysts from swearing they have caught sight of him and from elaborating on all the pathological things he is up to. Indeed in true fisherman fashion they compete with one another to tell the tallest story.

But what they have spotted is simply a normal human being – not a 'schizophrenic'. Philosophers from the beginning of time – both East and West – have argued that human beings and the cultures they create are fundamentally divided. So it would be odd if we could not find conflicts and divisions in Scotland and the Scots. In 'A Drunk Man Looks at the Thistle', Hugh MacDiarmid wants to advance the idea of the Caledonian antizysygy ('to pit in a concrete abstraction/My country's contrair qualities') but what makes this a great poem is the universal significance of the opposites he deals with: life and death; past and future; humankind and God; masculine and feminine; flesh and spirit; high and low.[13] Of course, some of the symbolism of division in the poem is particularly Scottish but it would be a queer country indeed that could not come up with its own version of the divided nature of human experience.

Arthur Herman made a similar point in his book *The Scottish Enlightenment*. Herman is an American academic with no Scottish connections and he was motivated to write about Scotland because he believes that the Scots have shaped the 'modern world'. Herman has read widely on Scotland and his last chapter is on modern Scotland so he is familiar with all the arguments about dichotomies and divisions. And he simply tries to present it positively, as an insight which Scots, like Sir Walter Scott, have into human experience:

> Scott was aware of . . . divisions in himself –
> between the romantic poet and the historical
> scholar, between the lover of nature and the
> student of science, between the sentimental
> Jacobite and the hardheaded lawyer, between the
> staunch Tory and the admirer of progress . . . And
> he was aware of the same split in Scottish culture

> . . . The credit for defining the artist as a person
> who can hold two inconsistent ideas at once goes
> to F. Scott Fitzgerald. The credit for realising that
> that is precisely what all modern men can do –
> indeed, must be able to do, belongs to Sir Walter
> Scott.[14]

As for Jekyll and Hyde, it simply does not make sense to argue that this has some exclusively Scottish meaning. Not only did Stevenson set the novel in London, he wrote it in 1885 during the height of Queen Victoria's reign – a period well known for its hypocrisy and the corrosive division between an outer show of public virtue and private acts of immorality. Undoubtedly, the book was inspired partly by Stevenson's personal experience of Edinburgh and the character of Deacon Brodie, but he could have found such inspiration in every other city in the British Isles, so deep was the hypocrisy of Victorian Britain.

In his book *The English* Jeremy Paxman devotes considerable space to charting the extent of male hypocrisy in Victorian times. Women were instructed to be chaste and 'respectable' while men went to prostitutes and were obsessed by 'foreign sexuality'. 'The sheer hypocrisy of many Englishmen, pretending morality, while debauching themselves,' writes Paxman, 'takes some believing.'[15] But Paxman does not then go on to argue that there must be something pathological about England or the English as a result of this behaviour.

In Scotland the notion of the Scots as a 'schizophrenic', pathologically divided people is a rather tired and inadequate analysis to describe or deal with some of our nation's problems. And, as we have just seen, this might be an attempt to analyse supposedly Scottish problems when there is not even a particularly Scottish problem to discuss.

Joep Leerssen has made a study of national identity and national stereotypes and he argues that 'countries are always contradictory in a specific way: their most characteristic attribute always involves its own opposite.' He also argues that 'the ultimate cliché that can be said of virtually any country is that it is "full of contrasts".'[16]

If we examine the notion of a fatal division between head and heart, the core of Tom Nairn's analysis of Scotland and the essence of Edwin Muir's idea of a split between thought and feeling, then we shall see there is nothing particularly Scottish about it. Indeed the term 'dissociation', much used by cultural analysts to describe the notion of division in Scottish literature, was first used by T.S. Eliot to describe a trend he perceived in English poetry. The head/heart divide – often portrayed as a split between masculine reason and feminine emotion – haunts all Western societies. It is present every time a voter enters a polling booth and feels torn between idealism and realism; public good versus immediate private interest. It is at play in our private lives when we opt for the security of a loveless marriage or a well-paid job rather than act on our deepest feelings and desires. The heart/head division is a deep, fundamental conflict which often manifests itself in our dreams. Whatever way we look at the divided Scot, whatever definition we use, one thing remains clear: there is nothing particularly Scottish about division of this type. We are not dealing with pathological monsters or divided selves, simply ordinary human beings.

The Scots are not any more divided than other people but

they do tend to think in either/or terms. And it is this, rather than the divisions themselves, which leads to an important insight about Scottish consciousness.

The 'Blight' of Calvinism

A similarly simplistic and polarising discussion underpins analysts' depictions of the influence of Calvinism on the Scots from the time of the Reformation of the Church in Scotland. As a Scot I am aware that there are certain traits in the Scottish character which can be attributed to a Scottish upbringing, such as a strong belief in the importance of principles, a highly developed work ethic and a sense of duty and social responsibility. All these qualities are part of Scotland's Calvinist legacy. Of course, these qualities can be overdone and have a negative side – a diminished interest in pleasure and a heightened sense of guilt, for example. But for me, and for many Scots, these are still positive features of the Scottish character. This is not the view taken by many Scottish analysts, many of whom lay at the door of John Knox and John Calvin everything they believe to be wrong with Scotland and the Scots.

A common theme in the literature is that the Scots have been contorted in some way by the religious fanaticism of the past. George Blake talks about Scotland being 'infected' by Calvinism and the notion that the Reformation ushered in some kind of disease of the mind is commonplace. For example, W. Gordon Smith writes:

> Four hundred years of bloody bigotry bitten deep
> into the bone. Centuries of self-righteousness and
> extreme unctuousness. Slavering hypocrisy and
> unrepenting smugness. The rape of logic and the

> murder of reason. Blindness, deafness, and
> beggared imagination. . . To think that in this age
> of penicillin and streptomycin there's no anti-
> biotic to cure such a pox of the mind.[17]

Willa Muir, the novelist and critic, maintained that 'the Reformation was a kind of spiritual strychnine of which Scotland took an overdose.'[18] Another common charge against Calvinism is that it made the Scots a guilt-ridden, joyless people, with few social graces. Continual quibbling over religious meaning also turned us apparently into a nation of 'nit pickers' and 'pedants'. According to many commentators, the ministers snuffed out art and culture of every kind. Edwin Muir, who was very influential on the literati's views of Scotland, was a stern critic of Knox and the Reformation. Indeed Muir saw John Knox and Andrew Melville's Reformation as largely responsible for Scotland's spiritual and artistic 'desolation'. In his poem 'Scotland 1941' Muir writes about this desolation crushing 'the poet with the iron text'.[19] Art critic Cordelia Oliver even blamed Calvinism for the 'rusty bedsprings', 'gin bottles' and the general 'ugly mess' that 'disfigures the natural beauty of so much of the west coast of Scotland and the Highlands'.[20] And Tom Nairn's most famous soundbite is that Scotland could only be 'reborn the day the last minister is strangled with the last copy of the *Sunday Post*'.[21]

The link between various aspects of Scottish society and Calvinism, the positive and the negative, are charted in the more scholarly works on Scotland, but many modern writers attribute everything – rusty bedsprings, pedantry, dourness or the lack of an indigenous dramatic tradition in Scotland – to the 'terrible' course Scottish history took following the Reformation. In other words, Calvinism is portrayed as having only a negative and disfiguring effect on Scottish culture and the Scottish people and heightens the notion of the Scots as deranged and 'schizophrenic'.

Harry Reid takes up this issue at the end of his book *Reformation: The Dangerous Birth of the Modern World*, arguing that in Scotland there is 'a tendency to blame anything that goes wrong in society on Calvin.'[22] As Reid charts in his book some of the positive aspects of Calvin's and Knox's thinking about the welfare of the poor, for example, he finds it difficult to understand why so many Scots are never prepared to 'praise them for what was so good and beneficial in their legacy'.[23]

Sentimental Scots

Another well-worn theme is that the Scots are particularly, and embarrassingly, sentimental. The novelist John Buchan claimed he liked the emotion and sentimentality of the Scots but he is almost alone for most share George Blake's diagnosis of the 'chronic Scots disease of nostalgia'.[24] Neil MacCallum spoke for a whole raft of analysts when he wrote: 'The Scot in tears is an appalling piece of human wreckage.'[25] Iain Finlayson argued that the Scots are 'deeply emotional' but they deny it with 'passion'. 'They don't much care for the heart freely bleeding on the sleeve,' wrote Finlayson, 'but have an insatiable taste for the artificial heart strapped to the forearm and made to beat by means of a rubber bulb, hidden in the pocket, pumping air into it so it palpates madly and inexhaustibly.'[26]

Commentators who decry the sentimental side of Scottish character also disparage the culture which, they say, it creates. They argue that Scots sentimentality has led to a national fascination with the Highlands and much of the iconography of Scottish culture – bens and glens, but and bens, mystic mountains, Bonnie Prince Charlie and over the sea to Skye. Much of our analytical literature paints the Scots as ridiculously sentimental about their supposed Highland past. Commentators repeatedly portray the Scots sniffing back the tears, maudlin', nostalgic, talking about their 'ain folk', remembering their 'granny's hielan' hame' or breaking into yet another verse of 'Roamin' in the Gloamin'.

One school of thinkers argues that Scottish sentimentality is unhealthy and sick because it shows the Scots, one of the most urbanised and industrialised people in the world, obsessed by a romantic Highland past which has no bearing on their current reality. Here are the Scots, they say, living in some of the ugliest slums in the world and in some of the most desperate conditions but instead of facing up to the reality of their conditions they escape into drink and sentimental fantasies about kilts and heather. Such nostalgia and sentimentality could be seen compassionately as an understandable 'opium' of a city-based people plagued by social problems and deprived of nature. But Scottish analysts are much more likely to castigate poor, sentimental city dwellers for their failings than to show them any empathy or compassion.

In reality there is nothing pathological or odd about the Scottish tendency to be sentimental. The Scots are first and foremost logical people and the development of logic in a person's character is inevitably at the expense of a mature and controlled expression of feelings and emotions. In other words, one downside of being logical is that it means you can easily become sentimental. The Scots have definite weaknesses and are imperfect beings, but that's life. There is nothing specifically Scottish about being flawed and imperfect.

The Kailyard

The view that much of Scottish culture, as one critic remarked, is 'rancid with false sentiment' also extends to that particularly unloved child of Scottish literature – the Kailyard. This is the name originally given to a genre of nineteenth-century Scottish novels which show Scotland as a land of idealised communities and couthy natives. Analysts argue that these books are completely devoid of literary merit and only became popular in Scotland because they were nostalgic and sentimental. The Kailyard is now a term of abuse used to cover anything of this ilk produced in Scotland – *Dr Finlay's Casebook, Take the High Road, The People's Friend, The Broons* and the Alexander Brothers. Anything which can be labelled 'Kailyard' is deemed worthless and is used as further evidence of Scotland as a cultural backwater where the natives have become sick on too much 'sugarally' water. In the words of one critic, literature of this sort is 'not so much drama as diabetes'.[27]

The Kailyard analysis also reinforces another negative image of the Scots – as an inward-looking people. A few years ago I attended a lecture in Glasgow given by a senior official of the World Bank who was putting forward proposals on how people from all round the world could come together to solve problems which can only be tackled globally. A senior official from Scotland's economic development community then got to his feet to give an initial response from a Scottish perspective. The speaker has the reputation for being lively, open and optimistic but on this occasion he began by saying how depressed he felt by the lecture as there was a genre of literature in Scotland, called the Kailyard, which highlighted how inward-looking the Scots are and how they do not see beyond their own cabbage patch.

But is this really true? The Scots have always been an adventurous, outward-looking people who explored the world. Before the Union with England, the Scots were much more international in outlook than the English or the Chinese, for example, whose insularity is well-known. Currently, Scotland is a small country within a bigger partnership and she does not have the same need for or possibility of entering into dialogue with other countries than she would if she were an independent state. But this does not make the Scots an insular people uninterested in what is going on outside their borders. Countless Scots still travel the world as migrants and tourists. The same cannot be said of that truly inward-looking nation – the United States. What I found most depressing at the lecture was that our Scotsman's first response was to be negative about the Scots when it would have been very easy to be positive and upbeat. He could have argued that the Scots were obvious candidates for involvement in global issues forums because we believe passionately in social responsibility.

The historian Tom Devine believes the Kailyard has attracted such criticism because the original writers of Kailyard novels had 'committed the unforgivable sin of being hugely successful'. But I think there is something else at work here – male pride. [28] As I shall argue later, most of the analysis on Scotland has been written by men and it is shot through with a male view of the world. Men tend to be more egotistical than women. A man will often over-react if he thinks his ego is being dented in some way, and when it comes to the Kailyard this appears to be the problem for some of our male critics. According to George Blake – the man who first led the charge – the Kailyard writers 'held up their fellow countrymen as comic characters for the amusement of the foreigner'. Later he complained of a 'betrayal of national dignity'.[29] And this notion found echoes in Tom Nairn's work many years later when he brought up the rearguard action. With the passage of time Nairn had more Kailyard targets to hit. He set his sights on *Doctor Finlay's Casebook* and its ilk rather than J.M. Barrie's *A Window in Thrums* but the point was generally the same. Nairn wholeheartedly agreed that the producers of such works are guilty of 'holding up our fellow-countrymen . . . to the ridicule and contempt of all sane and judicious human beings'.[30]

As the idea of the Kailyard has been a major supporting pillar in the notion of Scotland and the Scots as culturally backward, insular and pathological, I am pleased to report that it has been attacked from within the intellectual community itself; the edifice is starting to crumble. For example, Tom Devine in his much acclaimed history of Scotland points out that the three writers most accused of peddling crude, sentimental images of Scotland in their Kailyard novels – S.R. Crockett, Ian Maclaren and J.M. Barrie – only wrote 'a dozen books in . . . a single decade' and sold most of them to the upper middle classes in Scotland, England and abroad.[31] This means two things: first that the significance of the Kailyard novels to Scottish literature is greatly overdone. Quite simply it was no big deal. And second there was nothing particularly *Scottish* about the appetite for such sugary and unhealthy fare.

Authoritarianism

The Scots pride themselves on being democratic, yet another common theme to emerge from the literature is that the Scots are a people with strongly authoritarian tendencies. The Scots schoolmaster, or dominie, is commonly portrayed as a cruel and authoritarian figure. So too are the ministers and elders of earlier times who, we are told, took great delight in humiliating and punishing sinners for their misdemeanours. If we believe our analysts, no area of Scottish life escaped the icy blast of Scottish authoritarianism.

In the nineteenth century, Robert Louis Stevenson gave the Scots a sense of the authoritarian personality in *The Weir of Hermiston*, but the idea that the Scots have a particularly callous and authoritarian streak muscled its way into the Scots notion of themselves following the publication of *The House with the Green Shutters* by George Douglas Brown in 1901. This novel revolves round the twisted, callous, authoritarian personality of the central male character – John Gourlay. As the illegitimate son of a farmer, Douglas Brown felt he was a victim of a small Scottish community. He loathed the false portrait Barrie and others had painted in their works so his novel was designed as a deliberate 'counterblast' to the Kailyard. He too set his novel in a rural community and he adopted elements of the genre, but there the similarity ends. In place of couthy sentimentality we have what was once called the 'Scot malignant'. His novel is a pessimistic and melodramatic tale of Scottish village life. It is about malicious gossip, spite, weakness, pride and self-interest. John Gourlay and his family are ultimately destroyed by his authoritarian ways, his arrogance and his pride.

All the characters in *The House with the Green Shutters* are uniformly black. There is no white, or even shades of grey in them. Indeed George Douglas Brown's work may be as much a caricature of Scottish life as are the Kailyard novels. This is not a well-rounded picture of Scottish characters and communities – the good alongside the bad. He has simply gone to the other end of the spectrum. Yet even on publication a *Glasgow Herald* reviewer described it as 'True to the verge of being merciless. . . Overdrawn, but grimly true, and full of promise.'[32] The novel was greatly admired by commentators and intellectuals who saw it as 'compelling', an important rebuttal of the Kailyard and an insightful commentary on Scotland. It was highly praised by many well-known Scottish writers. Hugh MacDiarmid believed *The House with the Green Shutters* to be 'distinctively Scottish in the deepest sense', and it is still seen as an important landmark in Scottish literature.[33]

The character of John Gourlay himself has lived on as the man who epitomises an extremely harsh and authoritarian side of the Scottish character. Tom Nairn wrote: 'We all have a vital bit of John Gourlay inside us. . .' Nairn's belief that authoritarianism is bred in the bone of 'bourgeois' Scots led him to argue once that if the SNP ever came to power in Scotland they would be a 'junta of corporal punishers'.[34] Yet again we see this tendency in Nairn and others to pounce on any negative characteristics displayed by Scots and then claim them either as particularly Scottish or as more pronounced in Scotland. This is why Nairn comes up with the view that there is 'no Stalinist like a Scottish Stalinist',[35] when quite simply no Scottish Stalinist has *ever* been in the same league as the original Russian Stalinist.

Ironically once the SNP did come to power in Scotland its First Minister, Alex Salmond and Justice Secretary Kenny MacAskill, became famous worldwide not for their punitive views but for 'the compassionate release' of Abdelbaset Al-Megrahi, who had been convicted of blowing up the Pan Am flight 103 over Lockerbie.

Nonetheless it is true to say that the Scots are rather troubled by authority – simultaneously attracted to and repelled by it. But it simply is not true to say that the Scots are particularly authoritarian. Throughout the world we can see examples of the authoritarianism and potential sadism which easily flow from patriarchy and power. Often it is institutionalised in religion – not just in Calvinism but in Catholicism and Muslim fundamentalism. The priests depicted in many an Irish novel are as capable of tyranny and preaching 'hell-fire and damnation' as their Scottish Protestant counterparts. And John Gourlay and his ilk are nothing in comparison to some of the world's Ayatollahs. Nairn may sneer about the possibility of a 'junta' but the Scots as a people have never flirted with fascism or been attracted to political dictatorship of any kind. By contrast much of the world has physically suffered under the hands of real, not imaginary, tyrants – Germany, Spain, Italy, Chile, Argentina, Korea, Afghanistan – the list is long.

John Gourlay was a fictional tyrant who lorded it over his family, his workers and anyone else he could bully but there is nothing particularly Scottish in the authoritarian figure who rules the roost. He is the Yorkshire mill owner of many a novel, or Citizen Kane. Nor is there anything distinctly Scottish about the cruel husband or father who physically or mentally abuses his wife and children. English novelist D.H. Lawrence suffered cruelly at his father's hands, as did Beethoven. The Irish singer Sinead O'Conner has talked openly of the abuse she suffered as a child. So too has Brian Wilson of the Beach Boys.

Most authoritarian characters happen to be male – women rarely need to shore up their egos in this way, nor are they as often in positions of authority. But women are not immune and some recent cases have shown that women as mothers, or as nuns, are capable of authoritarian cruelty. Most authoritarian figures, male and female, are very similar to John Gourlay – they are insecure and arrogant, they detest weakness in any form, and they have to be right. They cruelly use and abuse their physical and economic power. There is nothing particularly Scottish about John Gourlay's malevolent spirit – sadly, it haunts the world. We may regret its existence, but we have no reason to brand it Scottish.

The 'Tartan Monster'

It was Tom Nairn who coined the phrase, much loved by our analysts, the 'tartan monster'. They extend the term 'tartanry' to cover any Scottish knick-knacks or particularly Scottish type of gathering. This could include the Edinburgh military tattoo or a Murrayfield Rugby International replete with kilts and pipers. And they hate it all. Some are particularly critical of 'tartanry' because it shows the Lowland Scots (the vast majority of the Scottish population) stealing the Highlander's kilt and other symbolism and using them to establish their own identity – an act of cultural theft which, they claim, is particularly reprehensible since Lowlanders used to denounce Highlanders as savage and barbaric.

Reading the literature, however, I cannot help feeling that more than anything else it is the 'vulgarity' of it all that our analysts particularly detest. For example, the journalist Neal Ascherson writes about 'the fringe of glaring tartanry on sale along Princes Street . . . the joke cards about shooting haggis, lifting kilts and tickling sporrans', and adds, 'nobody selling this stuff would be seen dead with it at home'.[36] But all that Ascherson is saying is that Scottish knick-knacks are 'Kitsch' –

cheap, plastic goods made for the tourist market. And Kitsch can be found all round the world – it isn't the monopoly of Scotland.

Nairn acknowledges this fact but still can't resist giving the Scots first prize. 'How intolerably vulgar! What unbearable crass, mindless philistinism!' writes Nairn, 'One knows that Kitsch is a large constituent of mass popular culture in every land: but this is ridiculous!'[37]

Yet again we see the formulation at work – Scotland = the worst. And once more the idea of the Scots as 'the worst' cannot be justified. If you have travelled at all you will have seen hideous Kitsch everywhere – day-glo holy water bottles in Lourdes which play a tune, leaning tower bookends in Pisa. Right round the world local people have 'commodified' their culture, inventing or embellishing where necessary, and then selling the resultant Kitsch goods to tourists to make money.

If I reflect on the beliefs and attitudes which I have learned in Scotland, examine the messages which I imbibed from an early age and then try to rank them in order of importance – tartanry, sentimentality and a modern version of the Kailyard would not even register on the scale. But it has been very easy for these ideas to exert a great influence.

Men to a Man

And finally, as you have no doubt noticed, there is another striking feature of the Scottish character, as described by our analysts – it is unquestionably male. 'You and I are Scotsmen, members of a famous race,'[38] writes John Buchan, and no modern woman reader can fail to notice that she is excluded from this early literary discussion on Scotland. Much of what was written on Scotland by Scots, up to the 1980s at least, was written by men for men. Unless they specifically state that they are talking about women, all the symbols, the topics, and the language these men use to talk about Scotland and the Scots are masculine. Everything is seen from a man's point of view – whole areas of life have simply been omitted or hardly mentioned. There is little about childhood or family relationships, nothing about maternity, almost nothing on sexual relations or sexuality. In fact there is hardly anything about personal relationships of any kind. However, there is nothing particularly Scottish about such myopia. The fate of women in every culture dominated by men is that they are either ignored, forgotten about, or mentioned as an afterthought.

There is little doubt that some of Scotland's 'great men', most notably Hugh MacDiarmid, were happy to keep women in their place:

> Now, I am not a misogynist by any means. I simply believe there is a time and a place for everything. . . And like a high proportion of my country's regular and purposive drinkers I greatly prefer a complete absence of women on occasions of libation. . . *no one* wants to be distracted from that absorbing business by music, women, glaring lights, chromium fittings. . . [39]

The entire thrust of MacDiarmid's views is quite simple – women's experiences and opinions don't count. We are no more than distractions from the serious business of drinking!

If women had contributed to the analysis of Scotland there might have been a more well-rounded portrayal. This point is exemplified by Catherine Carswell, the woman most often mentioned as part of the Scottish Renaissance of the 1920s and 30s. She was a successful novelist who wrote an acclaimed biography of Robert Burns. In the introduction to this book she makes some general comments about Scottish history and in these few pages she displays more warmth and willingness to understand the full impact of Calvinism, the good and the bad, than many of her male colleagues manage in entire volumes. In short, she is not out to attribute blame and she displays an abundance of empathy and compassion. For example, she dutifully charts the clergy's suppression of culture and talks about 'brutal persecution' but at the end of a section on Scottish poverty she writes: 'Through the darkest years the Scottish ministers, with all their faults, had truly been the leaders of the people, and they had done much to preserve and fortify the soul of the nation.'

She is able simultaneously to tell us about the 'fulmination' and fear preached from the pulpit and then remind us that 'other voices with more of pleasantness and peace in them were calling to the people of Scotland. For not all the ministers were stern evangelicals.'[40] Sadly Carswell did not make many general comments about Scotland and the Scots and this type of compassionate voice is missing in much of the diagnosis we get from male analysts.

So at the end of this tour through some of the literature dedicated to the analysis of Scotland and the Scots how can we best summarise what we have seen? One thing is certain, it is not a pretty sight; the archetypal Scot routinely portrayed in much of the literature by fellow Scots is a grotesque, inward-looking Harry Lauder figure dressed in a kilt, suffering from 'schizophrenia' and a Calvinist pox of the mind, simultaneously nasty and authoritarian and pathetically emotional and sentimental. I should, of course, add that our 'typical Scotsman' isn't feeling too good about himself. He has something of an inferiority complex. He lacks self-confidence. Surprising, isn't it?

Such views of Scotland and the Scots are now being routinely challenged. In 1989 Craig Beveridge and Ronald Turnbull published a highly influential and ground-breaking book called *The Eclipse of Scottish Culture*.[41] Drawing on Frantz Fanon's *The Wretched of the Earth*, they argue it is 'inferiorism', the type of mindset third world peoples develop as a result of colonisation, which leads some commentators to disparage Scottish culture and represent it as deformed or pathological. The Scottish literary expert Cairns Craig has undermined many of the negative arguments in his insightful book *The Modern Scottish Novel*[42] and the sociologist David McCrone has also tried to normalise the debate about Scotland. Even Tom Nairn has changed the tone of his language.

But it is quite wrong to believe that this type of negative portrayal of Scotland is history. It constitutes a significant part of the debate on Scotland in the literature – pick up a few Scottish volumes and you cannot help but see Scotland through this dark, negative glass. What's more, many of those who studied aspects of Scottish politics or culture at university at the height of the negativity in the 1970s and 80s are now teaching children in schools, writing for Scottish newspapers or are involved one way or another in Scottish public life. And this may be one of the reasons why negative views of Scotland continually seep into the Scottish press. So the intellectuals themselves may no longer indulge in this extremely negative discussion, but Scotland may well suffer from the consequences of such analytical self-criticism for some time to come.

From a confidence point of view I do not think that some of the counter-arguments are necessarily that helpful. While Beveridge and Turnbull's argument about the Scots having a colonial mindset holds some truth, the argument can easily be overdone. The Scots, outside the Highlands, have never been colonised in a way that is similar to third world peoples. In fact, the Scots were enthusiastic partners in the British Empire and were often the colonisers to which Turnbull and Beveridge refer. The Scottish political theorist, Tom Nairn, has always been scathing about any attempt to liken Scotland to a colony but in his speech to the seventieth anniversary conference of the SNP he nonetheless put forward arguments which give some credence to the theory of inferiorism. He argued that a central issue in the history of the Scottish nation is 'shame' and attributed some of his 'frankly nihilistic excesses about strangling Kirk ministers'[43] to the shame and feelings of hopelessness inspired by the Union and the political and cultural climate it engendered. He argued that for ordinary people these feelings often led to migration but that for the intellectual community, of which he himself is part, it meant trying to become someone else, or 'adopting and displaying a superior persona'.

The problem with arguing that Scottish negativity about Scotland is essentially about shame, or a colonial mindset, is that it puts the Scots in the position of hapless, helpless victims of English imperialism. 'It isn't our fault. They've done it to us and we didn't have the power to stop them.' Or it bounces back in the idea that there is something pathetic about the Scots to have been colonised in the first place. This is a notion conveyed dramatically by Irvine Welsh in Renton's famous outburst in *Trainspotting* when he says:

> It's SHITE being Scottish! We're the lowest of the low, the scum of the fucking earth, the most wretched, miserable, servile, pathetic trash that was ever shat into civilisation. Some people hate the English, I don't. They're just wankers. We, on the other hand, are colonised by wankers. We can't even find a decent culture to be colonised by. We are ruled by effete arseholes. [44]

This then leads to the view that Scots' negativity or lack of confidence can be cured easily by liberation from England. Some nationalists tend to argue that any problems with Scottish confidence, the Scottish Parliament, or anything Scottish for that matter, could be changed almost overnight if Scotland won independence. According to them, any faults in the Scottish psyche lie not with the Scots themselves, but are a direct result of the inferior position Scotland occupies in the United Kingdom. For them, a free Scotland would inevitably be a confident Scotland.

But for me the problems of Scottish confidence are much more complex than this. Of course, a substantial shift in political power is likely to boost Scottish self-confidence but I do not believe it would be enough to eliminate the confidence issues facing the Scots. A great deal of the Scots' negativity about Scotland, and lack of confidence, cannot simply be blamed on our political state or on the English – they arise from a particularly *Scottish* way of looking at the world.

Notes

1 John Grierson 'The Salt of the Earth' in Forsyth Hardy (ed.) *John Grierson's Scotland* (The Ramsay Head Press: Edinburgh, 1979), p.32

2 Moray McLaren *Understanding the Scots: A Guide for South Britons and Other Foreigners* (Frederick Muller: London, 1956), p.8

3 John Buchan 'Some Scottish Characteristics' in W.A. Craigie, John Buchan, Peter Giles & J. M. Bulloch, *The Scottish Tongue* (Cassell & Company: London, 1924), p.58

4 W. Gordon Smith *This is my Country: A Personal Blend of the Purest Scotch* (Souvenir Press: London, 1976), p.29

5 G. Gregory Smith *Scottish Literature: Character & Influence* (Macmillan: London, 1919)

6 Edwin Muir *Scott and Scotland* (George Routledge and Sons: London, 1936)

7 Tom Nairn 'The Three Dreams of Scottish Nationalism' in Karl Miller (ed.), *Memoirs of a Modern Scotland* (Faber and Faber: London, 1970), p.35

8 Tom Nairn 'Old Nationalism and New Nationalism' in Gordon Brown (ed.), *The Red Paper on Scotland* (EUSPB: Edinburgh, 1975)

9 Tom Nairn *The Break-up of Britain* (Verso: London, 1981), p.93

10 Tom Nairn *After Britain* (Granta Publications: London, 2000), p.101

11 Iain Macwhirter 'Scotland Year Zero' in Gerry Hassan and Chris Warhurst (eds) *The New Scottish Politics: The First Year of the Scottish Parliament and Beyond* (The Stationery Office: London 2000)

12 Douglas Dunn *Scotland: An Anthology* (Harper Collins: London, 1991), pp.5 –6

13 Hugh MacDiarmid *A Drunk Man Looks at the Thistle* (Caledonian Press: Glasgow 1953) p.71

14 Arthur Herman *The Scottish Enlightenment: The Scots' Invention of the Modern World* (Fourth Estate: London, 2002), pp.263-4

15 Jeremy Paxman *The English: A Portrait of a People* (Penguin Books: London, 1999), p.212

16 Joep Leerssen, internet document 'National Identity and National Stereotype', www.hum.uva.nl.

17 W. Gordon Smith *This is my Country*, p.262

18 Willa Muir *Mrs Grundy in Scotland* (George Routledge: London, 1936), p.165

19 Edwin Muir *Collected Poems* (Faber and Faber: London, 1960), p.97

20 Cordelia Oliver 'The Visual Arts in Scotland' in Duncan Glen,

Whither Scotland? A Prejudiced Look at the Future of a Nation (Victor Gollancz: London, 1971), p.220

21 Tom Nairn 'The Three Dreams of Scottish Nationalism', p.54

22 Harry Reid *Reformation: The Dangerous Birth of the Modern World* (Saint Andrew Press: Edinburgh, 2009), p. 363

23 Ibid., p.365

24 George Blake *Barrie and the Kailyard School* (Arthur Barker: London, 1951), p.18

25 Neil McCallum *It's an Old Scottish Custom*, (Dennis Dobson: London) p.180

26 Iain Finlayson *The Scots* (Oxford University Press: Oxford, 1988), p.231

27 G. M. Thomson *Caledonia: Or The Future of the Scots* (Kegan Paul, Trench, Trubner: London), p.65

28 See, for example, Deborah Tannen *You Just Don't Understand: Women and Men in Conversation* (HarperCollins: London, 2007)

29 George Blake *Barrie and the Kailyard School*, pp.66-75

30 Tom Nairn *The Break-up of Britain*, p.158

31 Tom Devine *The Scottish Nation 1700-2007* (Penguin: London, 2006), p.297.

32 Quoted in George Blake *Barrie and the Kailyard School*, p.93

33 See Beth Dickson 'Foundations of the Modern Scottish Novel' in Cairns Craig (ed.), *The History of Scottish Literature Volume 4* (AUP: Aberdeen, 1989), p.51

34 Tom Nairn 'The Three Dreams of Scottish Nationalism', pp.49-51

35 Ibid., p.44

36 Quoted in David McCrone, Angela Morris & Richard Kiely *Scotland – the Brand: The Making of Scottish Heritage* (Polygon: Edinburgh, 1999), p.56

37 Tom Nairn *The Break-up of Britain*, p.162.

38 John Buchan 'Some Scottish Characteristics', p.49

39 Hugh MacDiarmid 'The Dour Drinkers of Glasgow' in Hugh MacDiarmid, *The Uncanny Scot: A Selection of Prose* (MacGibbon & Kee: London, 1968), pp.93-94 My emphasis.

40 Catherine Carswell *The Life of Robert Burns* (Chatto & Windus: London 1951), pp.9-10

41 Craig Beveridge & Ronald Turnbull *The Eclipse of Scottish Culture* (Polygon: Edinburgh, 1989)

42 Cairns Craig *The Modern Scottish Novel: Narrative and the National Imagination* (Edinburgh University Press: Edinburgh, 1999)

43 Tom Nairn *After Britain*, p.104

44 Irvine Welsh *Trainspotting* (Mandarin Paperbacks: London, 1996), p.78

3. Sceptical Scots

A nation has a development: the things which
happen to it possess a logic in which is
concentrated. . . its national spirit.
                    Edwin Muir, *Scottish Journey*

Moray McLaren tells the story of a young couple who went to
visit an old uncle on their return from honeymoon, taking with
them a photograph album which they had carefully produced.
The old man looked through the album without saying anything
and then he slowly went through the pictures again. 'The young
couple,' writes McLaren, 'a trifle dampened by his silence,
awaited his verdict. At length it came. Putting a broad spatulate
finger upon one picture he uttered the words, 'That's the worst.'[1]

I am sure every single person living and working in Scotland
will be aware that the Scots find it much easier to be critical
than appreciative; negative rather than positive. In the last
chapter we saw just how negative and critical the Scots can be
about themselves, but the Scots' tendency to be critical is not
confined to self-criticism. The Scots have a highly developed
critical faculty. Why? One of the aims of this book is to establish
an alternative way to understand Scotland and the Scots better
– a way which encourages self-acceptance and builds genuine
self-confidence. And it is only possible to do this if we can
undertake a realistic assessment of national strengths and weaknesses.

This is a difficult and complex task but I believe it is possible if we utilise conceptual tools set out by the eminent Swiss psychoanalyst C.G. Jung in his ground-breaking book, *Psychological Types*.[2]

Understanding Cultural Preferences

In *Psychological Types* Jung argues that human beings use four mental functions. He calls these *sensing, intuition, thinking* and *feeling*. Sensing and intuition are the functions which structure how we take in information, whereas thinking and feeling are two different ways to evaluate. Individuals have the capacity to use all four functions, and do use them in their everyday lives, but they do not tend to use them equally. An individual's psychological type is defined by the way they prefer to use these functions and whether they prefer to use them in the introvert or extravert world. All four mental functions that Jung describes can help us to understand not just individuals but cultural preferences better. In this chapter I shall concentrate on the thinking/feeling dimension as it is 'thinking judgement' (see later in this chapter) which helps us to understand Scotland and the Scottish people better. For the purpose of this exposition, I shall not confine myself to Jung's original concepts but will elaborate from my own experience of the types.

Let us imagine there are two countries – near neighbours – who have certain cultural characteristics in common such as a similar language, a shared music tradition and a reputation for being friendly people with a strong belief in equality. Both our imaginary countries have citizens with individual preferences for thinking and feeling, but at a cultural level there is national respect and encouragement for one of the processes rather than the other. So our two countries differ in that one has a national preference for feeling and one for thinking judgement.

Types that prefer feeling judgement use their personal values to evaluate and make decisions and usually place great emphasis on harmony and appreciation. So the nation that prefers feeling judgement has an international reputation for being warm and friendly; its people smile a lot, their hospitality is legendary, and they are adept at seeing the best in things and being appreciative. For example, they may say 'it's a fine morning' even though it is raining. They have extremely good social skills and can be very persuasive and charming. Their way with words, their insight into their own and other people's feelings, and their general sensitivity, means they can be gifted writers. In fact, this nation has a world-wide reputation for its poets, playwrights and novelists. To these undoubted strengths we must add a few weaknesses. This nation is not noted for logic – it boasts few gifted philosophers and scientists, for example. The emphasis on personal values means it has been difficult for this nation to maintain standards in public life and it has been rocked by a few scandals involving brown envelopes. As this is a nation which encourages harmony, caring and compliance rather than independent-mindedness and questioning, the Church has dominated society and its abuse of power has also emerged belatedly in a number of scandals. Finally, the charm of its people is almost without equal but this charm can be overdone and when this happens they can come across as manipulative and insincere.

As thinking types use objective logic to evaluate, the people in the thinking culture, by contrast, have developed good analytical skills. They are quick to see the flaws in anything and their questioning, sceptical minds mean they are not easily taken in by others. They care deeply about principles and standards in all areas of life and they have an international reputation for honesty and integrity. In short, people from other nations trust what they say. This thinking nation has made a huge contribution to intellectual endeavour of all kinds – philosophy, science, social science and technology. A number of important inventions have been made by these people. Again, this country has undoubted weaknesses. These people are not very clued-up on feelings – their own or others'. Over the centuries this country has produced a few literary giants but is not now noted for the quality of its literary output. The tendency to criticise rather than appreciate has also created a cultural environmental which is rather negative and intimidating.

By now, many of you will have realised that I am not describing two fictitious nations. The nation which prefers feeling judgement is, of course, the Republic of Ireland and its thinking neighbour is Scotland – two nations where the indigenous culture has encouraged the development of distinctly different 'personality types', as pithily captured by the English poet Ewart Gavin:

> The Irish are great talkers
> Persuasive and disarming
> You can say lots and lots
> Against the Scots
> But at least they're never charming.

The Scots are not inclined to be 'charming' for they are too busy being critical, sceptical and logical. In other words, their attention tends to be taken up using the mental function Jung defines as 'thinking'.

Thinking Judgement

In everyday language we use the term 'thinking' to cover any kind of reflection or inner thought processes, but in Jungian psychology the term is confined to mental activity of a particular type. Thinking refers to the mental process which involves evaluating, drawing conclusions or prioritising on the basis of objective logic. Thinking therefore involves making a judgement or evaluation and making it as objectively as possible. Most thinking decisions involve the application of logical 'if. . . then' reasoning. As thinkers try to reach a conclusion objectively and logically based on the available evidence, they usually believe that any other reasonable person in their position would come to the same conclusion because it is 'right'. In Jung's scheme, the alternative way to evaluate is to use feeling judgement. This is also a rational way to evaluate, but instead of objectivity and logic, the feeling type uses his/her subjective value system to reach a conclusion. When a person uses 'feeling' he/she is not being 'emotional' for it is a mental process just as 'thinking' is. The difference is that when individuals use feeling judgement they evaluate on the basis of personal values and relationships. Everyone has the capacity to use both mental functions and will use both but it is impossible to use the two processes simultaneously. We are only able to use one and then the other, as we cannot be subjective and objective at the same time. Most individuals have a preference for one of the two ways to evaluate and use it more frequently. Repeated use then shapes the individual's personality and determines some of their strengths and weaknesses.

When assessing the evidence presented in the following pages to support my contention that Scottish culture heavily endorses the use of logical thinking, please remember that I am not arguing that individual Scots *all* prefer logical thinking. Many have an individual preference for feeling judgement but, in a culture which encourages the use of logical thinking, they are aware of being 'out on a limb'. For example, Scottish feeling types do not feel as confident as their Irish counterparts in expressing their values or in being openly appreciative. Even though feeling judgement is a mental process – a way of analysing and deciding on the basis of values and relationships – and not simply an emotional response, feeling types often berate themselves for being 'weak' and will often try hard to see the world through thinkers' eyes. In this way feeling judgement has been driven almost underground and logical thinking has been allowed to flourish. As thinking judgement plays down the importance of subjective values, emotions and relationships it is much more in tune with a conventionally 'male' way of looking at the world and so the dominance of this preference helps to account for the distinctly masculine character of Scottish culture. Scotland is not the only country where thinking judgement dominates in this way; we can see a similar pattern in Germany, for example.

A Very Logical People

Over the years various commentators have noted the Scots' liking for logic. For example, the author of a nineteenth-century book entitled *Scottish Characteristics* argues that 'One of the most essential attributes of the Scottish mind is its orderly, methodical, in a word its logical character'.[3] Many also point out how much the Scots love words like 'partly, nevertheless and outwith' – words that help to structure the thinking process. Given this love of logic it is no coincidence that the great master of solving problems by the application of logical reasoning, Sherlock Holmes, was created by Sir Arthur Conan Doyle who was born and brought up in Edinburgh. What's more, Doyle modelled Holmes on the eminent surgeon Dr Joseph Bell who taught him forensic science at Edinburgh University.

In the literature on Scotland there are countless examples of Scots who, despite their humble origins, were able to make a huge contribution to knowledge as a result of their ability to employ logical reasoning. One man sums this up. He is James Ferguson, a self-taught shepherd boy who eventually became a fellow of the Royal Society. He was a celebrated astronomical instrument maker and theoretician yet he had only three months of formal schooling in his whole life. While still a boy, he looked after sheep by day and studied the stars at night, and despite having no knowledge of elementary maths was nevertheless determined to explain the nature of the universe: 'Even before his voice had broken he devised a string threaded with beads. With this device . . . he went to the fields at night, and – lying on the ground – he laid his beads across the firmament.'[4]

Gazing at the stars can inspire human beings to all sorts of things; it may encourage them to dream, to write poetry, to feel spiritual, to contemplate God, or to speculate on the possibilities of life on other planets. It has inspired humans to ponder the effect of the heavens on their own personal lives, thus giving rise to astrology. Star-gazing led James Ferguson, and other Scots, to elaborate the principles of astronomy and to devise the instruments necessary for understanding the heavens.

A leading specialist on psychological type, Lenore Thomson, argues that all human societies, even underdeveloped ones, have to make sense of what is happening in their external world by relating their 'experiences to principles they can count on'.[5] So they use the thinking process to try to order the universe. The principles people devise are not always scientifically accurate but this does not matter, argues Thomson, for the function of thinking is to ensure that these 'principles are reliable enough to use as consensual bench-marks, thereby freeing us from the dictates of immediate experience'.[6] So it does not matter if other cultures use a different way of measuring time, for example, because what counts is that people in any given social group have an agreed, impersonal way of defining it.

From the seventeenth century on there was increasing pressure in the Western world not only to ensure that these organising principles were applied to more and more areas of life but also, where possible, for these principles to correspond with scientific fact. Much of this pressure came from Scotland and so did much of the ground-breaking work. Interestingly, the American academic, Arthur Herman, uses the subtitle *The Scots' Invention of the Modern World* for his book *The Scottish Enlightenment*. Scholars of this period showed how human beings were 'ultimately creatures of their environment' and that the changes which alter human beings' behaviour and character are not 'arbitrary or chaotic. They rest on fundamental principles and discernible patterns'. But, as Herman also points out, the Scottish Enlightenment project was much more than the creation of a proper study of history or the 'science of man', for it:

> . . . embarked on nothing less than a massive
> reordering of human knowledge. It sought to
> transform every branch of learning – literature and
> the arts; the social sciences; biology, chemistry,
> geology, and the other physical and natural sciences
> – into a series of organised disciplines that could be
> taught and passed on to posterity.[7]

The Scottish Enlightenment is a period in Scottish history from the Act of Union to the 1830s when Scotland had so many first-rate thinkers and intellectuals it was as if 'giants walked the land'. Even the great French philosopher Voltaire remarked that 'it is to Edinburgh that we look for our ideas'. The roll-call of scholars was certainly impressive and included such weighty figures as the philosopher David Hume; the author of the highly influential book *The Wealth of Nations*, Adam Smith; Adam Ferguson, the father of sociology; James Hutton the founder of geology; the eminent chemist Joseph Black; and the medical pioneer William Cullen, to name only a few.

It would be wrong of me to portray it as a movement where objective logical thinking reigned in splendid isolation. Thinking was not the only one of Jung's four mental functions to feature in this great period of Scottish intellectual life. Speculative ideas (intuition) played a large part in the Scottish Enlightenment and even feeling judgement had its place. Indeed the mental process Jung defines as 'feeling' had a central role in the early part of the movement thanks to the influence of the man generally credited as its father – Francis Hutcheson.

Hutcheson was an Ulster Scot and his intellectual work sprang, not from a desire to codify or understand, but from his personal conviction that human beings are essentially good, altruistic beings. Hutcheson was a hugely compassionate man and, according to Herman, his mission was to get the Presbyterian church 'to take on a more humane, comforting face'.[8] Hutcheson was, by all accounts, a brilliant lecturer who inspired a generation of students with his ideas. One of these students was Adam Smith, who talked about his mentor as 'the unforgettable Hutcheson'. And we can detect the influence of

Hutcheson's ideas in the role Smith assigned to sympathy in his moral philosophy, as well as in the works of some of the other great Enlightenment figures, such as Adam Ferguson, who also appeared to have been a compassionate man whose work is animated by his deeply-held values. But more commonly, feeling judgement made its presence felt in this movement, not as a sophisticated grown-up, but as a rather gauche teenager. Indeed the great sentimental work of this period, Henry MacKenzie's novel *The Man of Feeling*, was, in the words of Bruce Lenman, a 'lamentable tear-jerker'.[9]

There is little doubt, however, that the lasting legacy of these great Scottish intellectuals was their ability to use objective, logical thinking. Over the years many analysts and visitors to Scotland have passed comment on the Scots' ability to employ thinking skills. For example, the nineteenth-century English political theorist, Walter Bagehot, maintained that 'There appears in the genius of the Scottish people . . . a power of reducing human actions to formulas or principles'.[10] The Scottish Enlightenment era was one in which Scottish intellectual achievement was at its height, but even after this high-water mark had been reached, Scotland continued to produce some truly great scientists and thinkers such as the physicists Lord Kelvin and James Clerk Maxwell. Scottish science is still a credit to the nation and, per head of the population, Scotland ranks third in the world for the publication of science research papers.

As Bagehot pointed out, many Scottish scientists and intellectuals were particularly concerned to develop arguments and theories based on 'first principles'. And we can see that throughout history principles have mattered greatly to the Scots. Given the Scots' preference for objective thinking this makes sense – thinking types are greatly attracted to principles as they are derived from logic and founded on notions of universal truth. So it is hardly surprising that it is difficult to escape the word 'principle' in the evolution of Scottish intellectual life and institutions. For example, Scottish law is founded on Roman law and is concerned with establishing first principles. This is unlike the English and American legal systems, for example, where law is essentially judge-made and based on precedent.

The Historical Legacy

The love of the mental process defined as thinking is so strong and pervasive in Scotland that we can see its presence even in traditional song. Scotland was once noted for its rich ballad tradition – a ballad being simply defined as a folksong which tells the story of a 'crucial situation' by 'letting the action unfold itself in event and speech' and where the story is told 'objectively with little comment or intrusion of personal bias'.[11] In other words, the singer does not impose his or her personal values or morality on the tale.

The American historian Wallace Notestein, in his historical study of the development of this Scots characteristic, maintains that even in medieval times foreigners, like Erasmus, noted the Scots' love of logic and the 'dialectic'.[12] Alexander Broadie, currently Professor of Logic and Rhetoric at the University of Glasgow, has written numerous books and articles which illustrate that a strong and distinct philosophical tradition has existed in Scotland from the days of the philosopher John Duns Scotus in the thirteenth century.[13] Many other writers on Scotland have observed that it was the Scots' inclination towards logical thought which led them to support the Reformation with such enthusiasm. In England Protestantism had its beginnings in Henry VIII's desire to divorce his Queen, but in Scotland the roots of the Reformation were essentially ideological.

Life for the average Scot in the sixteenth century was fairly tough. Many lived in back-breaking poverty and no doubt resented the wealth of the Church. It is calculated that the unreformed Church in Scotland had control of about half the country's revenues. Many of the most educated and powerful in Scottish society despised the Catholic Church as it had become increasingly degenerate and corrupt and churchmen were notoriously ignorant. A growing number of Scots were also critical of the Church because they believed its 'mumbo jumbo' and religious ritual were obscuring the word of God.

Calvinism is an intensely rational religion and so it held great appeal for the logical Scots. John Knox and his followers fashioned out of Calvinist dogma a religion for the Scottish people which stressed the importance of *understanding*. The key to this new religion was education: the ordinary parishioners in Scotland were to be taught not only how to read the Bible but also how to understand its meaning so that they could enter into debate on the scriptures. The scheme to transform the Scots into a people capable of such understanding was set out in the *First Book of Discipline* written by a commission appointed by the General Assembly in 1560 and led by John Knox. The Book states that all children in Scotland, no matter how poor, should receive an education. It also set out a scheme for the development of the Scottish universities. Provisions were made for children to be publicly examined on the Catechism and every year the ministers and elders were to examine each parishioner publicly on the chief points of the Bible. The scheme envisaged by the *Books of Discipline* was never formally instituted, partly because of lack of funds, but Knox and his followers did ensure that for hundred of years Scotland educated her people along these lines. In the centuries that followed, visitors to Scotland were amazed that even the poorest peasants could not only read but also debate arcane points of religion. As Campbell Maclean, a Church of Scotland minister, points out in an article on the Scots' way of religion, Knox's vision for education 'produced the most knowledgeable and articulate lay theologians in the history of the Christian church'.[14]

Obviously this emphasis on understanding and debate has had huge implications both for the Scottish Presbyterian church and for Scots culture. As many commentators have remarked, in Scotland 'God is an intellectual'. The core of the Scottish service is the sermon – the singing, prayers and communion are mere appendages. The bareness of the Presbyterian service and the lack of ritual, candles, kneeling and so forth, obviously appealed to the reformers' taste for logic and understanding but inevitably they created a religion which caters for the mind at the expense of the emotions: there is little beauty in Scottish Presbyterianism – little balm for the soul.

More importantly, for the Kirk itself, by emphasising the importance of independence of mind – of each parishioner being able to debate the finer points of theology – it sowed the seeds of its own destruction. It would have been well-nigh impossible for there to have been one single Church in Scotland given the disputatious nature of the Scots. The fact that the Scottish Kirk survived intact for almost two hundred years is indeed remarkable. Infighting and disputes did become commonplace leading ultimately to the Great Disruption of 1843 when Thomas Chalmers and four hundred others walked out *en masse* from the General Assembly. As Campbell Maclean points out:

> It is true that many of the departures from the established church were undertaken more in a spirit of sorrow than anger and always with a high-minded disregard for the subsequent loss of privilege and property of the dissenters. But inevitably, once the flood began, it gave rise to a spate of self-indulgent sectarianism so farcically delicate of conscience that it could only be satisfied by every Presbyterian having a kirk to himself.[15]

Ultimately a Church which encouraged people to think for themselves was also paving the way for agnosticism and atheism and this is precisely what happened in Scotland. In urban areas, even by the nineteenth century, many Scots took the view that religion was a matter of personal belief and conscience.

Earlier I argued that many popular commentators on Scotland only portray the Reformation and Knox's legacy as a huge blight on Scotland. They will often hold this view while simultaneously praising the thinkers of the Scottish Enlightenment. But historians generally believe that the intellectual and economic activity of this period in Scotland would not have happened without the Reformation and the Presbyterian emphasis on education, independence of mind and logical thinking. Indeed Tom Devine argues that by the eighteenth century Calvinism had developed into a set of religious beliefs which stimulated 'an interest in moral, philosophical and scientific questions'.[16] Likewise Herman argues that it is impossible to understand 'the story of the Scots' place in modern civilisation' without 'an appreciation of Scotland's Presbyterian legacy'.[17]

Philosophy

The Scots and English education systems have traditionally differed in their approach, with the Scots being more in favour of generalism and the English preferrring specialisation. But, traditionally, there was another key difference between the Scots and English education systems and it could be summed up in one word – philosophy. The Scots believed that to be properly educated a student had to have a good grasp of philosophy. Before the Scottish universities were forced to adopt the English system, Scottish students started at university at the age of fifteen or sixteen – at least two years before English students – and were then given a general classical and scientific education in which philosophy was given pride of place. The Scots abhorred the idea of specialising too early and believed that it was better for students to get a broad, philosophical education in their first few years at university and then go on to specialise, in law or science, for example, at a later date. The Scottish approach was in line with what happened on the continent but it was out of step with the English tradition.

Nevertheless, as George Davie charted in his book *The Democratic Intellect*, the Scots were still forced to introduce specialised first degree courses along English lines. These changes meant that Scotland lost touch with an important part of her intellectual tradition – a tradition which had, at one point, led her to be one of the great intellectual centres of the world. There is little doubt that over the years Scotland has made a major contribution to philosophy. Not only is David Hume reckoned to be the most important philosopher to write in English but Scotland has produced a score of significant, albeit less well-known, philosophers such as the father of the Common Sense school, Thomas Reid, and the moralist John Macmurray.

A Nation of Logical Thinkers

Philosophy as such has dimmed within Scottish cultural life but logical thinking has not. Indeed the love of logical thinking is so ingrained within the Presbyterian tradition in Scotland it would have taken more than a change in university practices to eliminate it. Quite simply, the Jungian thinking process is still common currency within Scotland. It is the mental process we are expected to use. And this is true not just for Presbyterian Scots but for Catholics, atheists and Asian Scots as well, for the prevailing culture in Scotland encourages everyone to adopt this type of thinking.

Logical thinking still holds sway in contemporary Scotland. Viscount Stair enunciated the principles underlying Scottish law in the seventeenth century and three centuries later the Scots are still intent on putting principles at the heart of Scottish public life. The Scotland Act legislated for the establishment of a Scottish Parliament but its ethos and working practices were defined by the Consultative Steering Group – an all-party group established by Donald Dewar. This group determined that the Parliament's activities should be anchored by four guiding *principles* – power-sharing, accountability, openness and participation/equal opportunities.

Nowadays the Scots can still be described as an independent-minded, opinionated and sceptical people. As the Glasgow commentator and author Cliff Hanley once remarked, if Scotland were to have a slogan it should be 'aye that'll be right'. (For the sake of foreign readers, I should point out that these words sarcastically convey disagreement, not agreement!).

Even when the Scots appear outwardly to respect authority, few will accept others' opinions and views at face value. As I know very well from my training experience, many Scots turn up to courses feeling very sceptical and often sit, arms folded, waiting to be convinced. This need to see the logic and rationale behind something means the Scots are more likely to be questioning rather than accommodating.

However, many Scots do not want to draw attention to themselves (a theme I shall return to later) and this often stops them from being argumentative in formal or on public occasions. In more relaxed, informal surroundings like pubs, they are often extremely opinionated and argumentative. Stand at the bar in many a busy pub and you will soon be in no doubt that the Scots love exchanging opinions and arguing about football, politics or even the meaning of life. And they will often argue their point of view even in the face of higher authorities. John Buchan recounts a story which illustrates this well: 'I remember an old shoemaker in Fife who was a great theologian,' writes Buchan. 'He was always discussing points of theology, and on one occasion his opponent quoted St. Paul against him. "True," said the old man, "but that's just where me and Paul differ".'[18]

The Scots' love of logical thinking also means they have a highly developed critical faculty and are much more aware of what they think is wrong with something than what is right. It is this trait which can lead to the impression that Scotland is a 'can't do' or an 'ah. . . but' culture. As John Buchan once pointed out, there is also a tendency in Scotland to delight in 'pricking other people's bubbles' – to see others' enthusiasm as something to be dampened rather than encouraged. The predisposition for logical thinking also means that praise and appreciation tend to be squeezed out. Indeed anyone who lives in Scotland will be aware that if they want to criticise someone or put them down they have a veritable treasure chest of Scottish expressions to choose from. (Terms such as glaikit, hackit, sleekit and greetin-faced immediately spring to mind.) The Scot who wants to appreciate, compliment or praise has fewer expressions to convey positive thoughts and will also tend to ca' canny on compliments because he or she knows from experience that saying positive things to people in Scotland, outside the immediate family at least, easily causes embarrassment. So stinting can the Scots be with praise, that not being criticised is a bonus. Campbell Maclean maintains that any minister overhearing a parishioner saying of his sermon 'I've heard worse' should feel that his 'time was not wasted'. He also tells a very believable story of an English summer visitor of the evangelical tradition visiting a country church service in Scotland. After some very enthusiastic singing he started to:

> . . . punctuate the sombre-toned sermon with cries of 'Hallelujah! Praise the Lord!' At last, an aged worthy, unable to abide these intrusions any longer rose from his seat and addressed him in a cold, emphatic voice: 'We dinna praise the Lord here!'[19]

Traditionally, if the Scots wanted to show affection or liking in every day life they simply said 'wee' or stuck the letters 'ie' on the end of words and talked about 'lassies', 'laddies' or 'beasties'. This is a theme pursued in a fascinating article on the Scots' liberal use of diminutives published in the 1920s in which Miss Symon, a Scottish poet from Dufftown, is quoted as saying:

> Diminutives are our only emotional outlets. We have practically no endearments. The southerner spreads himself out on 'dears', 'darlings', 'beloveds' and such-like saccharinities. The tidal wave of passion

swamps the Scot. Even the mildest of ordinary, everyday loves remain unexpressed either directly or indirectly because there is no vocabulary for them . . . In a vague, unformulated fashion we consider tenderness a weakness, very nearly an indecency. At any rate we fight shy of it. We *are* shy of it. 'Love but dinna lat on' about sums up all the erotic philosophy of the hill plaid and the sleeved weskit. So in our soft moments – no dithyrambics, no little urbanities, or amiabilities. We just drop into diminutives.[20]

Of course, the advent of the mass media, and some would say the Anglicisation of Scottish life, means that terms of endearment are now used more routinely in Scotland. Nonetheless it is apparent that the Scots feel on more familiar terrain if they are criticising or pointing out what is wrong with something, rather than praising it or showing affection.

The logical thinkers' tendency to home in on what is wrong with something rather than to appreciate what is good about it was very much in evidence in the delicate bedding-in period of the new Scottish Parliament. Almost overnight many of the Scottish media corps went from being keen on the idea in principle to becoming the staunchest critics of the new Parliament. The Presiding Officer, David Steel, issued a public rebuke and even took the *Daily Record* to task for 'bitch journalism'. Newspaper columnist and television presenter Iain Macwhirter broke ranks to attack his colleagues for churning out such critical copy, yet in the process he simply added to the sense of despair and negativity by peddling well-worn images of Scottish deformity: 'The assault on the Parliament probably has something to do with latent philistinism and cretinism in the Scottish character,' wrote Macwhirter.[21]

Criticising the Critical Scots

Commentators on Scotland have not had the conceptual tools to allow them to see that the Scots have a penchant for what Jung defined as thinking, but they have been aware of the weaknesses which can easily flow from the use of this mental function. Edwin Muir lamented what he called a 'thoroughness in the Scottish character' due to the inability to compromise and the desire to take things to their logical conclusion. Sir Iain Moncreiffe likewise maintained it is independent-mindedness which means the Scots find it practically impossible to agree with one another on anything 'except Rabbie Burns'. 'The snag is,' writes Moncreiffe, 'having thought for themselves, they tend to carry things to their logical conclusion *ad absurdum*: so that they tend to be pretty intolerant of those who disagree with them'.[22]

George Blake believed that in 'the Scottish nature' there is 'a tendency to niggle over shades of meaning, the hesitation to accept large generalisations and make easy agreements'. Indeed Blake believes there is a great 'capacity' in Scotland 'to slice metaphysical sausages into the finest slivers'.[23] In a judgmental, critical culture which holds every individual to account those who feel called to express themselves artistically are often most fearful of exposing themselves or of not getting it 'right'. Various artists in Scotland have referred to such fears. According to film-maker Bill Forsyth, 'You are only allowed one chance in Scotland, and if you blow it, that's your lot'.[24] The poet Alan Bold once said 'Anyone who has the temerity to set up shop as a writer in Scotland is bound to attract hostility'.[25] Others just feel oppressed or ground down. 'The skin of a man of letters is peculiarly sensitive to the bite of the critical mosquito,' claimed Alexander Smith, a nineteenth-century Glasgow poet, adding 'and he lives in a climate in which such mosquitoes swarm. He is seldom stabbed to the heart – he is often killed by pinpricks'.[26] And more recently the novelist Alasdair Gray asserted:

> The curse of Scotland is these wee hard men. I used to blame the English for our mediocrity. I thought they had colonised us by sheer cunning. They aren't very cunning. They've got more confidence and money than we have, so they can afford to lean back and smile while our own wee hard men hammer Scotland down to the same dull level as themselves.[27]

The problem for artists in Scotland is not just the prevalence of a judgmental critical atmosphere, and people thinking their opinions are superior to others, but also, as Jung himself points out, thinking types are often poor in 'aesthetic activities, taste, artistic sense'.[28] In other words, logic can easily suppress imagination as well as feeling and so weaken literary expression – a process which may help account for why, in the words of Scottish literary expert David Craig, an ' "all-round" literature' did not emerge in modern Scotland.[29]

As this type of thinking can sometimes repress passion it can easily lead to the unenthusiastic, dour Scot. As logical thinkers do not routinely consult their feelings to make decisions, they can also become emotionally illiterate. In fact thinking types often fear emotions and believe that feelings, their own and others', get in the way of good (i.e. logical) decisions. This means that a logical thinker's feeling side often remains childlike and undeveloped. Thinking types usually like to believe that their tender side, their feelings, can be kept at bay, but inevitably, as human beings, they are not able to do this. Logical thinkers need to pay attention to their feelings and values and when they do they can easily become sentimental – attracted to cheap and easy expressions of emotion.

The Other Side

Which leads me to the one potential flaw in my argument about Scotland's great penchant for logical thinking and hence the critical and unappreciative Scot – Robert Burns. Burns is the most celebrated and famous Scot not only within his own country but also abroad and it would be impossible to describe him as critical, unappreciative, or unprepared to engage with his emotional, feeling side. Of course, Burns was a gifted intellectual, but his reasoning took place, not on the basis of objective logic, but on his personal values. Burns was aware of this himself and talked about being governed not by his 'head' but his 'heart'. Even when Burns was critical, for example in his bitingly satirical poems, his criticism rarely sprang from a cool, principled opposition but from deep feeling. Burns also differs from the typical Scot in that not only was he comfortable expressing emotion, he also passionately wanted to understand himself and his personal responses.

Accepting that Burns was a feeling type does not, however, undermine my argument about the contribution Jungian thinking can make to an understanding of Scotland. It strengthens it. Jung argued that all human beings have the capacity to use both the thinking and the feeling processes. They cannot completely ignore one and concentrate on the other. Through use, one will become preferred and developed, thus colouring the individual's personality, but the undeveloped process will still demand some expression. It will still make its presence felt in the individual's life. Burns is so important to Scotland because he encourages the otherwise logical, critical Scots to celebrate and appreciate what is important to them in their everyday lives – daisies, mice, simple family ways, a smile, a sweetheart. Since Burns's poetry is heartfelt but not deep it is easy for the Scots, who lack emotional sensitivity, to understand.

Burns's capacity to redress an important imbalance in the typical Scot and in Scottish life is best seen on Burns night. At Burns suppers, men who in normal life would never dream of expressing emotion in public, stand in front of an audience and declare 'my love is like a red, red rose'. They make all sorts of enthusiastic, positive statements about things they like – whisky, lassies, lines from Burns's poems, haggis. They talk in passionate terms about their homeland. The toast known as 'the Immortal Memory' is also known as 'the Appreciation' and the one rule a speaker must observe is that it must be positive about Burns, Scotland and humankind in general. Any speaker who is critical or accusatory strikes the wrong note. Indeed my *Burns Supper Companion* tells me that one of the key ingredients of this speech is its 'warmth'. Fairly tedious, predictable criticism is permitted in the 'Toast to the Lassies' and 'the Reply'. But even then, my *Companion* informs me, both should end on a 'conciliatory note'.[30]

There are few occasions in Scottish life where these are the terms of engagement – even the Kirk does not function like that. The Scots are much more likely to be argumentative than conciliatory. They are critical rather than appreciative. The Scots do not openly talk about love, relationships or emotions – except on Burns night.

There is hardly a commentator on Scotland who has not tried to fathom why Burns should be celebrated by the Scots to the extent he is; why Burns is not just an important national poet, but a demigod with a cult following. Some argue that Burns's popularity is intrinsically tied up with Scotland's relationship with England and how he galvanised nationalist sentiment. Others show how Burns carries important Scottish values. Another common argument is that Burns was a chameleon who could easily be 'all things to all men'. I have no doubt there is much merit in all these arguments. But there is another reason as well: Burns encourages a very logical, unemotional people to get in touch with their tender side. Remove Burns from Scottish life and it would be greatly impoverished. Without Burns to encourage us to consider our hearts, not just our heads, the Scots would be more aware of living in a world dominated by cold, impersonal logic. A world where scepticism reigns and where it is more acceptable to criticise than appreciate and where it is very easy for us to lose sight of what is important in life.

Notes

1 Moray McLaren *Understanding the Scots: A Guide for South Britons and Other Foreigners* (Frederick Muller: London, 1956), p.27

2 Carl Jung *Psychological Types* (Routledge: London, 1989)

3 Quoted in W. Gordon Smith *This is my Country: A Personal Blend of the Purest Scotch* (Souvenir Press: London, 1976), p.188

4 Neil McCallum *A Small Country* (James Thin: Edinburgh, 1983), p.128

5 Lenore Thomson *Personality Type: An Owner's Manual* (Shambhala: Boston, 1998), p.257

6 Ibid., p.258

7 Arthur Herman *The Scottish Enlightenment: The Scots' Invention of the Modern World* (Fourth Estate: London, 2002), p.54

8 Ibid., p.68

9 Bruce P. Lenman 'From the Union of 1707 to the Franchise Reform of 1832' in R. A. Houston & W. W. J. Knox (eds) *The New Penguin History of Scotland: From the Earliest Times to the Present Day* (Penguin Books: London, 2001), p.345

10 Quoted in Christopher Harvie *Scotland and Nationalism: Scottish Society and Politics, 1707-1977* (George Allen & Unwin: London, 1977), p.130

11 Quoted in Douglas Gifford *James Hogg* (The Ramsay Head Press: Edinburgh, 1976), p.11

12 Wallace Notestein *The Scot in History: A Study of the Interplay of Character and History* (Yale University Press: United States, 1947)

13 See, for example, Alexander Broadie *Why Scottish Philosophy Matters* (The Saltire Society: Edinburgh, 2000)

14 Campbell Maclean 'Who is Their God' in Alastair M. Dunnett (ed.) *Alistair MacLean Introduces Scotland* (Andre Deutsch: London, 1972), p.196

15 Ibid., p.202

16 T. M. Devine *The Scottish Nation 1700-2000* (Penguin Books: London, 1999), p.69

17 Arthur Herman *The Scottish Enlightenment*, p.10

18 John Buchan 'Some Scottish Characteristics' in W.A. Craigie, John Buchan, Peter Giles & J. M. Bulloch *The Scottish Tongue* (Cassell & Company: London, 1924), p.63

19 Campbell Maclean 'Who is Their God', p. 207

20 Quoted in J.M. Bulloch 'The Delight of the Doric in the Diminutive' in W.A. Craigie, John Buchan, Peter Giles & J. M. Bulloch *The Scottish Tongue* (Cassell & Company: London, 1924), pp.143-144

21 Iain Macwhirter *Sunday Herald*, 5 September 1999

22 Sir Iain Moncrieffe 'The Long Story – to Queen Victoria' in Alastair M. Dunnett (ed.) *Alistair MacLean Introduces Scotland* (Andre Deutsch: London, 1972), p.77

23 George Blake *The Heart of Scotland* (B.T. Batsford: London, 1934), p.69

24 Quoted in Angela Cran & James Robertson *Dictionary of Scottish Quotations* (Mainstream Publishing: Edinburgh, 1996), p.134

25 Alan Bold 'Dr Grieve and Mr MacDiarmid' in P.H. Scott & A.C Davis (eds) *The Age of MacDiarmid* (Mainstream Publishing: Edinburgh, 1980), p.38

26 Alexander Smith *Dreamthorp* (1863)

27 Quoted in Angela Cran & James Robertson *Dictionary of Scottish Quotations* p.150

28 C.G. Jung *Psychological Types* p.348

29 David Craig *Scottish Literature and the Scottish People 1680-1830* (Chatto & Windus: London, 1961), p.14

30 Nancy Marshall *Burns Supper Companion* (HarperCollins: Glasgow 2002)

4. The Pull of Possibilities

Speculative hard-headedness unites in the national character with a sublime and lofty enthusiasm concerning things altogether remote and intangible.

Paxton Hood, *Scottish Characteristics*

It is impossible to read Scottish history and not be struck by the fact that for centuries the Scots have been discontented with the *status quo*. John Buchan believed this 'unsettlement' to be one of the most important aspects of Scottish history. A decade ago Kirsty Wark highlighted the Scots' unsettlement in her TV series on Scottish politics, *Restless Nation*.

For centuries the Scots have dreamed of change and possibilities and have responded to a vision of a different future. A good example of this is the Scottish Covenant of 1949. This document was the brainchild of John MacCormick, a Scottish lawyer, who was instrumental in the formation of the Scottish National Party. MacCormick went on to set up the first Scottish Convention – an all-party group designed to exert pressure for 'reform of Scottish Government'. It held a 'Scottish National Assembly' in 1947 and over six hundred delegates from all walks of Scottish life attended. Ultimately this organisation supervised the creation of a Scottish Covenant to allow the Scottish people simultaneously to swear their loyalty to the United Kingdom and their commitment to the creation of a Scottish Parliament. The document was unveiled at a crowded national assembly meeting in the General Assembly building on the Mound in Edinburgh in October 1949. Over twelve hundred people attended what seemed at the time like a momentous Scottish occasion. John MacCormick recorded the event in the following terms:

> Unknown district councillors rubbed shoulders and joined in pledges with the men whose titles had sounded through all the history of Scotland. Working men from the docks of Glasgow or the pits of Fife spoke with the same voice as the portly business-men in pin-striped trousers. It was such a demonstration of national unity as the Scots might never hope to see, and when, finally, the scroll upon which the Covenant was inscribed was unveiled for signature every person in the hall joined patiently in the queue to sign it.[1]

As with earlier Scottish Covenants, copies were distributed around Scotland – in colleges, shops and cafés. Although two million people eventually signed, Westminster ignored the Covenant and a Scottish Government did not materialise. The vision remained unfulfilled until 1999 and the inauguration of the Scottish Parliament.

Other examples of vision playing a major role in Scottish life include the original Scottish Covenant of 1638, when 300,000 signatures were collected in support of Scottish religious independence. Another is the founding of an ill-fated Scottish trading colony at Darien in the late seventeenth century. On that occasion Scots did not simply sign their name in support of a vision but gave money to support a trading venture. Indeed it is estimated that a third of all Scotland's liquid assets were sunk into the proposal. On other occasions, particular sections of the Scottish community were involved in the furtherance of a vision: the nobles in the Declaration of Arbroath or the workers in Glasgow during the period known as Red Clydeside. And no doubt many of the millions who have chosen voluntarily to leave Scotland over the centuries did so animated by their own personal vision of a new life for themselves and their families.

One possible reason for the Scots' responsiveness to vision is that historically they have been unhappy with their lot. Lacking opportunities at home they have packed up and gone elsewhere. What's more, because Scotland is the junior partner in an incorporating Union, and an ancient state without sovereignty, the Scots are bound to feel discontented with the situation in which they find themselves. So the Scots may well be attracted to the vision of a different future because they do not care too much for the *status quo*. But I believe there is another reason as well.

The Scots are much more responsive to visionary ideas than the English, for example, not simply because they have a constitutional position they dislike, but because they are fairly comfortable with abstract ideas and potentially more open to the idea of change. Of course, there is a distinct backward-looking strain within Scottish culture. But such a strain is apparent in any modern society. The nostalgic longings of millions of Scottish emigrés have also strengthened what Sir Compton McKenzie once called 'the Lone Shieling Complex'. No doubt Scotland's proclivity for sentimentality, outlined in a previous chapter, has also encouraged the tendency to romanticise aspects of the past. But none of this gainsays the fact that there is a strong, progressive current within Scottish thought. In the last chapter I argued that the Scots are logical thinkers, but there is much more to it than that. Traditionally the Scots have also been bold, speculative thinkers who are comfortable with theories and abstractions. Vision, speculation, abstraction and theories may not seem linked but we can easily appreciate the connection if we return to Jung's tool box and borrow the two remaining mental processes he describes – sensing and intuition.

Sensing and Intuition

In everyday life we can see that some people are 'big picture' types whilst others are interested in 'detail'. We can also see that some people like change and innovation whilst others are conservative and prefer the known to the unknown. But while we can see these differences we cannot account for them. We have no idea why people vary in this way. Jung provides an explanation by describing the underlying mental processes.

Sensing is a way of taking in information from the five senses. When individuals use the mental process Jung defines as sensing, they pay high quality attention to real, concrete information. In short, they live in the moment, with their feet on the ground, noticing what is going on round about them, or they tap into their memory banks to access information based on real, lived experiences. Obviously, everyone has to pay attention to some sensory information, but the difference between sensing types and intuitive types is that the former *prefer* this kind of information. They concentrate their attention on what is real and on what they know from experience to be true. People who prefer sensing information also respect facts and care about practicalities and details.

People who prefer intuition, by contrast, are not motivated by what *is* but by *what could be* – they are pulled by what Jung calls 'possibilities'. So intuitives do not pay much attention to real, concrete information; they pay more attention to a vast array of information gleaned from their unconscious mind. Intuitives often describe this type of information as a 'hunch'. What this means is that the intuitive instinctively 'knows' something even though he/she cannot support it with concrete facts. So intuitives favour a type of information gathering which looks beyond or behind what is really there. The intuitive process encourages individuals to do a variety of different things – such as ask questions about meaning, construct theories, speculate, associate, or visualise a different future.

So sensing is a process which respects concrete facts and prefers to confine its attention to the real and the known, whereas intuition is more concerned with an abstract world of possibilities, theories and ideas. Each individual uses both processes to some extent in life and will move from one to the other, but one of the processes is usually preferred, and its use seems right and natural, just like when we use our dominant hand.

Again a preference for one of these two functions leads to significant personality differences in individuals. People who prefer sensing are down-to-earth, practical, realistic, good on detail and are motivated by facts and personal experience, whereas intuitives get bored easily and look for new possibilities and opportunities to theorise or innovate. Another key difference between people who prefer sensing and those who prefer intuition is that the former tend to be conservative, valuing the known to the unknown, whereas intuitives stress the importance of possibilities and vision and are drawn to change.

It is important to understand that intuitives do not completely disregard facts or believe they are unimportant; but their preferences often lead them to devise a theory based on their hunches and then work backwards to see how the facts fit.

The Scots' Intellectual Method

If we examine the work of those involved in the Scottish Enlightenment we shall see just how strong the preference for intuition was during the heyday of Scots' intellectual endeavour. In fact, the Scottish Enlightenment project, with its particular focus on 'progress', 'improvement', radical, social, economic and scientific change, was undoubtedly a movement dominated by intuitive thinkers. Of all the types it is those who combine thinking and intuition who are most intent on changing the world through new ways of thinking and conceptualising. This is what the Scottish Enlightenment was all about. It is tempting simply to say that as many intellectuals and radical thinkers have a preference for intuition then there was nothing special about the Scottish Enlightenment thinkers, but the English historian Henry Buckle helps us see that Scottish intellectuals, in the past at least, did differ from their English counterparts.

Buckle was a historian of ideas. Although his book is titled *The History of Civilisation in England*, Buckle died before writing specifically about England. But he did write a general introduction to his history, a study of Spain and a full history of Scottish ideas. In this volume, entitled *On Scotland and the Scotch Intellect*, Buckle compared the intellectual method preferred in England and Scotland. He argued that, following

Bacon, English scientists and intellectuals used 'inductive reasoning'. By that Buckle meant reasoning which takes place on the basis of concrete facts and that English intellectuals reason from the particular to the general.

'The inductive philosopher,' wrote Buckle, 'is naturally cautious, patient and somewhat creeping'.[2] According to Buckle, 'deductive reasoning', which the Scots intelligentsia preferred in the eighteenth and nineteenth centuries at least, proceeds from 'generals to particulars and from the ideas to the senses'.[3] Buckle's thesis does not fit precisely with Jungian definitions of sensing and intuition but it seems legitimate to argue that Buckle used concepts which overlap with three of Jung's four mental functions. Buckle maintained that the English, following scientific method laid down by Bacon, proceed from facts – that is, sensing – whereas the Scots either reason from first principles – thinking, or from abstract ideas – intuition. In either case, the Scots in their preferred intellectual method relegate sensing, e.g. paying attention to concrete facts, to second if not third place. Presumably this is one of the reasons why the Scottish universities traditionally gave weight to philosophy and were less concerned to engage in practical research.

Buckle gave many examples of the Scots' penchant for the deductive method. For example, he wrote:

> *The Wealth of Nations* . . . is entirely deductive, since in it Smith generalises the laws of wealth, not from the phenomenon of wealth, not from statistical statements, but from the phenomenon of selfishness; thus making a deductive application of one set of mental principles to the whole set of economical facts. The illustrations with which his great book abounds are no part of the real

argument: they are subsequent to the conception;
and if they were all omitted, the work, though less
interesting, and perhaps less influential, would,
from a scientific point of view, be equally valuable.[4]

Buckle was critical of the Scottish deductive method yet a great admirer of Scottish thinkers such as Adam Smith. He not only praised the bold sweep of the book and the 'prodigious' work Smith undertook, he also claimed it to be 'the most important book ever written'.[5] He also maintained that Smith realised that 'an inductive investigation (i.e. one based on facts) was impossible, because it would require the labour of many lives even to assemble the materials from which the generalisation was to be made'.[6] According to Buckle, Smith was influenced 'by the intellectual habits which prevailed around him' and argued on the basis of hypothesis and the 'intentional suppression of facts'.[7]

Buckle asserted that even the great empiricist David Hume, in works such as *The Natural History of Religion*, used a deductive method because he established principles to support his arguments without the use of facts and observation and then simply used facts as illustrations. 'In him a contempt for facts,' wrote Buckle, 'was merely the exaggerated result of a devotion to ideas'.[8] Again Buckle claimed that, 'If Hume had followed the Baconian scheme, of always rising from particulars to generals, and from each generalisation to that above it, he would hardly have written one of his works'.[9]

Buckle also maintained that the Scots used deductive reasoning in the natural sciences. According to Buckle, Professor Joseph Black, who was famous for his theory of latent heat, 'began to speculate concerning heat', and taught his theory a number of years before the necessary experiments were undertaken to prove it. Buckle claimed that James Hutton, whose theory on the evolution of the earth earned him the title 'father of geology', likewise proceeded from ideas and not from facts when coming up with his *Theory of the Earth*:

> It . . . appears that one of the chief parts of the Huttonian Theory, and certainly its most successful part, was conceived in opposition to all preceding evidence; that it presupposed a combination of events which no one had ever observed, and the mere possibility of which nothing but artificial experiment could prove; and finally, that Hutton was so confident of the validity of his own method of inquiry, that he disdained to make the experiment himself, but left to another mind that empirical branch of the investigation which he deemed of little moment, but which we, in England, are taught to believe is the only safe foundation of physical research.[10]

I have little doubt that Buckle is right – speculative ideas and theories have played an important part in the work of great Scottish thinkers throughout history and into our own time. One of the great strengths of the Enlightenment thinkers and other great intellectual Scots such as James Clerk Maxwell or Sir James Frazer who wrote *The Golden Bough*, a groundbreaking work on anthropology, is that the Scots are not content to study detail and confine themselves to facts. They are good at seeing the patterns in a mass of information and then coming up with new theories to explain what is happening. This does not mean that Enlightenment thinkers did not have a respect for inductive reasoning and use it where relevant, but that they were not constrained or limited by it.

Buckle's book on Scotland's preferred intellectual method is the only work I know which shows in detail how, if we look beneath the Scots' love of logical thinking, we often find attraction to abstract ideas and intuitive hunches. He helps us to see that the success of many past Scots thinkers is that they had the courage and confidence to build grand theories or take great intellectual leaps of faith. But this does not mean, as Buckle argues, that the Scots *underrated* the importance of concrete reality, facts or experience. As we shall see more fully in the next chapter, Scots intellectuals have always been drawn to the external, 'extravert' world and want their ideas to be relevant to that domain. Scots rarely fit the description of ivory-tower intellectuals who do not think it important to ground their theories in the real world. Scots intellectuals and inventors have been intent on coming up with theories and ideas and then working backwards to see how they could be supported by facts and made to work in the real world.

James Watt is a good example of this. A gifted instrument maker and good with his hands, he ultimately devised a steam engine which revolutionised production and transport, ushering in the technological age. Watt's invention did not result from inductive reasoning and observation in a laboratory or workshop. Watt's big idea for a separate condenser, which solved the limitations of the Newcomen engine, occurred to him one Sunday morning when he was walking across Glasgow Green. He was later to say that he 'had not walked further than the golf-course when the whole thing was arranged in my mind'. Neil McCallum wrote of Watt:

> After devising the separate condenser, there were
> years of work, of laborious make-shifts with

> imperfect materials. His ideas leaped ahead of the
> ability to translate them into mechanism. There
> was a succession of models, always amended and
> improved on paper before they were completed.
> But his essential idea was so sound, and Watt so
> persistently fertile with secondary ideas, that the
> harnessing of power to industry followed with
> logical certainty.[11]

What McCallum described is the working in tandem of the two mental processes Jung defined as intuition and thinking. Watt was not the only Scot to excel at generating ideas and then, mainly through the application of logical reasoning, make them practical. The Scots have come up with a number of hugely important inventions – the steam engine, the telephone, television, chloroform, penicillin, modern surgical methods, the commercialisation of gas lighting, tyres, tarmac, various agricultural improvements, ultra-sound scans and countless more. And there is little doubt that many of them came upon their new idea not by cautious, creeping observation but through an intuitive leap. Once they had the idea they not only worked backwards to see how it might work in real life but they also had the technical abilities and know-how to make it practical.

So it is not difficult to see why the British social scientist Havelock Ellis, who conducted an objective study of British genius, concluded that over the centuries, in proportion to their numbers, Scotland has produced more productive geniuses of the highest talent than the rest of the United Kingdom.

Buckle was simply wrong to argue that the English inductive method is superior to the Scots approach – science is a much messier process than he describes. Most great scientists, inventors and theoreticians, such as Einstein, follow their intuition – they make huge leaps – they do not simply observe concrete reality. They are not the cautious observers of fact that Buckle describes. Indeed the science he describes is the science of the school room. It is not the science that makes great discoveries and changes the world. As Jung himself observed, 'even physics, the strictest of all the applied sciences, depends to an astonishing degree upon intuition, which works by way of the unconscious'.[12] Though he adds that 'afterwards' it is possible to go back and demonstrate 'the logical procedures' that would have led to the same result.

Buckle's work was very influential in its day, throughout Europe. It was much quoted in Russia, for example, and in the UK George Bernard Shaw rated Buckle's influence on him and his generation alongside Karl Marx.[13] George Davie argued that Buckle's criticisms of the Scottish intellectual method gave impetus to those who wanted to restructure the Scottish universities along English lines. Yet Davie, in his celebrated book on the philosophy of Scottish education, wrote little about the substance of Buckle's theory though he did claim that the book was 'lively and authoritative'.[14]

In contemporary Scotland you are hard-pressed to find in books on Scottish history and culture a mention of Buckle, let alone any proper examination of his thesis. Even McCallum, in his detailed portraits of Scottish Enlightenment figures, did not mention Buckle's argument. And the only explanation I can find for this failure to see anything interesting in Buckle's claims is that Buckle used his argument to say some very unflattering things about Scotland and the Scots. Indeed Buckle's motivation to write the volume on Scotland largely came from his anti-clericism. Having witnessed the spectacle of the Great Disruption of the Church of Scotland in 1843, he believed that religious thinking and the Kirk played a hugely important part in Scottish life and that as a result 'there runs through the entire country a sour and fanatical spirit'.[15] As he also believed 'there is no country which possesses a more original, inquisitive and innovative literature than Scotland does',[16] he wanted to provide an explanation for this apparent contradiction.

The nub of Buckle's ensuing argument is that ordinary people are more likely to understand the inductive method (reasoning from observable facts) because it is similar to the way they view the world. So where this method predominates, as it did in England, a rift does not open up between intellectuals and ordinary citizens. Science and other types of intellectual endeavour can therefore have an impact on everyday life and lead to the development of a generally civilised and prosperous country. According to Buckle, in countries where deductive reasoning predominates, intellectuals 'consider things at too high an altitude' and so they are unable to 'influence the body of the people'.[17] This is what Buckle thought had happened not just in Scotland, but in ancient Greece and nineteenth-century Germany. According to Buckle, Scotland may have had brilliant intellectual thinkers but their ideas were so removed from the lives of ordinary people that they did little for economic prosperity and hardly dented religious fanaticism. In Scotland during the eighteenth century 'superstition and science', wrote Buckle:

> . . . the most irreconcilable of all enemies, flourished side by side, unable to weaken each other and unable to come into collision. . . The two forces kept apart, and the result was, that, while the Scotch thinkers were creating a noble

and most enlightened literature, the Scotch
people, refusing to listen to those great masters of
wisdom which their country possessed, remained
in darkness, leaving the blind to follow the blind,
and no one there to help them.[18]

It is these views which lead Buckle on to some of his most vehemently anti-Scottish statements.

But Buckle is misguided here too. Scottish thinkers were no ivory tower intellectuals, far removed from reality. They cared about everyday life and were immersed in it. They also wanted to come up with ways to improve society and did develop ground-breaking ideas and inventions. The Scottish intellectuals Buckle analyses *did* challenge superstitious religious thinking and managed to found 'the Common Sense School' of philosophy as well as the academic disciplines we now call 'social science'. And they did not just win over the Scottish mind in the process – they ultimately influenced the world.

Buckle was also wrong, for another reason, to maintain that the intellectual method in Scotland created a rift between the educated elite and ordinary people. For centuries Scottish culture has encouraged everyone to be much more open to speculation, theories and possibilities than they are south of the border. There is much more willingness in Scotland for people, even those who are not intellectuals, to speculate on the meaning of life; to construct personal theories and to think about possibilities for the future. In the words of William McIlvanney, Scotland is an 'intense talking shop' where 'the Ancient Mariner haunts many pubs and Socrates sometimes wears a bunnet, and women at bus-stops say serious things about the world'.[19]

The English writer Charles Jennings, in his book on Scotland, *Faintheart*, also remarked that, despite the constant swearing, there is a higher level of chat in pubs than is the case down south.[20] Indeed one of the things that irritates many Scots about the English is that they are happy to chatter on about topics of no consequence. In modern Scottish culture we can still find the existence of what George Davie called 'metaphysical Scotland' in unexpected places. Pick up a copy of *Trainspotting*, for example, and you will find the junkie 'Rent Boy' explaining to the court that he stole a volume by Kierkegaard because he is interested in the philosopher's 'concepts of subjectivity and truth'.[21]

The Conservatives Next Door

Clearly it is difficult to reduce the character of whole peoples to a few lines and to say the English are like this and the Scots like that, as there is scope for huge individual variation. However Jung's concepts of sensing and intuition can help us better to understand not just the Scottish intellectual method but some of the key differences between Scottish and English culture. Take the practice of law. Arthur Herman, when writing about the eighteenth century, encapsulates some of the differences in the legal system north and south of the border:

> Scottish advocates had been practising before the bar since the thirteenth century, and had formed their own guild, the Faculty of Advocates, in the sixteenth. The rules for admission had been increasingly strict, even scholarly. The Faculty required from its members a full course of study of philosophy and law at a university for at least two years, in lieu of formal experience for seven.

The contrast with England was striking. The English barrister received no formal academic training at all. Instead, he learned his trade at the Inns of Court in London entirely in the old medieval style of hands-on apprenticeship. Like his solicitor counterparts, the young English barrister learned to play follow-the-leader, and to obey the dictates of precedent, because there was no practical alternative.

But his Scottish counterpart was as much the product of rigorous scholarly erudition as of practical skills. Two years of overseas study, at universities in Holland or even in France, gave the Scottish bar a cosmopolitan air the English never achieved.[22]

So in law, as in intellectual life, the Scots appreciated the importance of practicality and observation but they did not revere this approach so much that they downgraded the importance of intellectual rigour or ideas. In contrast, it is commonplace for commentators on England to point out that the preference for the known and the practical in England has, over the centuries, led to a certain hostility to new ideas. This hostility is not confined to the legal and academic worlds but permeates English culture. The Irishman Edmund Burke, for example, was a keen observer on English life. When he wrote his famous *Reflections on the Revolution in France* in 1790 he had lived in England for the best part of forty years and deeply identified with their world-view. And in page after page of this book Burke described the English as a deeply conservative people who dislike ideas:

Thanks to our sullen resistance to innovation, thanks to the cold sluggishness of our character, we still bear the stamp of our forefathers . . . We

are not the converts of Rousseau; we are not the
disciples of Voltaire; . . . We know that we have
made no discoveries; and we think that no
discoveries are to be made, in morality; nor many
in the great principles of government, nor in the
ideas of liberty . . . In this enlightened age I am
bold enough to confess . . . that instead of casting
away all our old prejudices, we cherish them to a
very considerable degree, and, to take more shame
to ourselves, we cherish them because they are
prejudices; and the longer they have lasted, and
the more generally they have prevailed, the more
we cherish them.[23]

More than two hundred years on writers are still presenting
the English in a similar vein. For example, in 1998 Jeremy
Paxman, in his book on the English, asserts 'The English
approach to ideas is not to kill them but to let them die of
neglect'. Paxman also argues that the English approach to
problems is 'empirical' and that 'the only ideology' they believe
in is common sense.[24] Roger Scruton, too, argues that the English
are much more interested in 'concrete realities' than speculation. 'Empiricism' is how Kate Fox defines the country's basic
outlook in *Watching the English*. '"Empiricism",' she writes, 'is
short-hand for our down-to-earthness, our matter-of-factness;
our pragmatism; our cynical, no-nonsense groundedness; our
gritty realism. . .'[25]

As English culture does not just value but venerates the
tried and tested, personal experience and practicality, we can
see that the mental process most promoted in English culture
is what Jung defines as sensing. As we shall see in more detail
later, English culture is more introverted than Scottish culture
– more interested in the inner, rather than the outer world.
That is why English culture does not have the oral, energetic

and active quality which is so apparent in Scotland. The combination of introversion and sensing has certain undoubted strengths. An individual of these preferences is usually dutiful and hardworking, down to earth, and very good at attending to detail. Hence this type is good at creating and maintaining administrative systems. They are also fairly tolerant of others and good at creating an environment which allows individuals to get on with living their own lives. In England's case this has helped to create an environment which is reasonably sympathetic to cultural endeavours of all kind.

However, in Jungian typology it is the people who combine introversion and sensing who are the most traditional and conservative types. Their interior function, writes Jung, 'has an amazing flair for all the ambiguous, shadowy, sordid, dangerous possibilities lurking in the background' [26] – a characteristic of English culture that, over the centuries, countless observers have identified. Of course, there are many individuals in England who do not share this fear of change and who like new ideas, but they are going against the grain of traditional English culture. The innate conservatism of the English can be viewed as either negative or positive. Some take Burke's view that it is a source of great stability and strength. Others, like Paxman, are more critical. Much depends on the person's own preferences and attitudes to change and possibilities.

I certainly believe that England's love affair with the past is as big as, if not a bigger problem than, the Scots' obsession with logical thinking. England is a country with a great desire to preserve its traditions and institutions even though they are often at odds with her becoming a truly modern nation. It is for this reason that Black Rod lives on within the Mother of

Parliaments, as does much of the pomp and circumstance. It is this innate resistance to change which also leads to the type of deep structural problems which economic historians such as Martin Wiener and Corelli Barnett argue lie at the heart of the British economy. Of course, there have been occasions when significant sections of the English people yearned for change. One such occasion was the 1945 election and the Labour landslide. There have also been a significant number of great English radicals and visionaries such as Tom Paine, William Cobbett and William Morris. But such radical visions have rarely animated the spirit of the English nation as a whole. When Margaret Thatcher was Prime Minister she had a strong, if unattractive, vision of what she wanted to achieve. She was interested in possibilities. However, she understood the natural conservatism of the English people and that is why she based much of her appeal, not on a radical new vision of an enterprise culture, but on Victorian values, on the jingoism of the Falklands War and on a Little Englander mentality which devalues all things European.

As the world is now a fast-moving place, and we are in the midst of another great technological revolution, and facing major environmental challenges, England's Achilles heel may become more and more of a liability. And not just for the English. Scotland has hitched her wagon to a rather old-fashioned, if once elegant and sophisticated, vehicle marked 'England' and her ability to find solutions to problems, even with devolution, may be constrained by what the English will accept.

Other characteristics which are often described as 'quintess-entially English' also flow from the combination of introversion and sensing. Jung argues that this psychological type is the most likely to display 'rational self-control'. Another way to describe this quality in a person is to refer to their 'stiff upper lip'. The difficulty in seeing future possibilities in a positive light may also account for the inherent pessimism the English often display, not necessarily about their own individual lives, but about the future of England. Paxman gives many examples of this 'strong streak of natural gloominess'. He argues that not only are they likely to 'ignore the silver lining and grasp at the cloud' but also that they often believe the country has 'gone to the dogs' – that somehow England and the English are 'finished'.[27] And this may help us understand why Roger Scruton chose the title *England – an Elegy* for his book.

The picture which often emerges of England is of a fairly stable, but rather dull place. In Jung's scheme there is a need for balance – the attitudes and functions which have been repressed will still find an outlet. That's why in Scotland we see the otherwise logical Scots declaring their love and values through their celebration of that great compensatory Scottish hero – Robert Burns. The English seem to find compensation for their heavy emphasis on conservatism and convention in that great English characteristic – 'eccentricity'. In a scholarly work entitled *The Character of England*, Richard Law describes the phenomenon in the following terms:

> . . . the Englishman . . . has a great respect and liking for the eccentric, for the 'queer one' . . . Victorian Oxford swarmed with 'characters', from the top-hatted venerables and topers to 'the British Workman', last of the tribe. To this day the heretic, the grouser, or the crank is allowed full play in club or pub . . . (As is) the Sabbatical Orator in Hyde Park . . . But English eccentricity is always

> qualified. It is only permitted within the frame-
> work of the law or, at any rate, within the bounds
> which are laid down for it by social usage.[28]

At the end of the book, 'eccentricity' is listed as an essential English characteristic and the editor observes that in England there are even 'societies of cranks' and that English literature is 'full of pictures of oddities'.[29] As I write these lines I cannot help thinking about all those things which seem to emanate from English eccentricity and which make the toes of your average Scot curl: Mr Blobby, The Monster Raving Loonie Party, The Smurfs, Ken Dodd and his tickling stick, Barbara Cartland, music hall, Stanley Unwin, Punch and Judy shows, Boris Johnson, Kenny Everett and the Temperance Seven singing 'Winchester Cathedral.'[30] And, for me anyway, the items on this list are every bit as embarrassing as the Scottish Kailyard or the crocodile tears of the sentimental Scot.

Notes

1 Quoted in Andrew Marr *The Battle for Scotland* (Penguin Books: London, 1992), p.97

2 Henry Thomas *Buckle On Scotland and the Scotch Intellect* (The University of Chicago Press: Chicago, 1970), p.243

3 Ibid., p.243

4 Ibid., p.21

5 Ibid., p.264

6 Ibid., p.255

7 Ibid., p.256

8 Ibid., pp.283-4

9 Ibid., p.284

10 Ibid., p.337

11 Neil McCallum *A Small Country* (James Thin: Edinburgh, 1983) p.100

12 C.G. Jung *Man and His Symbols* (Arkana: London, 1990), p.92

13 For further information see H.J. Hanham's introduction to

Buckle in the 1970 Chicago edition of *On Scotland and the Scotch Intellect*

14 George Davie *The Democratic Intellect* (Edinburgh University Press: Edinburgh, 1961), p.321

15 Henry Thomas *Buckle On Scotland and the Scotch Intellect* p.394

16 Ibid., p.227

17 Ibid., p.392

18 Ibid., p.470

19 William McIlvanney *Surviving the Shipwreck* (Mainstream Publishing: Edinburgh, 1991), p.138

20 Charles Jennings *Faintheart: An Englishman Ventures North of the Border* (Abacus: London, 2001)

21 Irvine Welsh *Trainspotting* (Mandarin Paperbacks: London, 1996), p.165

22 Arthur Herman *The Scottish Enlightenment: The Scots' Invention of the Modern World* (Fourth Estate: London, 2002), p.76

23 Edmund Burke *Reflections on the Revolution in France* (Penguin Books: London, 1968), pp.181-183

24 Jeremy Paxman *The English* pp.192-93

25 Kate Fox *Watching the English* (Hodder: London, 2005) p.405

26 C.G. Jung *Psychological Types* (Routledge: London, 1991), p.398

27 Jeremy Paxman *The English* p.14

28 Richard Law 'The Individual and the Community' in Ernest Barker (ed.) *The Character of England* (Oxford University Press: London, 1950), p.41

29 Ernest Barker 'An Attempt at Perspective' in Ernest Barker (ed.) *The Character of England* (Oxford University Press: London, 1950), p.568

30 In 1936 Hugh MacDiarmid published *Scottish Eccentrics* (George Routledge: London). It is a series of essays on unusual Scots and ends with MacDiarmid's attempt to link such eccentricity to the 'Caledonian antisyzygy'. It suits MacDiarmid to characterise the Scots as 'idiosyncratic' as he wants to use this idea to help him portray Scotland as a land of extremes. But in all but the most repressive countries it is always possible to find oddballs, characters or social misfits of one kind or another. What is different about England is that eccentricity has a compensatory element and is institutionalised within the culture.

5. A Way with Words

To understand the character of a particular people
we must examine the objects of its love.
St Augustine, *The City of God*

Almost one hundred years ago, Carl Jung came up with the terms 'introvert' and 'extravert' to describe a basic difference between people and it is these terms which help us to grasp an essential feature of Scotland. 'Extravert' (or extrovert) and 'introvert' have entered our everyday vocabulary, but we now tend to use these terms to mean something other than Jung intended. We use 'extravert' only to describe someone who likes to be the centre of attention or is the life and soul of the party. The term 'introvert', by comparison, is used to describe people who are shy, and rather anti-social. But on both counts the Jungian definition is much more subtle and complex.

Introversion and Extraversion

The simplest way to grasp introversion and extraversion is to understand that as human beings we constantly move between two distinct and separate worlds. One is the extravert world, which exists outside ourselves – it is the world of people, things and activity. When we speak, communicate, act and pursue many interests or hobbies we are in extravert mode. In fact we are directing our attention outwards – extraverting as opposed to introverting – every time our attention is drawn to the outer world. The introvert world is the world which exists inside our heads. It is a world of inner reflection. Here we process thoughts, make decisions, mull over our experiences or whatever in a solitary manner. Our attention is drawn inwards.

Jung acknowledged that all individuals introvert and extravert and so the issue is which of the two worlds each of us prefers. For Jung an essential difference between introverts and extraverts is how they gather and use energy. Extraverts are energised, and turned on, by action and interaction. They are stimulated by talking, doing and being with other people. They allow their energy to flow into the external world. So extraverts are energised in the extravert world and expend most of their energy there. Introverts derive their energy from internal sources. They can easily feel drained by involvement with the external world and have to turn inwards to recharge their batteries. Introverts are people who reflect deeply on life, but as they often have no real need to communicate these thoughts to others, this depth is often hinted at but not fully revealed. The term, 'still waters run deep' was certainly coined to describe introverts.

Like individuals, cultures can and do exhibit a preference for extraversion or introversion – the outer world or the inner world. This is not about numbers in the population who prefer one or the other; it is about which preference has come to dominate within public life and which encapsulates the spirit of the people and their culture. So what is the preference in Scotland? The most obvious thing to say is introversion. After all, the Scots are often thought to be a dour, quiet, rather expressionless people and that seems more in tune with introversion than extraversion. So too does the fact that a frequent and continuing complaint the Scots make about the English is that they talk too loudly in public and too freely. (The Scots generally do not approve of idle chatter on topics of little consequence.) And, of course, the Scots are often portrayed either as an inarticulate people or as a people who prefer to keep their own counsel. I do not personally recognise the inarticulate Scot who has been much written about, but I am fully aware of Scottish reticence. Indeed the Scots are often shy and do not want to draw attention to themselves but that does not mean to say they have a preference for introversion. In fact, I believe the opposite to be true – Scottish culture exhibits a profound preference for extraversion and this preference helps us to understand an essential feature about Scotland.

An Active, Outward-looking People

The Scots have always been an outward-looking people greatly drawn to explore foreign lands. Even in medieval times the Scots were precocious sailors and traders and many Scots established themselves as military advisers to foreign governments. Many became teachers in foreign universities. Before the Union with England, Scotland had great ties to other European nations. For example, thousands of Scots studied at universities in France and the Low Countries. Indeed it is estimated that in the sixteenth century three thousand Scots studied at the University of Leyden alone. The historian and journalist Michael Fry argues that the Scots were the first 'global traders': tobacco, textiles, tea – these and other goods were carried around the world in Scottish ships. In fact, Fry argues that all 'the great Victorian shipping lines' – including Cunard and P&O – had Scottish origins.[1]

Exploring the external world has held such huge appeal to Scots that it seems appropriate that the famous explorer, David Livingstone, was a Scotsman, and the missionary, Mary Slessor, a Scotswoman. And of course the first man to set foot on the moon, Neil Armstrong, is an American Scot. Many of the books on Scotland portray the Scots as wanderers and adventurers and at some point feature some variation on the story of a Scotsman going to the ends of the earth – a Himalayan mountain top, the back streets of Calcutta, a survival hut at the North pole – only to discover that some bloke from Possilpark or Mallaig had not only got there first but had been there so long he was practically a native.

If you read books on Scottish history you will soon see that the Scots traditionally have been 'men of action'. Of course, we have produced our reflective philosophers, scientists and theologians, but Scotland's past demonstrates that the Scots have primarily been great activists. Fighting, exploring, colonising, inventing, engineering, building, preaching, shipbuilding, coal mining – for centuries these have been some of the main types of roles Scots have played in the world. As many of our analysts point out, not only have the Scots been great 'doers' they have also been 'out and about' types.

An 'Energetic' culture

A preference for introversion or extraversion can also be seen in a nation's culture. Nations which prefer introversion, such as Japan, manifest a cultural preference for calm, quiet and solitude. They like things to happen slowly and gracefully. Think about traditional Japanese music and drama (or even their flower arranging) and you will see what I mean. Now compare this with Scotland's traditional music and dance which have a real energy, enthusiasm and vitality about them. As someone once remarked, 'the best way to torture the Scots is to nail their feet to the floor and play a Jimmy Shand record'. Scottish music and dance is exciting – it demands from us an energetic, physical response. In its blend of formal structure, sociability and sheer extraverted energy it captures something fundamental about the Scottish spirit. This energy and sociability is also present in Highland Games, fiddlers' rallies, choirs and pipe bands. The only counterpoint I can think of to all this outward display of energy is the solitary piper and the pibroch, and even in the most extremely extraverted cultures there is still going to be some expression of, and a hankering after, introversion.

The Love of Speech

One of the paradoxical things about Scotland is that, despite these obvious extravert tendencies, the Scots have a reputation for being reticent and inarticulate. Screeds have been written over the years about how the loss of the old Scots tongue and the imposition of English has created a people who are unable to express themselves well, yet, in reality, the Scots are not only drawn to expressing themselves in speech, they are good at it. Preaching, discussing, debating, arguing, declaiming, entertaining – all are ways of communicating that many Scots find deeply attractive and at which they can excel. Scotland has more than its fair share of call centre jobs and so it is often a Scot chatting at the other end of the phone: companies set up in Scotland because a lot of people have the requisite skills. Over the years we have produced some of the United Kingdom's most gifted talkers in the shape of people like the theologian and lecturer

William Barclay, the comedian Billy Connolly, the barrister Helena Kennedy, or any of the numerous orators from the days of Scotland's militant past: John Maclean, Jimmy Maxton or Jimmy Reid. Indeed it is said of Maxton that he addressed more political meetings than any other person in the world. In nineteenth-century Scotland there were also impressive numbers of women orators such as Helen Lockhart Gibson, Jessie Macfarlane, Agnes Walker and A.S. Hamilton. In the present world of politics some of the finest speakers are Scots – Alex Salmond, Nicola Sturgeon, Gordon Brown, Menzies Campbell, Charles Kennedy and Liam Fox. And in the UK's broadcast media, where people have to talk for a living, many of the most successful figures are Scottish – Kirsty Wark, Andrew Marr, Jim Naughtie, Muriel Gray, Kirsty Young, Alan Little, Nicky Campbell, Andrew Neil, Kay Adams and Lorraine Kelly.

The Scots also have a strong oral tradition. Scotland is reputed to have the finest tradition of 'work songs' in Western Europe and both Highland and Lowland cultures have a rich history of folk-song and ballads. This is how James Hogg, the Ettrick Shepherd, described the importance of song when he grew up in the Borders in the late eighteenth century:

> In my young days, we had singing matches almost
> every night . . . song, and song alone, was the sole
> amusement. I never heard any music that thrilled
> my heart half so much as when these nymphs
> joined their voices, all in one key, and sung a slow
> Scottish melody.[2]

The Knoxian Presbyterian tradition, with its emphasis on formal education, encouraged the Scots to respect books and reading but it also played an important part in encouraging the

Scots to love the spoken word. These reformers abolished the ceremonies and displays of the Catholic Church and put 'the word of God' at the centre of religious worship. In the 1930s one churchman argued that this meant the Calvinists had difficulty in creating a religious service:

> Lacking in stately ceremonial, without the glory of the mighty utterances which the spirit of worship had fashioned, divested of impressive ritual and without the dramatic movement of the soul's ascent, without the poetry of devotion. . . It makes its appeal exclusively to the hearing ear. . .[3]

The sermon, which could often be up to three hours long, became the centrepiece of the new Kirk service. Churches were redesigned – in place of an altar was a centrally positioned pulpit where the 'hearers', as the congregation was often called, could listen to God's word. (Pulpits were only moved off centre in the late nineteenth century.) In the past, ministers were expected to extemporise and reading from a manuscript was greatly frowned on. It is commonplace for historians to portray Scottish worshippers as under the thumb of authoritarian ministers, but many a minister in Scotland felt tyrannised by his congregation's demand that he preach off the cuff for hours – notes of any kind were forbidden.

In Jungian terms, speech is the preferred mode of communication for extraverts. Introverts do not have the same need to communicate what is going on in the inner world and if they do decide to communicate many choose to write rather than speak. But in Scotland the extravert impulse is so strong that it even permeates the written word. The literary expert Roderick Watson argues that, from the early eighteenth century on,

Scottish literature shows the Scots' 'national preference for the speech act. . . over the written text, even if that speech is paradoxically written down.'[4] Watson gives numerous examples of how many Scottish literary works heavily rely on vernacular speech and how many Scottish novels use narrators and are essentially speech-based. For example, a number of Robert Louis Stevenson's novels are narrated (*Dr Jekyll and Mr Hyde*, *Kidnapped*, *Catriona*, and *Treasure Island*) as well as other Scottish classics such as James Hogg's *Confessions of a Justified Sinner* and John Galt's *Annals of the Parish*. Many of Burns's poems are addresses and a 'speaking voice' is also much in evidence in some of his famous works such as 'Tam o'Shanter' and 'Holy Willie's Prayer'. Hugh MacDiarmid's great Scottish classic 'A Drunk Man Looks at the Thistle' is also written in the first person. And that quintessentially Scottish novel, *Sunset Song* by Lewis Grassic Gibbon, intertwines the 'speak o'Kinraddie' with Chris Guthrie's interior monologue. Watson notes that the speaking voice is also a device used by contemporary Scottish novelists and poets, such as James Kelman and Tom Leonard, and that this 'oral energy' is even to be found in some of the more formal English texts written by Scots writers such as James Boswell and Thomas Carlyle.

Enlightening Conversations

If we turn to the philosophical types involved in the Scottish Enlightenment we find this same attraction to speech. Many of these figures came up with ground-breaking ideas but they were not rarefied intellectuals cloistered in ivory towers. When historians write about Enlightenment Scotland they describe it as a period characterised by discourse, discussion, debate and conversation. To use modern terminology, we could say that these men (and they were all men) were part of a self-conscious network – they flocked together to talk and learn from one another. And the purpose of this knowledge was not simply to understand the world but to improve on it. David Hume wanted to see philosophy conducted as 'conversation' – as an activity carried out with other people. He placed communication between people as the strongest of all social bonds. This is why Hume declares 'Be a philosopher: but amidst all your philosophy, be still a man.'[5] Indeed Hume and other Scottish Enlightenment figures believed it unwise for intellectuals to abandon the social world and spend too much time in solitary, introverted, reflection.

George Davie, in his book *The Democratic Intellect*, outlines Scotland's distinctive intellectual tradition and shows how, from the late nineteenth century on, the Scottish universities were forced to reorganise themselves along English lines. The Scottish university tradition emphasised the importance of a number of interrelated beliefs. Most relevant here is the belief in the efficacy of a general, rather than a specialist, education. Another is the importance of speech and face-to-face communication. It was the lecture, not individual research or study, which was therefore the keystone of Scotland's traditional universities. The lecture was augmented by 'examination hours' where the professor questioned and debated with students. Indeed Davie maintains that 'the catechising system', based on question and answer, was a central feature of the whole system. And it is for reasons such as these that Davie argues that the 'pedagogical tradition' in Scotland was 'full of energy and vitality'.[6]

All of this was in complete contrast to the values of learning inculcated in the traditional English universities where knowledge was seen as detached from everyday life. Indeed Roger Scruton even argues that 'The further the subject seemed from the day-to-day concerns of the student, the more worthy of study was it held to be'.[7] Over the years Scottish universities have come under increasing pressure to specialise and adopt an English model but vestiges of Scotland's old beliefs still remain. For example, the Scots' emphasis on the importance of generalism means that Scottish school pupils still follow a broader curriculum than those in England – hence the greater number of subjects studied at Higher level in Scotland than at A-level in England. And in the old Scottish universities it is still possible to take a general degree.

The Voice of Scotland

Donald Dewar, Scotland's first First Minister, was a great admirer of the Scottish Enlightenment. Dewar was well-known to be something of a scholar and had a great respect for books but he was a typical Scot in that he paid much more attention to the outer, extravert world than to the inner world. He was an extremely sociable man who loved nothing better than the opportunity to be actively and energetically engaged with others. A man who, on a good day, could be a fine orator. Happily for Scotland, one of the best days for Donald Dewar's oratory was on 1 July 1999 – the opening of the Scottish Parliament. In his role as First Minister, Dewar spoke for the Scottish people and in some passages of his address he encapsulated, as no-one has ever done before, the importance of speech to the Scots:

> This is about more than our politics and our laws.
> This is about who we are, how we carry ourselves.
> There is a new voice in the land, the voice of a

democratic Parliament. A voice to shape Scotland
as surely as the echoes of our past:
the shout of the welder in the great Clyde shipyards;
the speak of the Mearns, with its soul in the land;
the discourse of the Enlightenment, when
Edinburgh and Glasgow were a light held to the
intellectual life of Europe;
the wild cry of the Great Pipes;
and back to the distant cries of the battles of Bruce
and Wallace.[8]

Despite his position as a public figure, Donald Dewar was a reserved man. He did not like fuss or being in the limelight unless there was a good reason. Nor did he like talking in public unless he had something worthwhile to say. He was a shy, contained extravert and, in this respect, he admirably typifies a common Scottish inclination.

Unfortunately, many commentators have seized on this shy, reticent quality in the Scots and labelled them introverts. In the process they have failed to grasp an essential features of Scottishness – the importance of the external world, the sociability and the love of activity and speech. Sometimes our commentators have noted the reserve and the sociability and then used this as evidence of Scottish 'schizophrenia'. It is slightly unusual and quirky for extraverts to eschew the limelight in the way the Scots often do, but there is certainly nothing pathological or 'schizophrenic' about it.

A Calvinist Legacy

Writing this book has taught me one simple lesson about Scotland – it is almost impossible to say anything about Scottish culture or character without making constant reference to the influence of the Kirk. And it is difficult not to conclude that the extravert nature of Scottish life is to a large extent the product of Presbyterianism. Some religions, most notably Eastern religions like Buddhism, encourage individuals to turn inwards – they believe that individuals must look within themselves to find God. This is why isolation and prolonged periods of meditation are part of the religious practices of most Eastern religions and why these cultures often have a profoundly reflective quality. Christianity is a religion which encourages its followers to look outwards to find God. In this scheme, God is in every fibre of the external world. Some versions of Christianity stress that God also lies within all of us, but Calvinism, believing as it does in the monstrous nature of human beings, does not make much of the notion that God is to be found in the human heart (or any other part of the vile, loathsome body we all inhabit). Indeed Calvinism, the religious belief system which most influenced the Scottish way of Christianity, believes that it is dangerous for people to spend time idly for 'the Devil makes work for idle hands and idle minds'. So Scotland's religion is not simply a religion which stresses the importance of hearing God's word, it also incites its believers to action.

Strengths and Weaknesses

Scottish culture's preference for the extravert rather than the introvert world has led to some distinctive features and to marked strengths and weaknesses. As we have already observed, the essential characteristics of Scotland's culture are the strong oral tradition, the love of debate and discussion, and sociability. The Scots at their best are energetic, lively people who want to act on the world stage. By nature they are 'doers' rather than observers. The downside of this activity and attention to the outer world is that there is little about Scotland or the Scots which you could describe as 'deep'. The Scots are not a people noted for acute sensitivity; creative or imaginative thinking; spirituality; or literary insight. Such skills are more likely to be acquired by people who prefer to spend time in the inner, introvert realm – a world which the Scots, as a result of the cultural preference for extraversion, are not encouraged to inhabit. Of course, many individual Scots have a preference for introversion and some have given to the world the insights from their inner reflections – Hugh MacDiarmid and Edwin Muir are undoubtedly two such examples – but somehow they are going against the grain of Scottish life, as Scottish beliefs and culture encourage activity and speech rather than deep reflection.

A Balancing Act

Jung's theory of types is complex because he argues it is important for the psyche to balance itself. Extraversion and introversion are essential aspects of human life. Extraverts will still be drawn to introvert, though they will not do it as often, and introverts will still want to extravert. We can see this balancing mechanism at work in Japan – a culture with a pronounced preference for introversion. Japanese culture encourages its people to cultivate their inner world and to hold back on communication with others. For example, the Japanese believe that it is childlike for someone to make his or her wishes known directly in speech and they greatly favour indirect, subtle, non-verbal forms of communication. Japanese culture in this and other ways makes a virtue of privacy. Japan also encourages people not to draw attention to themselves. But, according to Jung, the impulse to extravert cannot be repressed too much and it will find an outlet. In Japan one of the bizarre ways

Japanese extraversion is expressed is in Karaoke bars, where normally quiet and reserved people make an exhibition of themselves.

So what is the equivalent of Karaoke for the Scots? There appear to be three main avenues of introvert expression in Scotland. One is 'the Lone Shieling Complex' – the urban Scot's fascination with remote crofts, misty mountains and solitary pipers. A second avenue is the Scots' predilection for secrets. In the present permissive age this is less apparent than formerly, but countless commentators have remarked that the Scots, despite their outward principles and piety, were a nation of secret drinkers and fornicators. Secrets are still at the root of that other great and enduring Scottish pastime – guilt. For Catholics, these guilty secrets can be expunged in the privacy of the confessional box, but for Presbyterians and atheists in Scotland there is no obvious outlet for them and they can be likened to a stagnant river which makes its presence felt on the edge of Scottish life, seeping here and there into literature.

And finally, there is Sabbatarianism. Historically, Presbyterians in Scotland believed that nothing should be done on a Sunday other than reading the Bible or worshipping the Lord. Sabbatarian practices are still to be seen in parts of Scotland, most notably in some areas of the Highlands and Islands. Sabbatarian beliefs were not part of the first phase of Scotland's Reformation but when they did arrive they gripped the country with a vengeance. Silence and stillness descended across most areas of the country. Even young children were stopped from playing. Although there is nothing exclusively Scottish about Sabbatarianism – the English, under the Puritan Oliver Cromwell, were strict observers of the Sabbath – it is true to say that

Sabbatarianism gripped Scotland as a country tighter, and for longer, than other Protestant nations. One possible explanation for this vice-like grip is that the reformers realised that their religion of action was going against the grain of human life; that reflection, stillness, even idleness, were essential human needs and that the fulfilment of these needs should not be left to individuals but had to be controlled by the church. So the Kirk dictated to the Scottish people that they should spend time one day a week in quiet contemplation and reflection.

Introvert and Extravert Nations

Most Western cultures display a preference for extraversion and most Eastern cultures a preference for introversion. This is why Western cultures believe that self-confident, well-adjusted individuals should be assertive and good communicators. So is my claim that Scotland is an extravert culture little more than the obvious statement that she is part of Western culture? I believe I am saying something substantially more than that for one simple reason – nations, like individual extraverts them-selves, vary in their strength of preference. Some extraverts are indeed the life and soul of the party; they talk a lot, and spend almost all their time with people. But there are other extraverts whose preference is far less marked and who try to maintain more balance in their lives. Italy and the Republic of Ireland are two countries where the preference for extraversion is a significant feature of the culture. A cultural preference for extraversion is less obvious in France as the French are much more reserved and laconic. So what about the English?

In his highly acclaimed book, *The English – Portrait of a People*, Jeremy Paxman never uses the word 'introvert' when describing the English but on almost every page the portrait he paints is of a people with a strong preference for introversion. Not only does he point out, as many commentators before him, 'the insularity' of the English, he also argues that historically they were 'inclined to see the rest of Europe as nothing but trouble'.[9] Paxman also describes the English as having a 'natural reticence' and being a 'diffident' and 'reserved' people with a 'curious reluctance to engage with one another'.[10] The critic Roger Scruton makes similar points in his book about England claiming that traditionally 'English society was a society of strangers, who kept each other at a distance'.[11] Both writers argue that 'privacy' is very important to the English. Paxman quotes many foreigners' views on the English and claims that most believe the English are 'impossible to get to know'. For example a nineteenth-century visitor to England maintained:

> If you remark to an Englishman, in a smoking
> compartment, that he has dropped some cigar-ash
> on his trousers, he will probably answer: 'For the
> past ten minutes I have seen a box of matches on
> fire in your back coat pocket, but I did not
> interfere with you for that.'[12]

Kate Fox goes even further in her book *Watching the English* arguing that 'social dis-ease' is 'the central "core" of Englishness'. She sums it up as 'our lack of social ease, discomfort and incompetence in the field (minefield) of social interaction.' She elaborates that this can be seen in the 'embarrassment, insularity, awkwardness, perverse obliqueness, emotional constipation, fear of intimacy and general inability to engage in a normal and straightforward fashion with other human beings.'[13] Indeed Fox argues that the English find ordinary social interaction outwith the home so difficult that they need rules or various ploys to facilitate it – mainly games, clubs and societies, pubs and drink. She also thinks the difficulty with social intercourse accounts for much of the unattractive underbelly of English culture:

> When we feel uncomfortable in social situations (that is, most of the time) we either become over-polite, buttoned up and awkwardly restrained or loud, loutish, crude, violent and generally obnoxious. Both our famous 'English reserve' and our infamous 'English hooliganism' are symptoms of this social dis-ease, as is our obsession with privacy.[14]

All these commentators on England make virtually no reference to geographical differences. Yet, at least from a Scottish perspective, the reticence which they describe is much more evident in the 'home counties' as many of those from the North – Geordies and Liverpudlians, for example – seem positively garrulous and are much friendlier than they seem to allow. However, the fact that the spirit and character of England has been defined largely by the upper classes in the south means that there is a prevailing sense in England that somehow it is vulgar and common to be over-friendly.

What is clear is that the English do not share the Scots' cultural fascination with talk and speech. These commentators all argue that the English are obsessed by 'the word' but it is the written word they mean, not the spoken word. In that quintessential English institution – the Civil Service – people will sit feet away from one another yet still prefer to communicate by memo, or nowadays by email, rather than speak.

The descriptions of the English advanced by critics such as

Paxman, Scruton and Fox are of a rather dull, inactive people enthralled by peace and tranquillity. It is a land of Elgar and Vaughan Williams rather than Jimmy Shand and pipe bands. What's more, the images the English use of their own country are of a quiet, reflective land. 'Somehow the English mind,' writes Paxman 'kept alive the idea that the soul of England lay in the countryside'.[15] John Major, the former Conservative Prime Minister, defined England as 'the country of long shadows on county grounds, warm beer, invincible green suburbs, dog lovers, and – as George Orwell said – old maids bicycling to holy communion through the morning mist. And. . . Shakespeare . . .'[16] Major was in fact trying to define Britain in these terms, not just England, but there is no way that any Scot could identify with such a picture.

I am not seriously arguing that England is an introverted culture along the lines of Eastern countries like Japan, but I believe there is a moderate preference for introversion in England. Comparing Scotland and England in this way brings into focus an important truth about Scotland – she is a nation with a strong preference for the outer, extravert world.

It is important to remember that the application of the concepts of introversion and extraversion to Scotland or any other nation is not about numbers of people in the population with that preference. It is about whether one of these preferences has, for whatever reason, come to be expressed more within that nation's culture. It is about the spirit and character of a people as a whole and we can see that Scotland and her southerly neighbour could not, in this respect, be more different.

Psychological type is, however, only a broad framework – a

template to understand the pattern of growth and development an individual, or a nation, chooses. But it does not tell us everything we need to know to develop a full understanding. The types of preferences which Scotland has cultivated are similar to America's, for example. Many commentators have noted some similarities between the two countries, but there are also profound differences. To understand an individual fully we need to know not just about their type preferences, but also about their upbringing, religious beliefs and education. And, of course, all individuals are greatly affected by the various things which happen to them in life. In other words, as nations or individuals we are to a large extent shaped, not just by our preferences, but also by our experiences.

Notes

1 Michael Fry *The Scottish Empire* (Tuckwell Press and Birlinn: Edinburgh, 2001)

2 James Hogg 'On the Changes and Habits, Amusements and Conditions of the Scottish Peasantry' in Judy Steel (ed.) *A Shepherd's Delight: A James Hogg Anthology* (Canongate Publishing: Edinburgh, 1985), p.41

3 Quoted in 'Worship Since 1920' in Duncan Forrester and Douglas Murray (eds.) *Studies in the History of Worship in Scotland* (T. & T. Clark: Edinburgh, 1984), p.157

4 Roderick Watson 'Dialects of "Voice" and "Place": Literature in Scots and English from 1700' in Paul H. Scott, *Scotland: A Concise Cultural History* (Mainstream Publishing: Edinburgh, 1993), p.99

5 David Hume *An Enquiry Concerning Human Understanding*, p.1

6 George Davie *The Democratic Intellect* (Edinburgh University Press: Edinburgh, 1961), p.19

7 Roger Scruton *England: An Elegy* (Pimlico: London, 2001), p.168

8 *The Donald Dewar Collection* (Stationery Office: Edinburgh, 2004)

9 Jeremy Paxman *The English: A Portrait of a People* (Penguin Books: London), p.31

10 Ibid., p.116

11 Roger Scruton *England: An Elegy*, p.54

12 Quoted in Jeremy Paxman *The English: A Portrait of a People* p.116

13 Kate Fox *Watching the English* (Hodder: London, 2005), p.401

14 *Ibid*, pp.401-2

15 Jeremy Paxman, *The English*, p.147

16 Speech to the Conservative Group for Europe, 22 April 1993. Quoted in David McCrone, Angela Morris & Richard Kiely *Scotland – the Brand: The Making of Scottish Heritage* (Polygon: Edinburgh, 1999), pp. 23-24

6. My Brother's Keeper

They will not leave me, the lives of other people.
I wear them near my eyes like spectacles.

Douglas Dunn, *The Hunched*

'Scotland is highly individualistic. Individualistic cultures tend to be more focused on individualistic achievement and gains than the betterment of the group.' This is how students at DePauw University, Indiana, describe Scotland in their internet based 'Cultural Portfolio Project'. They add: 'It is obvious that Scotland is highly individualistic because of the significant numbers of discoveries and inventions attributed to their culture.'[1]

In their comments on Scotland these students are consciously employing the 'individual-collective' dimension of Geert Hoftede's work on national cultures.[2] However, what they write on Scottish individualism is simply conjecture. Nonetheless it is reasonable to assume that Scotland is individualistic in Hofstede's classification as the vast majority of advanced, industrialised nations, including Scandinavian countries, score high on individualism. According to Hofstede's empirical research, Great Britain scores third highest in the world for individualism after Australia and the United States.

This evidence on English individualism is corroborated by

commentators on the country. For example, Jeremy Paxman in his book *The English* calls one of his chapters 'Home Alone' and argues that the English are a people with a 'curious reluctance to engage with one another'.[3] He also asserts that they are greatly motivated by individuality and individual rights. Indeed Paxman states, 'If I had to list those qualities of the English which most impress me . . . I think I would praise most this sense of "I know my rights".'[4] Roger Scruton likewise argues that traditionally the English 'were individualists who prized the rights and privacy and freedom of the individual above all political gifts'.[5]

England's individualism is often attributed to her Protestant heritage, early industrialisation and the development of a market economy at the end of the middle ages. But the historian Alan Macfarlane in his book *The Origins of English Individualism* takes issue with this widespread notion that it largely results from such economic and cultural developments. His reading of English history leads him to argue:

> . . . the majority of ordinary people in England
> from at least the thirteenth century were rampant
> individualists, highly mobile both geographically
> and socially, economically 'rational', market-
> oriented and acquisitive, ego-centred in kinship
> and social life.[6]

In other words, according to Macfarlane, long before the industrial revolution community played little part in English life, and social ties were weak. In this respect, England was quite unlike her neighbours or other countries in Europe and Asia. Only the English colonies were soon to display this degree of individualism.

And what of Scotland? Of course, Scotland is a highly individualistic society and has been since the Reformation, the advent of urbanisation, and the development of a market economy. There's little doubt that, following the Union, Scottish culture was greatly influenced by the practices and beliefs of its southern neighbour. But nonetheless, as we shall see, Scotland's individualism is muted by some strong collectivist impulses. In a later chapter on enterprise we shall examine Scotland's attitude to the state and what some call her 'dependency culture'. Here we confine ourselves to looking at various undercurrents in Scottish culture which encourage a collectivist stance and take the edge off Scottish individualism.

Scotland's legendary clan system may seem like a good place to start as it embodies what Hofestede identifies as the core of collectivist cultures – lifelong loyalty to an in-group. But I am not going to look at this for two reasons. First the clan system is a huge topic in its own right which I cannot do justice to here. Second, the clans mainly operated in the Highlands and this way of life was fatally eroded by developments in the eighteenth century, particularly the emergence of market forces and the clan chiefs' increasing interest in making a profit from their lands, thus weakening social ties. In other words, economic individualism undermined the Highlands' traditional, collective way of life. The clan system was further weakened by the determination of both England, and Lowland Scotland, to eliminate the Jacobite clans following the 1745 rebellion. Of course, the clan system lives on, but largely as a tourist attraction or sub-culture, and not, to my mind, in a way that has influenced mainstream Scottish thinking.

The Collectivist Mentality of the Presbyterian Church

Presbyterianism is often thought to be a deeply individualistic and democratic religion. It places each man and woman in charge of his or her own spiritual destiny, for unlike Catholicism there is no intermediary between an individual and God, and no hierarchy. But this individualism is kept in check by much stronger group values. For example, *The Book of Discipline* clearly states:

> . . . no one may be permitted to live as best pleaseth him within the Church of God; but every man must be constrained by fraternal admonition and correction to bestow his labours when of the Church they are required, to the edification of others.[7]

John Knox and his followers made much of the importance of hard work, but this is to be channelled, at least some of the time, towards the social good and not just be used for the betterment of an individual or his or her family. Even the rich and powerful 'may not be permitted to suffer their children to spend their youth in vain idleness'. Instead they must be 'compelled to dedicate their sons . . . to the profit of the Church and to the Commonwealth'.[8] As we have seen earlier, *The Book of Discipline* set out elaborate measures for the education of all, including the poorest members of society. It also exhorts everyone to 'have respect to the poor brethren, the labourers and manurers of the ground' and states that the poor should be catered for out of parish funds. This did not happen, but from the intention we can see that Knox's religious ideology is essentially antagonistic to American-style Calvinism which does not see the poor as the responsibility of society at large. Even the nineteenth century influential Scottish Church leader,

Thomas Chalmers, who was opposed to state handouts for the poor, argued strongly in favour of community support and urged the rich to honour their responsibilities to less fortunate members of society.

If we go on and look at other aspects of Church organisation in Scotland we shall see that its collectivist values have had both a positive and negative legacy. Positive because they encourage us to acknowledge our social responsibility and negative because they have encouraged conformity and strict social control.

Prying and Spying

The Book of Discipline encouraged the elders and parishioners to watch the behaviour of the minister, his wife and family, to ensure they acted with propriety and set a good example. The minister and neighbouring ministers were likewise to observe the elders. And the parishioners were to keep a careful watch on one another. As Notestein observes, the Scottish Church reformers:

> . . . organised the censoring of behaviour so that even trivial faults were a matter for criticism. They put a premium on spying. They arranged for continuous moral judgements. . . They raised the scrutiny of one's fellows to a public virtue.[9]

So paradoxically while *The Book of Discipline* elevated the role of ordinary parishioners in the running of the Church, the Kirk session ultimately became complete master of the individual parishioner, for it took on the role of regulating the behaviour of all its congregation.

Knox's scheme for the denunciation of misconduct was

indeed introduced in Scotland. How much people ate and drank, the kind of clothes they wore, the words they used, how they treated the poor, their sexual behaviour, and what they did on a Sunday – all came under legitimate public scrutiny. In *The Social Life of Scotland in the Eighteenth Century* a cleric writes of officers, beadles and deacons:

> There was not a place where one was free from
> their inquisitorial intrusion. They might enter any
> house and even pry into the rooms. In towns
> where the patrol of elders or deacons, beadle and
> officers, paced with solemnity the deserted cause-
> way eagerly eyeing every door and window,
> craning their necks up every close and lane, the
> people slunk into the obscurity of shadows and
> kept hushed silence.[10]

In the Catholic Church, discipline is mainly achieved through private confessional, supported on occasion with public rebukes or excommunication. In Knox's reformed religion this was reversed. *The Book of Discipline* allows for transgressions, which were not widely known to be dealt with in private Kirk sessions, but more commonly, alleged sinners were called before the minister, elders and congregation. The celebrated social historian, T.C. Smout tells us that for sexual misdemeanours the sinner was:

> . . . forced to stand dressed in sackcloth, bare-
> headed and bare-footed, first at the kirk door and
> then on the public stool of repentance in front of
> the congregation on every Sunday for six months
> or occasionally for several years, and sometimes by
> whipping and fining as well.[11]

Many of the sinners treated in this way were young woman

accused of fornication. Indeed as women were excluded from Church governance until the end of the nineteenth century, such discipline was always imposed by men and women were often the recipients.

The system of discipline did, however, allow for repentance. If the sinner did repent (and most did) he or she could be admonished. Unrepentant sinners could be excommunicated and in that case no one, except their immediate family, was allowed to talk or have any dealings with the sinner. Fines and excommunications initiated by the Church were backed by the civil authorities. For example, people who had been excommunicated were not allowed to give witness in court or hold land. The Kirk's power over the population was so great in eighteenth-century Scotland that anyone wanting to move from one parish to another required a 'testificate' from the minister certifying the person's good behaviour.

The Church authorities also used prying to ensure the people of Scotland observed the Sabbath. People could even be censured for 'idly gazing out of windows'. A minute from the Edinburgh Kirk session of 1727 describes how each session was instructed 'to take its turn in watching the streets on Sabbath . . . and to visit each suspected house . . . and to pass through the streets and reprove such as transgress and inform on such as do not refrain.'[12] Again people could be referred to the Civil Magistrates for punishment.

The Kirk had other ways of enforcing conformity. For example, the session appointed the parish school teacher and inspected their school and teaching methods. The Church also influenced the universities. As Smout shows, its reach and power was enormous:

The emphasis in every home and school on repeating and understanding the catechism impressed on every child the importance of holding the right belief. Since justification was by faith and faith must be orthodox, orthodoxy was a prerequisite for salvation. On the other hand, by believing in the priesthood of all believers the Calvinist also stressed that every man must find his own way to God in his innermost thoughts and prayers. But this required the individual to become a reflective and intellectual being, with all the dangers that he might reach an independent and unorthodox conclusion about God. To guard against this it was doubly necessary for the church courts to detect and call to heel a deviant before he imperilled his own soul and began to infect those of the rest of the flock.[13]

But for most modern Scots, the most significant reminder of the prying times comes via Robert Burns, himself a victim of such denunciation for his frequent sins of fornication. And, of course, Burns openly attacked the Church for such practices in his poems. In the 'Address to the Unco Guid' he writes:

O ye wha are sae guid yoursel,
Sae pious and sae holy,
Ye've nought to do but mark and tell
Your neebours' faut and folly.

Interestingly it is claimed that the Pre-Reformation Scot was also extremely interested in other people's business. For example, Notestein reports that even before Knox's time, the Scots were intensely curious about people and what they were doing. Indeed he thinks the Scottish curiosity about others is surely 'one of the most in-born Scottish traits'. He maintains that Scottish epics and ballads show the Scots always interested in other people's business and trying to find out more by asking questions. And Notestein, an American who has the benefit of perspective, adds:

> Here we may recognise the modern Scot who talks to one on railway trains and asks questions, often personal questions which the traveller not used to Scotland might resent. The Scot has long been interested in the stranger as well as in his neighbour, his place of living, his status in life, his occupation, and his success in it. He can hardly be turned aside from making inquiries.[14]

Countless other foreigners make similar points about the Scots. For example, Buckle maintained the Scots have 'a love of inquiring into the opinions of others, and of interfering with them, such as is hardly anywhere else to be found'.[15] Some share Buckle's view that the Scots' penchant for making inquiries is sinister; others put it down to friendliness. But, undoubtedly, the interest in others can amount to nosiness and can have a sinister aspect when it is twinned, as it often is, by that other Scottish trait, critical judgement – a point we return to later.

The Importance of Others

During the Scottish Enlightenment various Scots contributed greatly to understanding individual human beings better. David Hume's pursuit of 'the science of man' led him to look closely at the way the human mind engaged with the world. Thomas Reid, the philosopher of 'Common Sense' also looked inwards to see how the mind constructed reality. And the type of individualism which was ultimately to triumph in the United

States owed some of its thinking to Scottish Enlightenment figures. But one of the lasting legacies of these Scots is the creation of 'social' science. Indeed one of the key hallmarks of Scottish philosophy during this period is its emphasis on the social. This can be seen clearly in the Scots intellectuals' attitude to the evolution of the social and political order. English theorists such as Thomas Hobbes and John Locke believed that people had once lived as isolated, warring individuals in a 'state of nature'. This gave rise to Hobbes's famous claim that life for humankind was 'nasty, brutish and short'. The Scots were not impressed by such a line of argument, claiming it was ahistorical and simply did not correspond to the reality of human existence – at all times and in all parts of the world people had lived, not as individuals but as part of communities.[16]

As these thinkers were social theorists they were also interested in morality. Adam Smith has been claimed by the radical right in Britain and they have even set up a right-wing think tank in his name. The former Conservative Secretary of State for Scotland Michael Forsyth was a founding member. But Smith is no American-style individualistic thinker. He too stresses the importance of people as social beings and maintained that sympathy with one's fellow creatures is at the very core of society and morality itself.

'How selfish so ever man may be supposed,' wrote Smith 'there are evidently some principles in his nature which interest him in the fortune of others, and render their happiness necessary to him, though he derives nothing from it except the pleasure of seeing it'.[17] Smith went further and argued that the regulation of a person's behaviour is achieved because he/she has a sense of 'an impartial spectator' within. This spectator is 'the man within the breast, the great judge and arbiter' – a judge we consult on the right and wrongs of our actions. So, according to Smith, even our conscience is guided by others.

Another source, or example, of Scots collectivism concerns housing. Research carried out by Hofstede and others shows that people living in countries with high individualism scores are more likely than those with low scores 'to live in detached houses versus apartments or flats.' [18] What is interesting about this finding is that over the years various commentators have noticed differences in the English and Scottish approach to housing. For example, the Scottish thinker Patrick Geddes, the father of town planning, argued in *Cities and Evolution*, published in 1915 that 'ordinary old-fashioned English readers' will find it difficult to understand the Scottish approach to housing because the English were brought up with the 'national idea . . . of homes as separate houses, of each family with its own bit of ground, at least its yard, however small'.[19] In the Scotland of Geddes's day, by contrast, in both the cities and many burghs, over half the population were housed in tenements – an extremely communal form of living. In the majority of tenements it was common for members of a family to share one room (the 'single end') and for families to live side by side, sharing washing and sometimes cooking facilities. As shared toilets were commonplace many Scottish families did not even have the most rudimentary privacy and people often lived literally 'cheek to cheek' with neighbours. In such a set-up, getting on with the folks over the landing, and what they thought of you, must have loomed large in everyone's lives.

We may not be as aware of the underlying collectivist feature of Scottish housing today for the very reason that much of our housing policy has been 'Anglicised'. The social and economic historian Richard Rodger argues that once Scotland's momentum on slum clearance got underway in the 1920s the underlying design of the new council housing did not continue in Scotland's urban tradition of tenements, communal facilities or urban density which allowed for local shops and facilities. Indeed Scottish housing was forced to comply with English, largely individualistic, cultural norms:

> The dominant housing ideology was based on garden-city principles and influenced by English middle-class suburban values. Curved perspective and cul-de-sacs, open spaces and low building densities, broken building lines, rustic aspects, and individual garden plots were the crucial characteristics of garden-suburb design.[20]

The Thatcher Legacy

In recent times the Scots have become more aware of the collectivist, as opposed to, individualist, side of their value system thanks to the English – or, more specifically, to Margaret Thatcher. Ironically, it was the detested Iron Lady who helped the Scots define their values and emphasise some basic differences with the English. It was the programme and ideology of her Governments which gave a huge boost to Scottish nationalist sentiments. It is not difficult to see why.

Thatcher was a convert to American individualistic ideology and her guru was the American right-wing ideologue Milton Friedman. So strong was her attachment to the value of the individual, Thatcher went so far as to claim that 'there is no such thing as society'.[21] In 1988 she came to Scotland and addressed the General Assembly of the Church of Scotland. In her speech, now commonly known as the 'sermon on the Mound', she set out her belief in individualism and tried to link her ideology with Christian values. The ministers were not impressed. Indeed the Moderator promptly presented her with two Church reports on poverty and housing and urged her to study them carefully. It was her turn to be unimpressed. She had long harboured the view that the Scots had a dependency culture and had to be made to stand on their own two feet again. Erroneously, she thought this completely in line with the views of Adam Smith.

During her second term of office Margaret Thatcher's attempt to roll back the powers of the state and 'free' the individual were in full throttle. The Thatcher Government decided to abolish local rates, levied on property, and introduce instead a 'community charge', or 'poll tax'. Many Scots were outraged that a government, with no electoral mandate in Scotland, was muscling through a policy which ran against the grain of Scottish values. Here was a government who did not believe in society, putting a tax on democracy itself and taking little account of householders' ability to pay. Of course, the issue was not as clear-cut as that. The rating system itself was unfair, leading to a single-member household paying the same as the house next door occupied by five adults. But no matter, the Thatcher Government was seen to have attacked fundamental Scottish values. Anti-poll tax campaigns followed. Martyrs, like Tommy Sheridan who was jailed for his protests, became heroes.

The Scottish writer and novelist William McIlvanney was one of Thatcherism's most eloquent opponents. In an address to the SNP in 1987 he claimed that the Thatcher Government was unlike any other:

> . . . we have never, in my lifetime, until now had a
> government whose basic principles were so utterly
> against the most essential traditions and
> aspirations of Scottish life. We have never until
> now had a government so determined to unpick
> the very fabric of Scottish life and make it over into
> something quite different . . . Under this
> government, it is not only the quality of our
> individual lives that it is threatened. It is our
> communal sense of our own identity.[22]

Aspects of the Tories' policies were publicly condemned in Scotland but embraced by individual Scots. Council house sales, for example, proved popular with tenants. In Scotland 54 per cent of the population lived in council houses in 1979, when the Tories came to power, and this had fallen to 38.8 per cent in 1991 – much of this drop was to due to the Government sales policy. But despite the popularity of some of Margaret Thatcher's policies, the Tories' belief that individuals should cultivate their own lives and not think about the community or their responsibility to others was ultimately the rock on which the Party subsequently foundered in Scotland. Many civic, political and religious leaders in Scotland, such as Canon Kenyon Wright, led the charge against what they saw as 'an alien ideology' being imposed on Scotland by the New Right. They believed the only way Scotland could preserve her traditional ways of thought was by a measure of self-government. And so the Constitutional Convention and a successful campaign for devolved powers was born. Despite a solid tradition of Conservative support in Scotland (the Tories had 36 Scottish MPs in 1955), not one Tory MP was elected to the Westminster Parliament in 1997. In General Elections since then, the most they have achieved is one seat.

This prevailing sense of everybody's life being inextricably bound up with others is what I most like about the Scots view of the world. And it seems to shape the thinking of just about everyone who grew up in Scotland. Even Andrew Carnegie who acquired millions as an entrepreneur in America's highly individualist culture, believed that anyone who made money had a moral duty to spend it for the common good. By the time of his death in 1919 he had given away £325 million. In modern Scotland there is no shortage of people who have made something of their lives and who feel a great need to do something for the commonweal. Undoubtedly this is what motivated Tom Hunter to fund a business school at Strathclyde University or Ann Gloag, who made millions running buses, to charter hospital ships to treat poor children from the third world.

But there is also a dark side to the Scots' belief in people's lives being intertwined with others.

Gossip and Censure

The penitence stool is a thing of the past and the days of Church elders peering in your windows to see if you were observing the Sabbath are long gone but some of the old mentality remains. In Scotland there is still a strong sense that little is private and that we live under the gaze of others. Where we choose to live, how we make and spend money, how we dress, where we send our children to school, what we believe – are all part of the public realm in Scotland. Gossip is an important feature of Scottish life which has featured in many novels, and what is gossip if it is not an excessive interest in other people's business and a lack of respect for their privacy? The mentality which is still evident in Scottish life could be summed up in three words: 'my brother's keeper'. Yes, in Scotland we still act as if other people's business is public property and we are adept at doing two things: first keeping a watchful eye on others so that we know what they are up to and, second, being prepared to judge, criticise and censure their behaviour if we think it is warranted.

The Scots have a well-practised habit of finding out what others are up to and then criticising them or condemning them for it. Try eavesdropping, if you do not already indulge, on other people's conversations. Read Scottish novels and see how often authors present gossip as a central feature of community life. 'The speak o' Kinraddie' in Lewis Grassic Gibbon's *A Scots Quair* is a perfect example of this. Writing about nineteenth-century Scotland, Sydney and Olive Checkland pointed out 'that Scottish specialism, "pawky" humour.' And they add, 'This was a dry, sly, cynical affair, never far from the frailties of neighbours and colleagues'.[23] Much of this criticism of others' behaviour is not said directly to the person's face and often happens behind the person's back.

If you are unconvinced of this sense of public intrusion into private lives, spend a few weeks reading the letters pages to Scottish newspapers and you will soon see what I mean. For example, in the midst of an acrimonious correspondence in *The Herald* about 'Nimbys' and wind farms, one man felt prompted to write: 'I have been married for 30 years and have two children, one grandchild, a dog, a cat, a mortgage on my ex-council house, and I consider myself to be happy.' Another included in his reply, 'Oh, and by the way, we do have a small conservatory, but my wife's "burr" comes not from coffee clubs, but from Castle Douglas – dear me, another "monied area".'[24]

The tendency to pry and criticise creates a culture which gives other people power over you and your actions. It is no coincidence that Adam Smith argued that our conscience is even dictated by other people – 'by the spectator within'. Nor is it any coincidence that one of Robert Burns's most quoted poems, 'To a Louse', deals with the issue of observing others and making judgements on them. In this poem Burns famously wrote 'oh wad some Power the giftie gie us/to see oursels as ithers see us!'. Judging from how often these lines are quoted in Scotland it is a sentiment which the Scots hold dear.

Little of this is as evident in English life. If anything the English are seen as lacking interest in other people. Paxman, however, argues that this does not suggest 'indifference', as some people claim, but illustrates what he sees as 'one of the country's informing principles' – the love of 'privacy'.[25] South of the Tweed 'an Englishman's home is his castle', for the English, by all accounts, believe passionately that they should be able to 'please themselves in their own lives'. There is also a great resentment at being 'overlooked and controlled'. At one point Paxman even argues that the English dream is 'privacy without loneliness'.[26] Scruton, too, stresses the importance of privacy and argues that in England, traditionally, there was no more valuable freedom 'than the freedom to close a door'.[27] 'The great English characteristic is the ability to leave you alone, to let you live your own life,' is how one man summed it up in Harry Reid's book on England.[28]

The Tyranny of Public Opinion

The combination of the Scots' strong preference for extra-version, the importance of community and the experience of

Presbyterianism, particularly its reliance on prying as a form of religious control and its system of public punishment, means that the Scots are overly concerned about what other people think of them. Over the years some discerning visitors to Scotland have observed this fact. In the early nineteenth century an English commercial traveller observed:

> A cautious reserve appears to pervade the breast of
> every Scotsman; he answers a question as if he
> were undergoing a cross-examination; the
> mysterious habit grows upon him, till he makes a
> secret of things which it would do him no manner
> of harm although all the world knew them.[29]

Notestein also remarked that, given their history, it is no wonder that the Scots became 'sensitive to public opinion'. Ronald Mavor, son of the playwright James Bridie, also observed that 'a holy dread of what the neighbours may say' does little to encourage young artists in Scotland.[30]

It is more common, however, for commentators on the Scots not to notice this fear of what others may think and to claim instead that the Scot is a great 'individualist'. It is not too difficult to understand why the Scots can, on the surface, appear individualistic. There are two basic reasons why people choose to toe the line, conform and let others' opinions of them rule what they say and do. The first is that a person can be genuinely concerned to maintain harmony in their personal relationships. They are keen to curry others' favour; they do not want others to think badly of them as people; and they do not want to upset others or offend them in any way. The second reason why people may conform to accepted forms of behaviour is that they are worried they may make a mistake or are seen to be 'wrong' and so make a fool of themselves. They may also be concerned that their conduct may lead others to denounce or damn them in some way. And it is this second type of fear which tends to have the upper hand in Scotland.

In other words, it is not fear of disharmony and giving offence to others but the fear of 'getting it wrong' which is likely to keep people in check in Scotland. If we examine the occasions when Scots do take a stand and appear 'individualistic' we shall see that it is when they are operating on fairly 'safe' Scottish ground – they are being sceptical of something which appears illogical or unproven; they are arguing from first principles; or they are arguing on the basis of a fairly well-defined Scottish value such as equality or democracy. So, with a strong 'Scottish' wind at his or her back, a Scot will often appear bolshie or individualistic. Indeed the temptation to channel arguments into fairly safe, uncontentious territory helps us to understand why Scots often acquire the reputation for being pedants and nitpickers – people who argue about fine print and detail, rather than big issues. It is a courageous Scot indeed who battles against the prevailing wind of Scottish public opinion. Hence my claim that Scottish individualism is tempered by enduring collectivist beliefs and practices.

In a culture which elevates others' opinions in this way, and which has a tendency to sit in judgement on other people's behaviour, we are all tacitly encouraged from birth to be somewhat fearful of drawing attention to ourselves. Having the spotlight upon you is dangerous because it leaves you open to scrutiny and criticism. Like Scots in the days described earlier by a cleric, we still have a tendency 'to slink into shadows and keep hushed silence'.

Notes

1 Retrieved from http://academic.depauw.edu/mkfinney_web/
teaching/Com227/culturalPortfolios/SCOTLAND/
TypologiesPage.html

2 Geert Hofstede, Gert Jan Hofstede, Michael Minkov *Cultures
and Organizations: Software of the Mind* (McGraw Hill:
USA, 2010).

3 Jeremy Paxman *The English: A Portrait of a People* (Penguin
Books: London, 1999), p.116

4 Ibid., p.133

5 Roger Scruton *England: An Elegy* (Pimlico: London, 2001),
p.204

6 Alan Macfarlane *The Origins of English Individualism* (Basil
Blackwell Oxford, 1978), p.163

7 'The Book of Discipline' in William Croft Dickinson (ed.) *John
Knox's History of the Reformation in Scotland, Volume 2*
(Thomas Nelson: Edinburgh, 1949), p.316

8 Ibid., p.296

9 Wallace Notestein *The Scot in History, A Study of the Interplay
of Character and History* (Yale University Press: United
States, 1947), p.128

10 Quoted in Lewis Grassic Gibbon & Hugh MacDiarmid,
Scottish Scene (Hutchinson: London, 1934), pp.315-6

11 T.C. Smout *A History of the Scottish People 1560-1830*
(Collins: London, 1969), p.181

12 Quoted in Lewis Grassic Gibbon & Hugh MacDiarmid,
Scottish Scene (Hutchinson: London, 1934), p.316

13 T.C. Smout *A History of the Scottish People 1560-1830*
pp.510-11.

14 Wallace Notestein *The Scot in History* p.82

15 Henry Thomas Buckle *On Scotland and the Scotch Intellect*
(The University of Chicago Press: Chicago, 1970), p.394

16 See Christopher J. Berry *Social Theory of the Scottish
Enlightenment* (Edinburgh University Press: Edinburgh,
1997)

17 Adam Smith *The Theory of Moral Sentiments* D.D. Raphael
and A.L. Macafie (ed.) (OUP: Oxford, 1976), p.7

18 Geert Hofstede et al *Cultures and Organizations* p.115

19 Quoted in Douglas Dunn *Scotland: An Anthology*
(HarperCollins: London, 1991), p.105

20. Richard Rodger 'Urbanisation in Twentieth Century Scotland'
in T.M. Devine and R.J. Finlay (eds) *Scotland in the
Twentieth Century* (Edinburgh: EUP, 1996), p.136

21 Interview with Margaret Thatcher *The Woman's Own*, 31 October 1987

22 William McIlvanney *Surviving the Shipwreck* (Mainstream Publishing: Edinburgh, 1991), pp.245-6

23 Sydney & Olive Checkland *Industry and Ethos: Scotland 1832-1914* (Edward Arnold: London, 1984), p.134

24 Correspondence published in *The Herald*, 3 –11 August 2001

25 Jeremy Paxman *The English,* p.117

26 Ibid., p.118

27 Roger Scruton *England: An Elegy*, p.51

28 Harry Reid *Dear Country: A Quest for England* (Mainstream Publishing: Edinburgh, 1992), p.208

29 Quoted in W. Gordon Smith *This is my Country: A Personal Blend of the Purest Scotch* (Souvenir Press: London, 1976), p.45

30 Ronald Mavor 'Art the Hard Way' in Alastair M. Dunnett (ed.) *Alistair MacLean Introduces Scotland* (Andre Deutsch: London, 1972), p.239

7. Knowing Your Place

What though on hamely fare we dine,
Wear hoddin grey, an' a that?
Gie fools their silks, and knaves their wine –
A man's a man for a' that.
> Robert Burns, 'A Man's a Man for a' that'

The centrepiece of the opening of the Scottish Parliament in 1999 was undoubtedly Sheena Wellington's beautiful rendition of Robert Burns's famous lines. In the speech which followed, First Minister Donald Dewar reminded us that 'At the heart of the song is a very Scottish conviction: that honesty and simple dignity are priceless virtues not imparted by rank or birth but part of the very soul'. Like many Scots I felt proud of my country that day as I stood in July sunshine and listened to these words.

But more than a decade on as I write this book, I wonder if as Scots we pay a huge price for this passionate belief in simplicity and equality. Before looking at what's written on that price tag, I want to explain where this commitment to equality springs from. For the sake of clarity, I should also point out that this chapter only looks at the inequality arising from wealth and rank and I shall look at other aspects of inequality, such as gender, in the following chapter.

We're A' Jock Tamson's Bairns

One of the reasons why the Scots have a strong belief in equality is that Scottish Presbyterianism is a deeply democratic religion. It may have taken hundreds of years, and the spilling of blood during Covenanting days, but the Scots managed to separate their Kirk from the King and state and build it on thoroughly democratic foundations. The power of the Pope was abolished. Bishops were done away with. Church governance was put in the hands of ordinary parishioners who elected the ministers and elders. *The Book of Discipline* encouraged ministers not to pay too much attention to the rich or to important members of the parish. Their funerals, for example, were just to be carried out like any ordinary person's. As we have already seen, the reformed Church aimed to educate every child, irrespective of wealth or rank and *The Book of Discipline* encouraged respect for the poor. Only 'stubborn and idle beggars' were singled out for criticism.

The reason for such equal treatment of rich and poor was not superficial but sprang from the deep Calvinist belief that God is not influenced by a person's rank as it is by their deeds or their faith that people will be judged. In his own lifetime Knox was well-known to be no respecter of rank. He denounced from the pulpit his critics and enemies, both rich and poor, high-bred and humble. He reduced Mary Queen of Scots to tears on more than one occasion and sent critical letters to Queen Elizabeth of England. Knox was not alone. Other Scottish religious figures also showed lack of respect for formal authority. Many have noted that Scottish Presbyterians even address their God in informal and almost irreverential terms; a style that was satirised to good effect by Burns in 'Holy Willie's Prayer': 'O

Thou, that in the Heavens does dwell/Wha, as it pleases best Thysel. . .

Over the years the Scots have also acquired a reputation, even as servants, for not being obsequious. This was brilliantly demonstrated in the film *Mrs Brown*, which showed the Scots ghillie John Brown talking to Queen Victoria as if she was nobody special. In fact, an oft-quoted Scottish proverb proclaims 'Jock is as good as his maister'. Another is 'we're a' Jock Tamson's bairns'.

It is important to put the democratic instincts of the Scottish Kirk in perspective, however. Presbyterianism was a strongly patriarchal religion and women were completely excluded from Church governance until the late nineteenth century. Within the Kirk itself most members were aware of distinct class divisions. Even in the 1950s and 60s Church congregations were often divided along strict class lines. The most well-off, respectable Church members occupied the best pews and did not mingle much with the lower orders who sat at the back.

Nonetheless it is still true to say that John Knox and his followers sowed the seeds of Scottish egalitarianism by establishing the new Kirk along fairly democratic lines. Once sown, these seeds were fed and watered by Robert Burns for it was he, in particular, who ensured that egalitarian beliefs established deep roots within Scottish culture. Indeed Burns spoke not just for ordinary people in Scotland but for ordinary people round the world, for his poem 'A Man's a Man' is nothing less than an international anthem for the basic, irreducible equality of human beings. 'The rank is but the guinea's stamp/The man's the gowd for a' that.'

But more importantly for our purpose, Burns became the carrier of the fundamental belief that *the Scots* are a people with deep democratic, egalitarian and humanitarian instincts: not only was Burns 'one of us', but by celebrating him in the way we do we annually pay homage to these democratic beliefs.

Just Plain Folk

It makes sense for people who believe in a common humanity and who dignify the poorest members of society in their thought, to uphold the values of ordinary everyday life. 'Common decency', 'honest poverty', 'plain talking' – in Scotland these are morally as good as more sophisticated, refined ways of living. 'High' culture usually emerges in societies which are wealthy enough to support a cultural elite, through patronage, for example, so Scotland, for centuries an exceedingly poor though well-educated country, was likely to be excluded from such sophisticated ways. John Grierson sums up this idea when he wrote:

> The secret of it is that we're a peasant and a proletarian people and have never had courtly affairs to strait-jacket us. Our songs are the songs of the common people, our practicality is of a people with a living to make, and a daily job to do, and no fine airs to impose on anybody. . . We never had anything but what we got out of our common doings as working people.[1]

If we examine Scotland's history we can find other reasons why the Scots were likely to be unimpressed, if not actually hostile, to the development of manners or cultural refinement. First, Scotland lost her King and royal court to England in 1603 with the Union of the Crowns. In European countries the court was generally responsible for the development of art, culture and manners. So when Scotland lost her court in Holyrood to the south of England, she lost this refining influence. Secondly, simplicity is at the very core of Presbyterianism. This can be seen in its church service which is supremely simple and easy to understand. This is no small matter as the Covenanters fought and died for the right to simplicity in their service and against the imposition of English High Church ways, such as kneeling, candles, choir singing or even the prayer book. The interiors and exteriors of Scottish churches also display the desire for such simplicity. Historically Presbyterianism was opposed to cultural and artistic expression in theatre, for example – and so another refining influence was blocked in Scotland.

Pretentious? Moi?

For a variety of reasons, then, the Scots came to value the simplicity of ordinary people. Hugh MacDiarmid put the matter simply when he wrote of the Scots: 'we feel no necessity whatsoever to indulge in any airs and graces'.[2] Pomp and circumstance, frippery, finery, posh words, anything that can be dismissed as 'all meringue and nae mince' is easily suspect in Scotland as it suggests pretension – the desire to pretend you are something you are not. And it is in avoiding pretension that many Scots try to display their deep attachment to egalitarian and Presbyterian values.

The nineteenth-century Scottish thinker and writer Thomas Carlyle is a perfect example of this. He was born in humble circumstances on a farm in Ecclefechan, Dumfriesshire. After a stint in Edinburgh and a farm outside Dumfries, he and his wife

Jane moved to London where he had more opportunity to make a living as a writer. In his day, Carlyle was seen as the cleverest man in the United Kingdom and dubbed the 'sage of Chelsea'. Carlyle is often decried by the Scottish literati for selling-out Scotland and going to live an affected life amidst English intellectuals and writers, but the old Presbyterian spirit triumphed in the end and he ultimately redeemed himself and proved his Scottish credentials. The Prime Minister, Benjamin Disraeli, offered Carlyle a state pension and an honorary title in recognition of his contribution to British cultural life. Carlyle refused both. On his deathbed he knew there were plans for an elaborate funeral and for an imposing grave among the great and good in Westminster Abbey. Again he refused and, according to his wishes, he was buried with no service in Ecclefechan, beside other members of his family.

One of the reasons Burns became such a Scottish folk hero is that he died penniless and unhonoured on a farm in Dumfries. It is the same mindset which helps us to understand why Sir Walter Scott, a figure of huge importance in the making of modern Scotland and a man with a massive international reputation, should be thought so little of by ordinary Scots. As a friend of mine who grew up in a council house in the Borders once explained, Scott was 'a toff'. So Scott's baronetcy and his big house at Abbotsford effectively deprived him of an affectionate place in the hearts of ordinary Scottish people.

In contemporary Scotland we can still see this respect for ordinary, unpretentious ways. It is exactly these sentiments which underlie aspects of former Prime Minister Gordon Brown's behaviour. A son of the manse, he refused to wear the customary evening dress to deliver the annual speech the

Chancellor of the Exchequer gives at the Lord Mayor's Banquet at the Mansion House. To avoid seeming ostentatious, he served £12 bottles of champagne from a supermarket at his wedding reception.

In an article on Glasgow, William McIlvanney argues that at the 'core' of Glasgow speech lie two central features – 'deflation of pomposity and humour'. Later he distils the essence of Glasgow to two words – 'human irreverence' – and adds:

> Those who are, for me, the truest Glasgwegians, the inheritors of the tradition, the keepers of the faith, are terrible insisters that you don't lose touch for a second with your common humanity, that you don't get above yourself. They refuse to be intimidated by professional status or reputation or attitude or name. But they can put you down with a style that almost constitutes a kindness.[3]

Openly 'taking the piss' out of people in this way is very Glaswegian, but I believe that the basic underlying belief, that getting above yourself is a bad thing, is essentially Scottish. In other parts of Scotland the criticism may remain unexpressed, but still be thought, or it may be said but with less humour or 'kindness'.

These basic values often lead to reverse snobbery. For example, it is common for Scots who have risen in the world to take pride in their proletarian roots. Indeed this is something which English commentators often deride. 'Nothing appeals so much to Scotch sentiment as having been born in the gutter', wrote T.W.H. Crosland. At the end of his book on the unspeakably loathsome Scots, Crosland suggested ten rules to improve the Scots' conduct. Rule number 4 reads: 'There is nothing specially creditable in having been born in a muck heap. Do not boast about it.'[4]

The Scots and the English share many attitudes in common but, historically, there are marked differences between their views on culture and manners. The editor of *The Character of England*, published in 1950, argued that 'position' is very important in England and that there is a great deal of 'snobbery'. He also argued that 'It is impossible to think about the character of England without also thinking about the character of the gentleman'.[5] The passage of time, particularly the ideology of the 1960s, has obviously eroded such a fascination with manners in English life and I cite this book to illustrate the historical difference between the two cultures. Most middle class Scots have never been preoccupied with 'position' and manners to the same extent as their English counterparts.

With the impetus for cultural refinement and manners less strong in Scotland than in England, anyone who acted in such a way, or who was particularly attracted to high culture, was easily seen as 'Anglicised'. Even today, Scottish aristocrats come across as very English. And with good reason. The landed classes in Scotland are likely to have been educated at English public schools, many attended English universities and have strong ties to the establishment in the south of England. Many do not even speak with a recognisably Scottish accent or act in ways which make them 'one of us'. So the Anglicisation of the Scots aristocracy has in this way reinforced the idea that anything 'upper crust', or even cultured, is essentially English and not authentically Scottish.

Toffs and Traitors

In contemporary Scotland there is still a quiet, and often unacknowledged, contempt for people who have been born into wealth or rank. They are often viewed as people who just 'don't know the time of day'. At the first sign of a silver spoon in someone's mouth, many a Scot will be thinking, albeit privately, 'there's someone who has had it easy, so what does she or he know about life?' Such disrespect is evident in Burns's poem 'A Man's a Man':

> Ye see yon birkie ca'd 'a lord'
>> What struts an' stares, an' a' that?
> Tho' hundreds worship at his word,
>> He's but a cuif* for a' that. (*ninny)
> For a' that an' a' that,
>> His ribband, star an' a' that,
> The man o' independent mind
>> He looks an' laughs at a' that.

It is common for Scots to believe that wealth and position protect people from 'the real world of hard knocks' and undermine their credibility as people. Nonetheless such toffs are often tolerated and treated with polite disdain because they may have power over you as employers or landlords. And their existence can to some extent simply be shrugged off as proof, if any was needed, that 'the warld is ill-divided'.

In Scotland the real venom is saved for 'the poachers turned gamekeepers' – for those of ordinary birth who seem to be enthralled by wealth, possessions, rank, or who have developed manners or affectations of any kind. People who are seen to have got on and turned their backs on their ordinary Scottish upbringing are particularly resented. 'Ah ken't his faither', 'who does she think she is?' or 'I knew him when he didn't have two pennies to rub together'. Whatever the formulation the meaning is the same: 'Here is someone from our own stable who is acting like he or she is better than the rest of us'.

It is this sentiment exactly which underlay the comedian Billy Connolly's fall from grace with sections of the Scottish press and many of his fans. Once lionised for his original humour and complete lack of deference, this one-time shipyard worker had the temerity freely to admit that he not only consorted with English nobs and royalty but actually liked them! Sheena Easton, the wee girl from Bellshill who made it big in the pop world, went to America and loved it so much she was deemed to have turned her back on Scotland. She even started to speak with a mongrel American accent. During an appearance in Glasgow in the 1990s her 'disloyalty' was repaid in boos and hisses. And then there is Ann Gloag, one of the founders of the Stagecoach empire. A former nurse who grew up in a council house, she then spent some of her millions on a castle in Perthshire and was allegedly spat at when she made an appearance on the streets of Perth.

The Scots poet Alexander Scott brilliantly satirised the Scots attitude to equality in two lines:

Scotch Equality
Kaa the feet
Frae thon big bastard.[6]

So we can see how the 'man's a man' sentiment can be something of a double-edged sword. On one side it is positive because it forces us to realise that people are human beings, and should be respected as such, irrespective of their economic circumstances or 'refinement'. In Scotland, we do not believe 'manners maketh the man'. And it is surely good for the rich, honoured or famous to realise that, despite all the trappings of their material success, deep down they are just likely everybody else. But these sentiments have a negative side in that they can easily be used to try to keep people in their place. It is ironic that a country which upholds egalitarian values should also communicate to ordinary people that they should be careful not to get 'above themselves'.

This sentiment is also prevalent in some English working class communities. The tabloid press in Britain as a whole is often accused of having an 'anti-success' mentality. But such attitudes are more powerful in Scotland because we are not just open to the charge of being pretentious and putting ourselves above our community if we get on; our very right to call ourselves 'Scottish' is called into question. What's more, for reasons set out in previous chapters, there is little sense of privacy in Scotland; it is very easy to feel that we live our lives under the glare of comment and with the threat of critical judgement and censure. By 'getting on' in life we can easily feel that we are setting ourselves up for criticism. In fact, the pressure just to be one of the crowd in Scotland can be so great that doing anything different can make people feel exposed. Sometimes the fear is not simply about being criticised but that age-old fear of being 'cast out'. Of course, such a fear is quintessentially human, but in a critical, judgmental society like Scotland, where other people play such an important part in our lives, it has much more power and resonance.

Getting On

It is not uncommon for societies to espouse communitarian values which keep people in their place. In Nordic countries, for example, the 'Janteloven' (Jante law) operates – dictating a moral and social standard which keeps individuals in check. This set of laws was first set out in 1933 by the Danish writer Aksel Sandemose in a novel about the imaginary community of Jante, but most Nordic countries recognise its relevance to them. The Jante law reads like the Ten Commandments and includes dictates such as:

> You shall not think that you are special;
> You shall not think you are the same standing as us;
> You shall not think that you are smarter than us;
> You shall not think you know more than us;
> You shall not think that you can teach us anything.

While there is obviously some overlap between the Jante law and what I have been describing, these statements do not describe the motivating force in Scottish culture. The Jante law is far too limiting and prescriptive. And it is not difficult to see why. In Scotland the pressure to be just like everybody else is just one side of the story. One of the great Scottish paradoxes is that existing alongside this notion that we shouldn't get above ourselves is the contradictory pressure to make something of ourselves and to show that we are at least as good, if not actually better than other people. Confused? You certainly are on the issue of self-advancement if you were brought up in Scotland.

Indeed one of the characteristics of Scottish culture is that it is extremely competitive and there is a huge pressure in Scotland for us to prove ourselves in some way. Intellectually the Scots may disagree with 'status' but they will often strive to be in the one-up position. Indeed one-up-manship is something of a Scottish pastime. Consult a *Broons* annual, the strip comic documenting the life of Scotland's most famous fictional family, and you will see that a regular storyline features family members competing with one another. Granpaw will even roll up his trouser legs and show he is better at water skiing than youngsters like Joe and Hen.

H.M. Paterson, in a book on Scottish education published in 1983, argues that schools uphold:

> the ferocious stress on social conformity so characteristic of Scottish society (as well as) the easy acceptance of a ruthless search for advancement to some position of reward, power and status within the undeniable social hierarchy – in the Kirk, in business, in politics, in sport, or in the professions.[7]

In Scotland we are reared to feel that we should be a nobody like everybody else, *and* that we must prove our worth by becoming a somebody.

A couple of years ago a young relative of ours called Janice came over from Nova Scotia to work in Scotland for a few months. She took a job as a waitress in a local hotel. When she was a student Janice had worked as a waitress in various places in the United States and Canada and she couldn't believe the difference in attitudes between Scotland and North America. 'Over there,' Janice told us, 'people just accept you as a person no matter what job you are doing. Even if it is a menial job they think you are trying to get your act together to do something with your life. Over here, people just look down on you if you are serving them. They treat you as if you are a nobody.' What else was there to say except, 'Welcome to Auld Scotia, Janice, the land that celebrates Robert Burns and "simple dignity".'

Traditionally, the most legitimate channel for competition and upward mobility has been the education system. Indeed, over the years when people have made the case for Scotland being an egalitarian country, they would often cite as evidence the fact that it is possible for people from lowly backgrounds to get on. The Scottish education system, they will argue, by being open to poor people has always been an important conduit for self-advancement. The theme of the clever but poor country lad (and they were all lads) rising through the education system is so well-worn in Scottish literature it is almost threadbare. What's more it is trotted out so often it is now simply referred to as 'the lad o'pairts'. In the mid 1970s, however, Scottish academics started to call this 'the Scottish Myth'. In the introduction to a book *Social Class in Scotland: Past and Present*, Allan MacLaren maintained that there has always been social inequality in Scotland and that to allow the brightest from the lowest order to advance cannot be termed 'egalitarian' – it is in fact 'elitist'.[8] In previous centuries, a few may have risen through the education system but the rest, the vast majority, had little opportunity for advancement. Indeed MacLaren argued that the opportunities for poor, Scottish boys were extremely limited but since they were better than the opportunities in England it fed 'the myth' that Scotland was genuinely an egalitarian society.

Scottish Egalitarianism

Scottish sociologist, David McCrone, in a textbook on Scotland looks in depth at studies which could support or contradict the myth of 'Scottish egalitarianism'. McCrone is at pains to point out that myths are never based on facts and simply shape the way we see the world, so the Scottish myth cannot be proved or disproved. However, he concludes that the most striking factor to emerge from the data is that the pattern of class mobility in Scotland is very similar to other parts of the United Kingdom and that this is due in large part to a shared industrial heritage and to similar access to higher education north and south of the border. He also states that these surveys show that:

> Scotland has a slightly smaller middle class, a slightly larger manual working class, but the processes of social mobility which created these structures of opportunity are remarkably similar on both sides of the Tweed.[9]

McCrone does not think this means that egalitarianism in Scotland is based on nothing, as there is a reasonable amount of upward mobility, but he argues that in this respect Scotland is not substantially different from other parts of the United Kingdom. Earlier I argued that the English are more concerned with 'position' than the Scots, but that does not mean that they are opposed to the idea of social advancement for those born at the bottom of the social ladder if they have talent and ability. 'The ladder,' writes Ernest Barker, editor of *The Character of England* 'has always been a ladder of possible ascent'.[10] McCrone, however, argues elsewhere that in Scotland the belief that the Scots are more egalitarian than the English is a fundamental part of Scottish identity. It is, he claims, 'an ideological device for marking off the Scots from the English'. And, he adds, 'it becomes the essence of Scotland.'[11]

David McCrone also argues that 'the man's a man' sentiment can lead to two different political interpretations. The first is 'an activist one' which seeks 'the resolution' of the contradiction between aspiration and reality. It is, therefore, a call to political action or support of some kind. The other is, according to McCrone, a 'more conservative interpretation of the myth, that if man is primordially equal, then social structural inequalities do not matter, and nothing needs to be done. It is sufficient that "we're a' Jock Tamson's bairns".'[12] Traditionally, Scottish politicians, at least of Labour or nationalist persuasions, have supported the activist interpretation and it is the more dominant interpretation in Scotland. In reality, however, we have done little to eradicate such inequalities and have had to fall back on the idea that somehow class and wealth do not matter too much in Scotland; it is respecting people's basic humanity which counts. Not much comfort for the casualties of Scots inequality such as men dying in their 50s in Shettleston.

The Class Divide

Gerry Rice grew up in the Gorbals and now works for the World Bank in Washington. In 2000 he returned to Scotland for a year to work at Scottish Enterprise. We used to meet regularly to talk about Scottish culture. Every time we met Gerry would reel off some of Scotland's appalling poverty and health statistics and express dismay that middle class Scots just seemed to accept these facts and do nothing to bring about change. 'Why are people not talking about it much, or trying to do something about it?' Gerry would keep asking me. Every time he raised the subject of poverty I felt uncomfortable. I knew he was right and I felt guilty. But, eventually, I decided to mount a defence.

'You live in Washington. That city has some of the worst deprivation in the Western world. Some poor people do not even have basic health care and America is a much richer country than Scotland.' His answer was unforgettable: 'That's America for you. That's what they believe in. But the Scots are always proclaiming to the world what decent, egalitarian people they are.'

It may be painful for modern Scots to accept, but Scotland is a society deeply divided by social class. Educational attainment, life expectancy, physical health, mental health, crime – all are affected by wealth and postcode. This is a real, physical divide. Stand at the railway line which separates the affluent Glasgow suburb of Bearsden from Drumchapel, one of Scotland's poorest housing estates, or go to countless other points round Scotland and you will see this divide with your own eyes.

Poverty and inequality in Scotland

- Around 25% of Scottish children live in low-income households. This is significantly better than it was in 1998/9 (32%) and is better than other regions in the UK.[13] However, the figure is still high by international standards.[14] Save the Children's research shows that 9% of Scottish children live in 'severe poverty'.[15]

- A 2006 Scotsman report analysing NHS data shows that 'A child born in Calton, in the East End of Glasgow, is three times as likely to suffer heart disease, four times as likely to be hospitalised and ten times as likely to grow up in a workless household than a child in the city's prosperous western suburbs.'[16]

- The poorest tenth in Scotland have 2% of total income and this has not changed since devolution in 1999. The richest tenth have around 29%.[17]

• Scotland has extreme differences in life expectancy between rich and poor. The difference between rich and poor postcodes in Edinburgh is 22 years. While life expectancy is generally rising in Scotland it is falling for people in the poorest areas.[18]

• A 2007 OECD report into Scottish education was impressed by the quality of education in Scotland but identified the biggest challenge as the country's 'achievement gap' between pupils from different socio-economic backgrounds – a gap which is wider than it is in other equivalent countries.[19]

The UK as a whole has become more unequal, not less, in the past few decades. Professor Danny Dorling's work shows that progressive taxation and various government policies meant that from 1918 to 1980 the income gap in the UK narrowed substantially.[20] However, this then changed from the 1980s on with the expansion of the economy, and the 'greed is good' philosophy unleashed by Thatcherism and apparent in the big bonuses paid to top executives. Dorling calculates that we are now back to levels of income inequality last seen in the mid-nineteenth century when Charles Dickens wrote *Hard Times*. Scotland performs slightly better but it is marginal: the top ten per cent of earners in Scotland have 29 per cent of the total income whereas in the UK as whole the figure is 31 per cent. In advanced, industrial societies only three countries – the US, Portugal and Singapore – are more unequal than the UK.[21] According to academics such as Professors Richard Wilkinson and Kate Pickett, who wrote *The Spirit Level*,[22] these figures matter profoundly. They present evidence to show that more equal societies have better health and social outcomes and less violence and attempt an explanation for why this is the case. In my book *The Tears that Made the Clyde: Well-being in Glasgow*

I use their theory to help explain why the city is the most violent city in Western Europe, has acute health inequalities and pronounced social problems.[23]

As Scots cleave to the idea of Scotland being an egalitarian country we are often blind to the great class divide. However, it is often very apparent to visitors. Here is how the New Zealand academic H.J. Hanham described it a few decades ago in his book *Scottish nationalism*:

> To the outsider, Scotland, with its aristocracy still largely in being and the gracious living of its big town houses . . . with the workers tucked away in their tenements out of sight, often seems much more of a traditional society than does that of England. It is the sense of social hierarchy that the outsider notices, not the native democracy . . . Scottish democracy may be a powerful force as a myth, but it is a myth base on style, not on the absence of income or class differentiations.[24]

A Paradox

So how can we account for this paradox at the heart of Scotland – the fervent belief in social equality yet the reality of a real, palpable class divide? Poverty cheek by jowl with wealth; advantage and opportunity flourishing alongside deprivation? There are lots of possible explanations, including the fact that since 1707 Scotland has not been a sovereign nation able to pursue her own political agenda. But I think this is too easy an explanation and the answer seems to lie at a much earlier point in Scottish history. T.C. Smout tells us that the early Church reformers saw themselves as champions of 'the impotent poor and of the peasant and labourer'. One of the first acts of the reformers was to nail a 'Beggars Summonds' to the doors of the friaries 'calling on them to surrender their possessions to the poor "to whom it rightfully belongs".'[25] *The Book of Discipline* also outlined a scheme of funding poor relief from the patrimony of the Kirk and intended to make offences against the poor part of ecclesiastical discipline. None of this happened, prompting Smout to remark, 'the complete failure of Knox's followers and successors to carry out any part of this programme makes the most depressing reading of anything in the history of the Godly Commonwealth.'[26]

There were various reasons for lack of progress, including practical difficulties with appropriating the funds of the old Church. Ultimately, once the new religion was established and was supported by lairds, merchants and tradesmen, the Kirk 'became blind and silent before the prospect that the economic self-interest of landlords and the middle classes could be sinful.'[27] In short, the Kirk was not prepared to rock the boat, named 'economic self-interest'. Idealism was tripped up, and rendered impotent, by practicality – a sequence we can see on various occasions in Scottish history.

There is also a paradox at the heart of Scotland's commitment to equality: Scotland is a deeply unequal society. For centuries Scotland has been a country where landowners have incredible rights and privileges. Indeed Sir John Sinclar author of the first *Statistical Account* of Scotland in 1814 observed that 'in no other country in Europe are the rights of proprietors so well defined and so carefully protected.' [28]

Andy Wightman is a celebrated Scottish land reformer and his latest book *The Poor Had No Lawyers* underlines the powerlessness of common people in Scotland *vis à vis* landlords who not only had money but also the support of the old Scottish Parliament to cement their authority and rights.

What's more, for centuries Scottish land ownership has been concentrated in very few hands. Wightman maintains that this is still true today: 'Evidence is yet to reveal a country anywhere in the world with a more concentrated pattern of private land ownership,' he writes. Indeed 57 per cent of Scotland's land is owned by just 0.001 per cent of the population. [29]

Ownership of land matters as it has the capacity to affect the wider social and economic culture. The Scottish historian, John Major, noted its impact on housing and popular attitudes in Scotland as early as 1521 in a passage which presages the 'dependency culture' and lack of enterprise in contemporary Scotland:

> In Scotland, the houses of the country people are
> small, as it were cottages, and the reason is this:
> they have not permanent holdings, but hired only,
> or in lease for four or five years, at the pleasure of
> the lord of the soil; therefore do they not dare to
> build good houses, though stone abound, neither
> do they plant trees or hedges, for their orchards,
> nor do they dung their land; and this is no small
> loss and damage to the whole realm.[30]

In our own times Professor Bryan MacGregor has drawn attention to the major influence that land tenure has on a nation and its people, citing 'the distribution of power and influence' as well as matters such as population size and distribution, 'labour skills and entrepreneurial experiences' and thus the pattern of migration, and access to housing and the resultant social structure. [31] Land ownership matters profoundly and in

Scotland we have not made nearly enough of the fact that for centuries the land has been owned and administered by a tiny clique of people and the vast majority have been disempowered.

The Scots' myopia on equality issues – the fact that we tenaciously cling to a myth – is not due to some kind of 'divided self' or fatal flaw in the Scottish character. It is not that uncommon for a people to uphold a myth of this type – that is exactly what millions of ordinary US citizens do when they cherish 'the American dream'. Despite a wad of statistics to the contrary, Americans still believe that anyone, if they work hard, can become President or live in a lovely house in the suburbs with a swing seat on the porch. In reality, success is largely determined by family background. The English too are hypocritical with their emphasis on 'fair play' and support for the underdog while maintaining a rigid class society.

So it is for a variety of reasons, then, as I sit and think of the opening of the Scots Parliament, and play back in my memory Sheena Wellington's haunting voice singing 'A Man's a Man' and hear Donald Dewar's fine words about 'simple dignity' being 'part of the soul', that I see Scotland's commitment to egalitarian values as double-edged. Of course, we are right to affirm human dignity; right to be unimpressed by wealth and rank. But such sentiments all too often lead to an unwitting desire in Scotland to keep people in their place. And, no matter how much we may pay homage to such sentiments, they have done little to diminish inequality. In fact, they may even stand in the way of our being honest with ourselves about the extent of inequality and deprivation in contemporary Scotland.

Notes

1 John Grierson 'The Salt of the Earth' in Forsyth Hardy (ed.) *John Grierson's Scotland* (The Ramsay Head Press: Edinburgh, 1979), p.33

2 Hugh MacDiarmid 'The Dour Drinkers of Glasgow' in Hugh MacDiarmid *The Uncanny Scot: A Selection of Prose* (MacGibbon & Kee: London, 1968), p.99

3 William McIlvanney *Surviving the Shipwreck* (Mainstream Publishing: Edinburgh, 1991), p.183

4 T.W.H. Crosland *The Unspeakable Scot* (Stanley Paul: London), p.196

5 Ernest Barker 'An Attempt at Perspective' in Ernest Barker (ed.) *The Character of England* (Oxford University Press: London, 1950), p.567

6 *The Collected Poems of Alexander Scott* David S. Robb (ed.) (Mercat Press: Edinburgh, 1994) p.147

7 H.M. Paterson 'Incubus and Ideology: The Development of Secondary Schooling in Scotland, 1900–1939' in Walter M. Humes and Hamish M. Paterson (eds) *Scottish Culture and Scottish Education, 1800 – 1980* (John Donald: Edinburgh, 1983), p.198

8 A. Allan MacLaren *Social Class in Scotland: Past and Present* (John Donald: Edinburgh)

9 David McCrone 'We're A' Jock Tamson's Bairns' in T.M. Devine & R.J. Finlay *Scotland in the 20th Century* (Edinburgh University Press: Edinburgh, 1996), p.112

10 Ernest Barker 'An Attempt at Perspective' in Ernest Barker (ed.) *The Character of England* (Oxford University Press: London, 1950), p.564

11 David McCrone *Understanding Scotland: The Sociology of a Stateless Nation* (Routledge: London, 1992), p.120

12 David McCrone 'We're A' Jock Tamson's Bairns' in T.M. Devine & R.J. Finlay *Scotland in the 20th Century*, p.114

13 Figures retrieved from 'The Poverty Site' http://www.poverty.org.uk/s16/index.shtml

14 See House of Commons Scottish Affairs Select Committee's Third Report of Session 2007-08, 'Child Poverty in Scotland'

15 Save the Children Briefing, 'Severe Child Poverty in Scotland' February 2011

16 Fraser Nelson, 'A nation still divided by poverty and inequality', *The Scotsman*, 4 January 2006

17 Figures retrieved from 'The Poverty Site' http://www.poverty.org.uk/s16/index.shtml

18 Fraser Nelson, 'A nation still divided by poverty and inequality'

19 OECD, 'Review of The Quality and Equity of Schooling in Scotland: Diagnostic Report', 2007. Retrieved from http://www.oecd.org/LongAbstract/ 0,3425,en_33873108_33873870_39744145_1_1_1_1,00.html

20 Danny Dorling *Injustice: Why social inequality persists* (The Policy Press: London, 2010)

21 Retrieved from the Poverty Alliances' website http:// www.poverty.org.uk/s09/index.shtml

22. Richard Wilkinson and Kate Pickett *The Spirit Level* (Allan Lane: London 2009)

23 Carol Craig *The Tears that Made the Clyde: Well-being in Glasgow* (Argyll Publishing: Argyll, 2010)

24 H.J. Hanham *Scottish Nationalism* (Faber and Faber: London, 1969), p.27

25 T.C. Smout *A History of the Scottish People 1560-1830* (Collins: London, 1969), p.91

26 Ibid., p.91

27 Ibid., p.92

28 Quoted in Andy Wightman *The Poor Had No Lawyers* (Birlinn: Edinburgh, 2010), p.40

29 Andy Wightman, Written Evidence to the Justice 2 Committee of the Scottish Parliament on the Land Reform (Scotland) Bill

30 Quoted in David Hackett Fisher *Albion's Seed: Four British folkways in America* (Oxford University Press :New York, 1989), p.656

31 Quoted in Andy Wightman *The Poor Had No Lawyers*, p.297

8. More Equal Than Others

> I want to see. . . (Scotland) as the most open, the
> most open-minded and the most tolerant wee
> country in the world.
> Jimmy Reid, *Power Without Principles*

I have little doubt that Jimmy Reid spoke for many people in
Scotland when he wrote these lines. But is Scotland as open
and tolerant of difference as many of her citizens would like?

Anglophobia and Racism

Many English people have reason to believe the Scots are not
that tolerant and open-minded: if they venture north of the
Tweed they often feel the Scots are prejudiced against them,
not just as a nation but as individuals. As the journalist and
critic Joyce McMillan once remarked, anti-English passion in
Scotland 'gives the nationalist movement a poisoned strength
that can only lead to racism and chauvinism'.[1] The Englishman
Charles Jennings, after a recent tour round Scotland, argued
that while the Scots have historical reasons to hate the English
he can't understand why they haven't managed to let it go:

> After all, Denmark co-exists with Germany, Portugal
> with Spain, Canada with the USA – yes with
> frictions, misunderstandings, irritations. But they

> don't see it as an essential pre-condition of
> nationhood to characterise their larger neighbours
> always and forever as predatory, hypocritical, self-
> obsessed bastards.[2]

This certainly chimes with my experience: it is common in Scotland for educated Scots to stereotype the English as people who are morally inferior or less compassionate than those living north of the border.

Anti-English sentiment is also ritualised in sport and most evident in the 'anyone-but-England' phenomenon which sprung to life in 2006 with remarks made by the Scottish tennis star, Andy Murray. In 2010 these slogans were put on T-shirts and even made it to the high street, though the number of complaints about the inherent racism and 'potential to cause a disturbance' led to their speedy removal.

Anti-English prejudice is often little more than a southerner getting a frostier reception in shops and pubs than other foreigners. But it can turn nasty. People have been beaten up for wearing England tops. In 2009 a young woman was severely punched in the face by a stranger in the centre of Aberdeen and told 'Get back to England'.[3]

The Scottish writer Ian Rankin once remarked: 'the Scots aren't racially prejudiced – they're much too busy being bigoted.' And Rankin's line illustrates that the Scots like to see themselves as much less racist than the English. But in the mid-1980s a BBC Scotland Radio series *It Doesn't Happen Here* exploded this myth. Numerous Scots from ethnic minority backgrounds all over Scotland testified that they were often victims of harassment and prejudice: that the Scots were quite capable of being racist.

Until a few years ago this everyday prejudice against the English was anecdotal but various surveys have shown that it is commonplace. For example, a 2003 Glasgow University study found that one third of the English people living in Scotland who took part in the research reported that the Scots were 'basically Anglo-phobic or anti-English'.[4] Interviewees did not think this prejudice was on the same level as sectarianism but nonetheless they were aware of what the lead academic researcher, Professor Bill Miller, calls 'a nagging antagonism'. A 2005 ESRC study concluded that 38 per cent of the Scottish population were 'Anglophobic' and that this prejudice was greatest in people with 'a strong/exclusive Scottish identity'.[5] Anglophobia was reduced to some extent by higher education and by having an English friend. The study also reported that more than a quarter of English people in Scotland had experienced 'ethnic harassment'.

In 1999 one black respondent in research undertaken by the Rowntree Trust maintained: 'As far as casual, unprovoked verbal racism is concerned, we just take it as part of living in Glasgow'.[6] That same year the Commission for Racial Equality produced figures showing that 'Scotland's black/minority ethnic groups were at least three times as likely to suffer racist incidents as black/minority ethnic people in England and Wales'. Such racism is not confined to verbal assaults. Just how racist the Scots can be was demonstrated tragically by the murder of Imran Kahn, a Glasgow schoolboy, and by the murder of a Kurdish refugee, Firsat Yildiz Dag, in Glasgow. In the wake of this murder the Scottish newspapers were full of quotes from refugees, some of whom had escaped persecution in their own lands, saying that they did not feel safe in Scotland.

In April 2002 Rowena Arshad, Director of the Centre for Racial Equality, and the Equal Opportunities Commissioner for Scotland, claimed that Scotland is inflicted by a 'polite and insidious racism' and is uncomfortable with the notion of diversity.[7] She also argued that one of the biggest barriers to tackling the problem is that the Scots liked to pride themselves on being a tolerant people who believe in equality. As with class inequality, denial is the name of the game.

Since the first edition of this book in 2003 there has been a plethora of reports on racism in Scotland – far too many to summarise here. It is worth nothing that since 2006, as a result of new laws, 'hate crimes' have been monitored in Scotland and that from 2006/7 to 2010/11 there were, on average, 4350 race crimes reported each year.[8] There was a welcome drop of 3.6 per cent in the most recent figures. The decrease may simply be a blip in the figures but it may be the beginning of a positive trend. Some of those involved with race relations in Scotland see some improvement and report that those from ethnic minority backgrounds are now less likely to be asked 'where they come from'. What's more, Scotland has not witnessed the radicalisation of young Muslims in the way that England has. Some attribute this to the fact that it is easier for these groups to feel that they belong – that they are 'Scottish' in a way that their counterparts down south don't feel they are 'English'. This fillip to race relations has been further enhanced by the Scottish political climate particularly the SNP's stridently anti-Iraq war stance which found resonance with many Scots.

Those involved in equality issues in Scotland also welcome the approach taken by successive Scottish governments. The McConnell administration, for example, adopted two campaign slogans proclaiming 'Scotland, No Place for Racism' and 'One Scotland: Many Cultures'. They also welcome the SNP's position on 'civic nationhood' particularly Alex Salmond's instance that their 'ambition is to see the cause of Scotland argued with English, French, Irish, Indian, Pakistani, Chinese and every other accent in the rich tapestry of what we should be proud to call. . . "the mongrel nation of Scotland"' – a quote from the novelist William McIlvanney.[9] The fact that the SNP is pro-immigration has reinforced the impression that they are not ethnic nationalists.

Interestingly, the 2005 ESRC study reported that there was less Islamophobia in Scotland (49 per cent) than England (63 per cent) and that unlike England where the most Islamophobic respondents were those who identify with English nationalism, Scottish nationalism 'does not exert any substantial impact' on Islamophobia.[10] However, the report draws attention to the fact that there is only a 11 per cent difference in Scotland between those displaying Islamophobic as opposed to Anglophobic attitudes.

Homosexuality

Shortly after devolution Scotland was plunged into controversy as a result of the proposal to repeal Section 2a of Clause 28 of the Local Government Act which prohibited local authorities from intentionally promoting homosexuality. In the midst of the debate, Tim Luckhurst, former editor of *The Scotsman*, described Scotland as a 'backward, repressed and socially conservative country.'[11]

Homosexuality was legalized in England in 1967 but Scots law did not catch up till 1980 so in an earlier period there was some truth in Luckhurst's views. But by the new millennium Scottish attitudes towards homosexuality and other sexual morality issues were no longer that different from the rest of the UK and the Scots were as likely as the English to believe that homosexuals should have the same legal rights as hetero-sexuals.[12] But this does not mean that it is easy to be a gay man, lesbian, cross-dresser or transgender person in Scotland. As a result of new 2009 legislation it is an offence to act in a prejudiced way towards people as a result of their sexuality. The first tranche of figures show that there were 448 people charged in Scotland for harassment linked to sexual orient-ation.[13]

What's more, homosexuals and lesbians have little presence in Scottish culture: there are no famous Scottish icons of homosexuality or gender bending – no Scottish Eddie Izzard, David Bowie or Boy George. Scots in the public eye are reluctant to 'come out' and openly acknowledge their sexuality. In 1993, Bob Cant, a Scottish gay social historian declared:

> Lesbians and gay men are, for the most part,
> invisible in modern Scotland. The few public
> references to us – by teachers, by preachers, by
> politicians, by pundits – imply that we are Other,
> that we are 'these people', that we do not belong.[14]

Almost twenty years have elapsed yet Cant's words still resonate.

Gerry Hassan writes frequently on sexuality and gender issues. In one piece headed 'The Slow Revolution of Gay Scot-land', he argues that progress has been made, pointing to the fact that Edwin Morgan, once Glasgow's Poet Laureate and Scotland's Makar, was openly gay and that James Robertson's

And the Land Lay Still, one of the central protagonists is a gay character. But nonetheless Gerry Hassan argues:

> Not being 'out' and comfortable about being lesbian and gay in Scotland is still part of our uncomfortableness about difference, diversity and the body. Some of this is related to the anxieties and hang-ups which many Scottish men have about themselves, sex and emotions, which is then magnified in unease about the issue of sexuality. It is also about our yearning and need for conformity, and our secret fears that Scotland might be a land of homophobes: a society of cultural ayatollahs (always ready) to persecute gays and anyone different up and down the land.[15]

At the height of the storm over the repeal of Section 28 (2a) it appeared as if homosexuality is a divisive issue in Scottish life, but it is a small fissure in comparison with that yawning chasm – religion.

Being Catholic

As Scotland is a small country which likes to proclaim its egalitarian ideals to the world, when the composer James MacMillan got to his feet at the 1999 Edinburgh International Festival and gave a lecture about a 'prevalent, if not unspoken bigotry' against Catholics in Scottish national life he did not just spark off but ignited a blazing controversy. The following year Tom Devine edited a book of essays about the controversy, *Scotland's Shame? – Bigotry and Sectarianism in Modern Scotland* and yet another debate ensued.

Does the Catholic minority have reason to feel aggrieved at

their treatment by the Protestant majority? It is undoubtedly the case that Scotland was once an anti-Catholic land. In 2002 the Church of Scotland even apologised for the sins committed in the early part of the twentieth century by some of their ministers who preached the virtues of forcible repatriation of Irish Catholics. Many Scottish intellectuals in the 1920s and 30s were likewise guilty of anti-Catholic prejudice as it was all too common for them to fret about Irish Catholic 'contamination' of Scottish Presbyterian culture. In employment too anti-Catholic discrimination was commonplace.

Scotland is an increasingly secular society and only a minority care very much about religion these days. Making recruitment more professional and the extensive use of 'person specs' and 'job specs' has also meant that while anti-Catholic prejudice may still exist in some quarters, it operates at the margins of Scottish life. The presence of Catholics in a large number of high-profile jobs testifies to the fact that being a Catholic in Scotland is no longer the barrier to professional, or political, advancement that it once was.

There's little doubt that MacMillan would have set off a less noisy pyrotechnic if he had acknowledged this change in Scottish life. But it is also true to say that the media ignored much of the spirit of MacMillan's remarks and focused on whether *discrimination* against Catholics is still a significant feature of modern Scotland. As MacMillan points out in the conclusion to Tom Devine's book, in his original speech his concern was not with 'discrimination' as such but with 'prejudice'. He maintains that his lecture was 'a plea for social inclusion' in the wake of the brave new Scottish Parliament being established. It was his attempt to 'call for pluralism and diversity'.[16]

Despite some flaws in MacMillan's original lecture, there is much in his argument with which I agree. Indeed many of the points he makes are similar to those I have advanced repeatedly in this book, for at the core of MacMillan's argument is the belief that in Scotland there is a strong tendency 'to restrict, to control and to enforce conformity and homogeneity'. An important strand in MacMillan's argument here is that Catholicism is not respected in Scotland; not seen as a conduit to Scotland's pre-Reformation history or part of the rich tapestry of Scottish life. Even liberals, he claims, at best tolerate Catholics only if they don't do anything too overtly Catholic like send their children to separate Catholic schools. In one of the most powerful passages in *Scotland's Shame?* Patrick Reilly, a retired professor of English at Glasgow University, writes:

> Scotland has ceased to be a Protestant country without ceasing to be an anti-Catholic one and it is a change that no Catholic will applaud. Catholics are still made to feel that their habit of kicking with the left foot is, at best, an inconvenience, at worst, a disaster. To do anything on or with the left, the sinister, side has long been a synonym for perverse, crooked, aberrant . . . From 1872 onwards there was pressure upon Catholics to stop kicking with the left foot and to switch to the right. Today the pressure is for them to kick with no foot at all, to purge their schools of religious education other than as a purely academic discipline sanitised of faith commitment. Once the wish was to make them Protestant; now it will suffice if they stop being Catholic. They were formerly criticised for being Catholic; they are presently criticised for being religious by Protestant atheists (they do exist) and by those who have deserted Calvin for Marx. But whatever else changes, one thing abides: the animus against Catholics and their schools.[17]

For me, one of the most challenging aspects of the MacMillan camp's argument concerns this defence of separate Catholic schools. It is commonplace for Scots to argue, including the EIS, the main teachers' union, that Catholic schools should be abolished; that religion should play no part in education. Essentially this argument is about the assimilation of the Catholic minority into the 'mainstream'. Some academics in Scotland argue that this process of assimilation has already happened. For example, sociologists Michael Rosie and David McCrone argue in *Scotland's Shame?*:

> Whatever may have been the case in the past, the evidence from studies in the 1990s indicates an acculturation and assimilation into mainstream Scottish society. While others . . . are exploring directly the thesis that Catholics are systemically discriminated against in Scotland, our evidence here makes that a very difficult argument to sustain. Scottish Catholics at the start of the new millennium are not the people they were. Their past is indeed history.[18]

With one high-handed swipe these two authors simply try to brush aside and render irrelevant the whole question of whether there is anti-Catholic prejudice in Scotland. Yet even on the subject of discrimination they are not standing on rock-solid ground. Fellow social scientists, Patricia Walls and Rory Williams, argue in the same volume that there simply is not enough evidence for academics to draw such categorical conclusions. More importantly, Rosie and McCrone are simply not prepared to engage with the argument MacMillan and others advance because, in this instance at least, they are only interested in what can be measured objectively. They just don't seem to understand that MacMillan's argument is largely about human feelings. MacMillan and others *feel* that their Catholicism is an important part of who they are as people but they do not simultaneously feel that this aspect of themselves is valued by the wider Scottish society in which they live. And no one, not even number-crunching sociologists, can deny these feelings or the importance people attach to them.

One of the central issues here is about assimilation. Rosie and McCrone apparently see assimilation as the pinnacle of equality – once this peak has been scaled and no differences can be identified there is no longer a problem to address. Next case. But assimilation usually means that a dominant group has absorbed a minority into its culture at the expense of that minority's own culture and differences.

Essentially James MacMillan and his supporters are saying they feel that Catholicism is not respected in Scotland. The idea that religion has no real place in school is largely a Protestant view, though undoubtedly a number of (assimilated?) Catholics now hold this view as well. So every time some well-meaning Scot argues that separate schools should be abolished, a significant number of Catholics, like James MacMillan, feel their point of view is being undervalued. The sensitivity has become even more intense in recent years because Catholic schools are now performing very well.

Earlier in the book I argued that in Scotland the love of objective, logical thinking means there is a tendency to reduce issues to first principles. For many Protestant-minded Scots, including myself until I read some of the essays in Tom Devine's book, a first principle is that religion and education should be separate. But if we move into the realm of *realpolitik* it is easy to see that no political party which hopes to win power will put the abolition of Catholic schools on its election manifesto for the simple reason that they would stand to lose votes and engender huge splits within the Party.

Scotland faces some huge educational challenges. To my mind, the issue of separate schools does not even register on the scale of problems to be tackled. Even if you still think *in principle* that religion and education should be separate – that the 1918 settlement should never have taken place – is it not about time to let the matter go? Undoubtedly sectarianism is an issue but should we not try to tackle the mindset that creates it rather than enforcing conformity, suppressing diversity and alienating those Catholic Scots who are passionate supporters of separate schools?

In the 2003 edition of the book I do not go on to talk about other manifestations of sectarianism in Scottish life such as in football, street violence or harassment. This was a reflection, no doubt, of my own lack of interest in football; my unwillingness to extrapolate from what happens in Rangers and Celtic football matches to the general culture of Scotland; and because I was aware that Professor Steve Bruce, an academic at Aberdeen University, argued that there was little evidence to show that football-related sectarianism was any different from the rivalry between clubs evident elsewhere in the UK and indeed Europe.

Eight years on and sectarianism has become a huge issue not just in the media but in Scottish political life. The legislation on hate crime extends to religious bigotry and so there is now annual figures for incidents reported to prosecutors. The latest figures were the highest in five years.[19] What's more, 2011 saw a number of worrying incidents involving parcel bombs and death threats sent to the Celtic manager and other prominent

Catholics; angst over the level of sectarian bigotry and abuse on the internet; and the amount of violence at Rangers and Celtic matches, including aggression between players and scuffles involving coaches. In the aftermath of the latest games police estimate that domestic violence rose by 81 per cent. The level of hate and violence has forced the SNP administration, who were not pursuing a high-profile anti-sectarian agenda, to follow Jack McConnell's example and hold a 'summit' to discuss what can be done to tackle the culture of 'booze and bigotry'. Legislation is now planned.

Professor Steve Bruce is unconvinced, arguing much of this is media hype and that 'Scotland's disgrace is not religious bigotry. It is the unthinking way in which sectarianism is assumed.'[20] To support his views Bruce says that he has undertaken considerable research in Northern Ireland and knows 'what sectarianism looks like'. When he set out his argument on *The Guardian* website in April 2011 it elicited almost 200 responses. Some agreed that Scottish sectarianism was blown out of all proportion in the media and did not extend into wider Scottish life. Many disagreed, wondering what 'planet he was on' and going on to give their personal stories of bigotry and intolerance. One particular entry caught my eye. It was written by a young man from Derry who came to study in Dundee. He was brought up a Catholic but is now an atheist and he writes with little malice, even recounting an act of kindness towards him by a man taking part in an Orange march. Nonetheless he gives various examples of routine sectarian abuse and aggression in various parts of Scotland involving both Catholics and Protestants before going on to comment on Professor Steve Bruce's article:

I'm sure there are a million similar stories regarding sectarianism in Scotland, but I find it shocking that this particular author is willing to downplay it all. The little examples above are fairly innocent (compared to the shite I grew up with in NI) but its positively simmering beneath the surface at all times, particularly in Glasgow. Its certainly much more regularly apparent than it was in my home town of Derry.

Women's Experience in Scotland

Finally what about that other great 'minority' in Scottish life – women?

In 2006 I was introduced to Tari Lang who has worked throughout the world, particularly in the Middle East, with corporations and individuals as a consultant, coach and mentor. Tari was partly based in Scotland as her husband was at that time principal of one of Scotland's universities. Over lunch Tari revealed that what shocked her most about Scotland was the visibility of women in public life. Indeed she maintained that women were more prominently involved in public life in the United Arab Emirates, Jordan and Qatar than they were in Scotland. What she found particularly puzzling was that the figures for women in management and leadership positions in Scotland were superficially reasonable, at least in comparison with other parts in the UK; what was most troublesome was that very few women's voices were being heard in the media, at events and on public platforms. This is a complaint I have heard from various women moving to Scotland from abroad or even the south of England. What these outsiders say is that they find the culture excessively macho and male-dominated.

In 2010 author and former editor of *The Herald*, Harry Reid wrote a column in which he noted that all the great icons of modern Scotland – Jimmy Reid, Sean Connery, Billy Connolly, Alex Ferguson are all men and representative of a 'macho hard Scotland'. He then goes on to ask:

> where are the female iconic figures? The nearest I can think of over the past couple of generations is that redoubtable nationalist Winnie Ewing, who was once dubbed Madame Ecosse, and managed, just about, to act as if the soubriquet was merited. But Winnie never really impinged on our national consciousness as a truly iconic figure. Where are the emerging Scotswomen of charisma, character and eloquence?[21]

In this small section of the book I cannot possibly do justice to the enormous, and important, topic of women in Scotland. I simply aim to help explain why Scottish culture does not encourage women's full participation in public life. I begin by looking at how traditionally women were kept in their place as a result of the country's religious views.

Calvinism postulates the spiritual equality of the sexes as it makes both men and women responsible for their own salvation. But Lesley A. Orr Macdonald, in a comprehensive review of women in the Scottish Kirk, argues that this 'potentially liberating' aspect of Calvinism for women was not realised for centuries. Indeed Macdonald argues that the Scottish Reformation ushered in a religion which was deeply masculine in both belief and practice.

Catholicism had allowed for female religious communities, making it possible for some women to live almost independently of men. The cult of the Virgin Mary and the plethora of female saints also meant that Catholicism offered women role-models and emphasised the importance of female compassion.

All this was swept aside by the Reformation. The Reformers' God was an authoritarian male figure and absolute masculine authority was considered appropriate not only for Church governance but also for family life. The Kirk believed it was right and proper for women and children to be under the rule and supervision of a patriarch. Indeed they believed that it was unnatural and 'disorderly' for women to have any authority. As only men could become ministers or elders, the Church discipline was the discipline of men, with women and girls often on the receiving end. So harsh was this discipline that the poet John Keats once remarked, 'I would rather be a wild deer than a girl under the dominion of the Kirk'. As Macdonald shows, much of the Kirk's discipline attempted to keep women submissive and in a subordinate position:

> For a range of offences, from gossiping and slander, to adultery, harlotry and witchcraft, women in the 16th and 17th centuries were subjected to punishments which were intended to silence, to humiliate, to shame, to demonise and above all to control them for behaviour which was not in keeping with the submission required by the defenders of the faith. Those who committed sexual misdemeanours, or who chose to live on their own and not in a male-headed household, were liable to particular pursuit and censure. This atmosphere of repression, abuse and contempt reached its nadir in the periodic witch hunts of the period. In 1727, the last of thousands of Scottish women were tortured and burned.[22]

The complete domination of women in the Scottish Kirk

continued until the first few decades of the nineteenth century. As the evangelical movement within the Kirk took off and encouraged a whole series of mission works to help build the Church, relieve the poor or convert natives and savages to Christianity, women were increasingly seen as particularly suited to carry out much of this activity. But while the Kirk changed its views on women's social role, it still saw women as subordinate to men. Even the women's organisations set up within the Church, such as the Women's Guild, were initially controlled by men. Not only were women still deprived of exercising any authority, they were also prevented from expressing their opinions. In 1847, Thomas Chalmers, the man who led the Great Disruption, said in response to the subject of women's rights: 'I have always looked upon this as a very paltry and distasteful question; I think that it is revolting to the collective mind of the Free Church.'[23]

But in encouraging women's mission, the Kirk had let the genie (or more precisely Jeanie) out of the bottle. As Macdonald shows so conclusively in her book, once women started to play a more public role their attitudes started to change. They soon began to acquire skills, knowledge, contacts and confidence which changed their lives irrevocably. It was these skills which they were later to utilise in proper, paid employment. It was their growing understanding of inequality and oppression, learned in their work with the poor and in anti-slavery campaigns, which helped women to see that they themselves had no rights and were victims of oppression. Before long, some women in Scotland, as elsewhere, were beginning to agitate for rights – not only in the Kirk but also in education and in politics.

Knox's vision of a literate and educated Scottish people

included girls and women yet Scotland has never produced one female intellectual or scientific figure of national, let alone, international renown – no Mary Wollstonecraft, Madame de Stael, Rosa Luxemburg, Simone de Beauvoir, Madame Curie, Hannah Arendt or Iris Murdoch. The absence of women's presence in Scottish intellectual and cultural life until the mid-twentieth century is not only striking in Scottish history books but unmissable by anyone visiting the Scottish National Portrait Gallery in Edinburgh. Leaving aside the section dedicated to the twentieth century, the few women on display are mainly queens, and duchesses – women who have made their name through birth or marriage. The main exception is the celebrated Flora MacDonald whose only claim to fame is that she helped Bonnie Prince Charlie.

In the past decade this has begun to change. There's now a thriving organisation called 'Women's History Scotland' and in 2006 the first *Biographical Dictionary of Scottish Women* appeared containing 830 entries.[24] Nonetheless in any society dominated by men, women's lives, and achievements, remain unrecognised. This is the argument Joy Hendry advances in an article on Scottish women's writing. 'Scottish women writers, of all forms and genres, have had a pretty raw deal,' writes Hendry. But she also says she doubts 'if any Scottish woman writer has felt that her environment was encouraging, sympathetic or favourable to her achieving the full extent of her potential'.[25] Indeed, Hendry adds, 'those who succeed are those who thrive in an adverse climate.'

Hendry is aware that Scotland's political status and Scottish culture as a whole have not been sympathetic to writers of either gender, but she maintains that Scottish women writers have been doubly disadvantaged – have had what Hendry calls 'the double knot in the peeny'. In a culture which undermines rather than builds individual self-confidence and which expects people to conform to rigid norms of behaviour, Scottish women have had good reason not to feel ambitious for themselves and to conform to the limited life which has, at least until recently, been on offer.

At various points so far in this book I have argued that what other people think of you is crucially important in Scotland and that, in an extremely critical culture, this combines with the fear of negative judgements to keep people in their place and limits individual initiative and action. These constraints affected, and continue to affect, both men and women but women are not just shackled and disadvantaged by them – they are more likely to be stopped dead in their tracks. It certainly stopped Susan Ferrier: the nineteenth-century Scottish novelist even abandoned novel writing because she felt the activity was 'socially unacceptable'.

Scotland's emphasis on respectability has weighed particularly heavily on women. Many social historians and sociologists have argued that 'respectability' has been a guiding principle in the lives of ordinary Scottish people. In 1936 the novelist Willa Muir, in her book *Mrs Grundy in Scotland* argued that 'respectability' had become a widespread Scottish disease. 'Behave yoursels before folk,' writes Muir, 'has taken the place of the Ten Commandments.'[26]

The social historian Richard Finlay argues that the Kirk's definition of respectability 'revolved round sobriety, temperance, thrift, hard work, religiosity, and self-improvement'. Finlay argues that there was 'widespread adoption' of such values in

Scottish society and that they had a particular hold on the working class. He also points out that 'perhaps the greatest propagators of these values were members of the labour movement and trade unionists who sought working class social and economic advancement'.[27] Finlay also argues, with much legitimacy, that the importance of these values in Scottish working class life had less to do with aping 'bourgeois ideology' than with 'human dignity': life was tough for poor, working class people in Scotland – if they practised restraint they could lead decent, if exhausting, lives. If they were not careful with money, if they did not work hard to maintain certain standards of cleanliness or worse still if they if gave into the temptations of drink, then there was nothing surer than that they would end up living in the most abject slum.

R.F. Mackenzie, the liberal educator, grew up in Aberdeenshire and reported how the quest for respectability was acted out in his household:

> We were brought up to be 'respectable', doing the
> right things, not being uncouth in any way,
> throwing under a cushion the socks that were
> drying at the kitchen fire when somebody knocked
> at the door. I wouldn't have admitted that we slept
> four to a room and that we had a dry privy at a
> corner of the garden. We maintained the façade
> that was considered respectable. I felt vulnerable,
> dependent on the good opinion of neighbours.[28]

These words chime with my own 1950s childhood. Having a clean, tidy house was very important in the respectability stakes. If we ever had visitors, a huge amount of time would be spent cleaning and polishing. If the door-bell rang unexpectedly on a Sunday the Craigs would rush about stuffing newspapers under cushions just in case it was the minister or an uninvited visitor! In England too, particularly in the poorer areas, respectability was important but the nature of Scottish tenement housing and the elevation of others in everyday life meant that being 'respectable' had even more importance in the lives of ordinary people than south of the Tweed.

Mackenzie argued that in Scotland the working and middle classes were obsessed by such respectability and that only the 'local aristocrats' could afford 'the luxury. . . of being themselves'.[29] He then tells a wonderful story about a Scottish baroness who was giving a talk to the Women's Rural Institute when she felt her bra come loose. According to Mackenzie, 'without fuss or concealment' the doughty baroness continued to give her talk while making a manoeuvre which allowed her to deposit the offending bra in her handbag. No doubt any Scotswoman of more modest upbringing would have been 'black affronted', to use Maw Broon's phrase, at the very idea of people knowing of her embarrassing predicament.

In the past, everyone in Scotland, bar the real aristocracy, felt the pressure to be respectable, but a family's respectability was often seen as the responsibility of the mother – it was up to her to ensure high standards of cleanliness and order in both the house and its occupants. Poverty, poor living conditions and large families meant that lives were particularly hard for many Scottish working class women. As is the case in many male-dominated societies, any laxity in women's moral standards was judged much more harshly than men's. I am not arguing, however, that women's behaviour was, and is, only controlled and limited by men – that women are inevitably victims of *male* power. Often the pressure on women to conform, in the past as well as the present, comes as much from other women as it does from men.

Some readers may be wondering why in a book on understanding the Scots, their culture and confidence, I am devoting time to analysing the experience of particular groups within Scottish society. And the answer is quite simple: it is very difficult for people to feel confident if they do not feel valued. It has been very hard in Scotland for women – more than half the population – to feel valued for being themselves. Indeed in many respects women have been ignored.

In cultures where there is a pronounced separation of heart and head women can still be given respect as they are seen as more in touch with feelings and the tender human side of life. This was the case to some extent in the Scottish Kirk in the early part of the nineteenth century. But, as I argued earlier, in Scotland the emotional aspect of life has been institutionalised in the work and cult following of Robert Burns. Indeed not only is Burns a man but the Burns cult itself is deeply male and, until recently, women were even routinely excluded from Burns suppers.

In the early 1970s the feminist Sheila Rowbotham argued that throughout the world women had been 'hidden from history'. Look at historical texts and you will see just how much they dwell on the activities of men and forget the lives of women altogether. Historians are now beginning to address this imbalance but Elizabeth Ewan and Maureen M. Meikle argue in the introduction to their edited volume *Women in Scotland* that 'Women's history has developed fairly late in Scotland in comparison with other Western countries'.[30] They acknowledge a complexity of reasons for this but maintain that in Scotland 'the focus' has been on identity and this means that 'political history' has tended to squeeze out social history – the branch of history which is more likely to examine women's role and contribution to society. As Lynn Abrams points out in an article on the need to 'gender Scottish history', 'these preoccupations' with national identity and national politics 'have never led historians to examine how women have intersected with the discourses on nationalism and nation-state formation in Scotland'.[31]

Leaving aside politics and constitutional history, the type of Scottish issues and events historians and cultural analysts tend to focus on are exclusively male. Take the Scottish Enlightenment – there is a huge roll-call of names to mention, but they are all male and there are not even one or two minor female figures to consider. The 'lad o' pairts' and the issue of social mobility in Scotland has likewise been analysed repeatedly and, as David McCrone points out, there is no female equivalent – no 'lass o' pairts'.[32] The Labour Movement has also been responsible for marginalising the role of women in Scotland. Since the industrial revolution women have played an important part in the Scottish economy. Indeed whole industries – such as jute in Dundee and cotton in Ayrshire – were largely dominated by women. Nonetheless the most celebrated aspects of Scotland's industrial past are heavy industries – shipbuilding, engineering, mining and steel – where men dominated. Even though women did work in some of these industries their labour is often forgotten. Women also played a part in the Scottish Labour Movement, organising rent strikes for example, yet they are not accorded an important place in the story: unlike the heroes, the heroines are largely unsung. Given these last few points it is unsurprising that the images of Red Clydeside are resolutely male. Indeed the only statue in Scotland commemorating the activities of a female socialist figure is on the banks of the Clyde and it is to La Passionara – a Spanish leader.

For decades I have been interested in the masculine nature of Scottish culture and I could write extensively about it here. But for the sake of brevity I simply intend to hold up for inspection two straws to illustrate that the wind blowing through much of Scottish culture is cold and hostile to women's lives and values. The first concerns the way women are routinely portrayed in an unflattering light in the highly influential Scottish working class novels penned by men like William McIlvanney or James Kelman. The women characters in these novels often have aspirations for a better house or more money, and these writers regularly depict them as the carriers of alien middle class (and therefore English) values. In one of his novels McIlvanney mounts a vicious attack on '*genus surbanus*'. 'After mating,' McIlvanney writes, 'two offspring are produced at intervals mathematically calculated by the female, whereupon the female swallows the male whole and re-emits him in the form of a bank-balance.'[33] Neil McMillan, in an article about women in Kelman's fiction, asserts that the author is within a tradition of male Glasgow fiction which 'persistently identifies womanliness with negative bourgeois aspirations'.[34]

The second, and final, straw illustrating a decidedly anti-feminine wind blowing through Scottish culture, is the life and work of Hugh MacDiarmid – the man the Scottish historian Christopher Harvie claims 'stood guard over the Scottish intellect' in the first half of the twentieth century.[35] Alan Bold in his biography of MacDiarmid asserts that the author 'changed

Scotland' and that in the course of his life gave 'the nation an ideal made in his own image'.[36] But what is the image of Hugh MacDiarmid? For me, it is of a churlish, critical patriarch who downplayed the importance of human relationships and exaggerated the importance of art – a viewpoint summed up in his memorable line that he 'would sacrifice a million people any day for one immortal lyric'.[37]

Of course, I feel dazzled by some of MacDiarmid's language and imagery and can appreciate how he managed to raise the level of Scottish culture, but as a woman, and a mother, I do not care for much of his philosophy of life. It is hard to find a more certain or authoritative Scottish voice than MacDiarmid's. It is true that he changes his opinion over time, but when he makes his judgements he speaks with such certainty and authority that his voice is not only intimidating it is tyrannical. Indeed MacDiarimid does not just express opinions – he writes in tablets of stone. It is he, the Great Man, who sits on high deciding how to rank the work of his competitors or what views are appropriately Scottish. In the article I referred to in Chapter 1 where he complains about distractions, such as women, in pubs, MacDiarmid writes:

> It is the old story of those who prefer hard-centre chocolates to soft, storm to sunshine, sour to sweet. True Scots always prefer the former of these opposites. That is one of our principal differences from the English. We do not like the confiding, the intimate, the ingratiating, the hail-fellow-well-met, but prefer the unapproachable, the hard-bitten, the recalcitrant, the sinister, the malignant, the sarcastic, the saturnine, the cross-grained and the cankered, and the howling wilderness to the

amenities of civilization, the irascible to the affable,
the prickly to the smooth.[38]

No doubt he was exaggerating for effect, but even so every time I read these lines I want to shout – 'speak for yourself Hugh MacDiarmid. You certainly don't speak for me or any Scottish woman I know'. If women had managed to make their views and presence felt over the last hundred years in Scottish culture, Alan Bold could not have confidently asserted that somehow MacDiarmid has given Scotland 'an ideal made in his own image'.

In the first edition of the book I ended this section on women being positive and upbeat. I recounted that when I was young in the 1950s I was hard-pressed to come up with the name of any famous Scotswomen other than Mary Queen of Scots, Moira Anderson and Maw Broon. But nowadays there are a growing number of Scottish females who are making their mark in literature and the arts, the media, sport, politics and business. Nowadays any young Scots girl can be inspired by women like Liz Lochhead, Kirsty Wark, Janice Galloway, Hazel Irvine, Margo MacDonald, Kirsty Young, Anne Gloag, Liz McColgan and Nicola Sturgeon. I also pointed out that the Scottish Kirk's views on women have changed so much in the past few decades that they seem progressive in comparison with other Churches and then went on to quote from a 2002 article by Fiona Mackay, 'A Slow Revolution? Gender Relations in Contemporary Scotland'. This points out that for years girls have been outperforming boys in Scottish schools and beginning to make 'significant inroads into many professions.'[39]

Of course, if we compare women's position in Scotland with

decades ago then we can detect real changes but as a 2011 EHRC report lamented: 'The progress of women to positions of authority in Scotland, and in Britain, has been tortuously slow'.[40] The report argues that women's progress is not steady – 'it is a trend of waxing and waning; not one of constant upward movement.' This is why the UK's figures as a whole continue to compare unfavourably with other European nations, particularly Scandinavian countries. The 'waxing and waning' can be seen, for example, in the fact that there were more female MSPs in Scotland in 2003 than 2011; that the number of women leading Scottish local authorities halved between 2007 and 2011; and that there are now fewer women holding public appointments than there were in 2003.

If we compare Scotland and England's progress there is a great deal of similarity with the Scottish data being worse in some areas and better in others. But this then returns us to the observation made by Tari Lang at the beginning of this section: it is not that Scotland's figures are particularly bad in comparison with other parts of the UK when it comes to women in senior jobs. The problem is that women's voices are rarely heard and this inevitably means they are not making sufficient impact on Scottish life to influence and change the country's macho culture. As Harry Reid reminds us 'too often Scotland seems caught in a time warp, forever trapped in memories of its industrial past.'

Harry Reid rightly concludes that to get out of this trap 'We need new icons . . . softer, gentler articulators of fresh values.' Inevitably this means 'We need women who can speak for Scotland, who can tell us not just what Scotland is or was but what it might yet be.'[41]

Not that out of the ordinary

We may talk a lot about common humanity in Scotland, and share Jimmy Reid's aspiration to be the most 'open minded' and 'tolerant' country in the world but there is little doubt that Scots, like people in many other cultures, are prejudiced and capable of marginalising and even dehumanising others who are different from them. Indeed it is no exaggeration to say that for many people in Scotland 'a man's a man' as long as he is not English, a homosexual, a Muslim, an asylum seeker, or kicks with the wrong foot. But this does not mean that we should go to the other extreme and berate ourselves for being hopeless, intolerant, prejudiced people. Just look at the international news and you will see how challenged human beings are by difference; just how many societies are trying to grapple with discrimination issues. Some countries, particularly Scandinavian countries, are much better than we are but many are worse. We do ourselves no favours if we hold to the Scottish myth of equality so much that it blinds us to the reality of our circumstances. But neither is it beneficial for us constantly to indulge in thinking that ends up with the equation: Scotland = the worst or with notions of Scottish pathology.

Notes

1 Joyce McMillan 'Tartan Special' in *Scotland on Sunday*, 15th July 1990

2 Charles Jennings *Faintheart: An Englishman Ventures North of the Border* (Abacus: London, 2001), p.43

3 John MacLeod 'The ugly truth about the Scots and our shameful anti-English bigotry', *Scottish Daily Mail*, 15th January 2009

4 Angus Macleod 'Anti-English prejudice rife in Scotland, survey finds', *The Times*, 6th October, 2003

5. ESRC 'Towards a multicultural nationalism? Anglophobia and Islamophobia in Scotland', Devolution Briefings, Briefing No 24th March 2005

6. Quoted in Rowena Arshad 'Social Inclusion' in Gerry Hassan and Chris Warhurst (eds) *A Different Future: A Modernisers' Guide to Scotland* (The Centre for Scottish Public Policy/The Big Issue: Glasgow, 1990), pp. 221-2

7. *The Herald*, 26th April 2002.

8 'Hate Crime in Scotland 2010-11', Official Statistics Publication for Scotland, retrieved from http://www.copfs.gov.uk/sites/default/files/Hate%20Crime%20-%20publication%20-%20final%20version.pdf

9 Quoted in Steve Reicher, David McCrone and Nick Hopkins ' "A strong, fair and inclusive national identity": A viewpoint on the Scottish Government's Outcome 13', Equality and Human Rights Commission research report 62, 2010, p.5

10 ESRC 'Towards a multicultural nationalism? Anglophobia and Islamophobia in Scotland'

11 Tim Luckhurst *The Independent*, 7th July 2001

12 For information on the Scots' attitudes to homosexuality see John Curtice, David McCrone, Alison Park & Lindsay Paterson *New Scotland, New Society?* (Polygon: Edinburgh, 2001)

13 See note 8 above

14 Bob Cant *Footsteps and Witnesses: Lesbian and Gay Lifestories from Scotland* (Polygon: Edinburgh:1993), p.1

15 Gerry Hassan 'The slow transformation of gay Scotland, *The Scotsman*, 2nd October, 2010

16 James MacMillan 'I Hadn't Thought of It Like That' in T.M. Devine *Scotland's Shame?* (Mainstream Publishing: Edinburgh, 2000)

17 Patrick Reilly 'Kicking with the Left Foot: Being Catholic in Scotland' in T.M. Devine *Scotland's Shame?*, p.38.

18 Michael Rosie and David McCrone 'The Past is History: Catholics in Modern Scotland' in T.M. Devine *Scotland's Shame?*, p.217.

19 See note 8 above

20 Steve Bruce 'Scottish sectarianism? Let's lay this myth to rest', *The Guardian*, Comment is Free, 24th April, 2011

21 Harry Reid 'Where are the women to speak for Scotland?' *The Herald*, 24th August 2010

22 Lesley A. Orr Macdonald *A Unique And Glorious Mission: Women and Presbyterianism in Scotland 1830-1930* (John Donald: Edinburgh, 2000), p.25

23 Quoted in Lesley A. Orr Macdonald *A Unique And Glorious Mission*, p.178

24 Elizabeth Ewan et al (eds) *The Biographical Dictionary of*

Scottish Women, (Edinburgh University Press: Edinburgh, 2006)

25 Joy Hendry 'Twentieth Century Women's Writing: The Nest of Singing Birds' in Cairns Craig (ed.) *The History of Scottish Literature: Volume 4* (Aberdeen University Press: Aberdeen, 1989), p.291

26 Willa Muir *Mrs Grundy in Scotland* (George Routledge: London, 1936), p.62

27 Richard Finlay in Michael Lynch *The Oxford Companion to Scottish History* (Oxford University Press: Oxford, 2001), pp.522-3

28 R.F. MacKenzie *A Search for Scotland* (Fontana Paperbacks: London, 1991), p.259

29 Ibid., p.259

30 Elizabeth Ewan & Maureen M. Meikle *Women in Scotland c.1100-c.1750* (Tuckwell Press: East Linton, 1999), p.xx.

31 Lynn Abrams 'Gendering Scottish History: An Agenda for Change' in *Women's History Magazine* Issue 40, February 2002, pp11-12

32 David McCrone *Understanding Scotland: The Sociology of a Stateless Nation* (Routledge: London, 1992), p.97

33 William McIlvanney *A Gift from Nessus* (Eyre & Spottiswoode: London, 1968)

34 Neil McMillan 'Wilting, or the "Poor Wee Boy Syndrome": Kelman and Masculinity' in *Edinburgh Review* No.108, p.49

35 Christopher Harvie *Scotland and Nationalism: Scottish Society and Politics, 1707-1977* (George Allen & Unwin: London, 1977), p.193

36 Alan Bold *MacDiarmid: Christopher Murray Grieve – A Critical Biography* (John Murray: London, 1988), p.438

37 Lewis Grassic Gibbon & Hugh MacDiarmid *Scottish Scene* (Hutchinson: London, 1934)

38 Hugh MacDiarmid 'The Dour Drinkers of Glasgow ' in Hugh MacDiarmid *The Uncanny Scot: A Selection of Prose* (MacGibbon & Kee: London, 1968), p.96

39 Fiona Mackay 'A Slow Revolution?: Gender Relations in Contemporary Scotland' in Gerry Hassan and Chris Warhurst (eds) *Anatomy of the New Scotland: Power and Influence* (Mainstream Publishing: Edinburgh, 2002), p.279

40 'Sex and Power 2011 Scotland', EHRC, August 2011, p.1

41 Harry Reid 'Where are the women to speak for Scotland?', *The Herald*, 24th August 2010

9. The Utopian Streak

Och aye, it's the New Jerusalem! It's a land of milk
and honey they're building up there in Scotland,
laddie. They'll nae be doing it with your horrid
Anglo-Saxon devil-take-the-hindmost approach.
No, they're just more socialist than us sour-
mouthed Sassenachs.

This is how Boris Johnson, the Mayor of London and former
Tory MP, satirised the Scots' attitude to politics during the debate
about the Scottish Parliament's support for free personal care.
I am no fan of the maverick Johnson, but I think he is right –
the Scots are a people with an inclination to Utopian dreams.
These dreams may seem harmless, or even laudable, but they
can be dangerous for they undermine our self-confidence.
Indeed I believe one of the main reasons why we Scots are so
self-critical is because we harbour dreams which are destined
not to come true. And when they don't, the sense of failure
catapults us to the other end of the scale and we end up knee-
deep in feelings of shame, inadequacy and worthlessness.

Of course, as rational, logical Scots we know that Utopia,
or perfection, is unachievable, but lurking behind the logic is
the belief that it should be achievable; that this is what we must
strive for. It is worth noting that it was a Scot, Andrew Young,

who penned 'there is a happy land, far, far away'. And that happy land still haunts the Scottish consciousness. Given what happened in Scotland less than four hundred years ago it would be remarkable if such Utopian tendencies were not evident in Scottish life, for the most striking feature of our religious past is the sheer scale of what the nation tried to achieve.

Religious Revolutionaries

In Scotland, the Reformation was not a one-off event but a series of changes which occurred from 1560 to 1690. Knox and his contemporaries did not simply overthrow Popery and Catholic ritual, they attempted to create the Kingdom of Heaven, to build the New Jerusalem. In his acclaimed work, *The History of the Scottish People*, T.C. Smout argues that the Protestant reformers in Scotland were trying to create 'a perfect mirror of the Kingdom of God in Heaven'.[1] In this respect, as Campbell Maclean argues, the Scots were nothing less than religious revolutionaries:

> Most nations, however Christian, have retreated from this dangerously Utopian hope and have been content with more realistic and attainable ends. Where it has been tried, the communities have either been territorially smaller, as in Calvin's Geneva, or have opted out of general life in society, like Catholic monastics or like some of the Puritan primitives in the United States. But this is the single instance of a whole nation over centuries, being absorbed by the vision of communal attainment of such ambitious proportions. Only the great Communist states of the twentieth century have shared a like vision.[2]

One of the main obstacles to the creation of the Godly

Commonwealth was the monarchy. King Charles I tried to re-establish royal supremacy by forbidding the General Assembly to meet and abolishing the presbyteries. But his attempt to impose a new common prayer book was the last straw. Rioting ensued. Churches were boycotted. In 1638 the Scots drew up a National Covenant requesting the King to respect the Presbyterian church. The Covenant was first signed in Greyfriars Kirk in Edinburgh but copies were made and dispatched round Scotland for the populace to sign. An astonishing three hundred thousand signatures were collected.

The National Covenant may read like a moderate and legalistic document but for many signatories it was much more than that. It was a vital step in Scotland's creation of the Godly Commonwealth. Archibald Johnston of Warriston, one of the document's creators, considered it to be 'the glorious marriage day of the Kingdom with God'.[3] He also drew a parallel between Scotland and Israel – 'the only two sworn nations to the Lord' – a view which underpins the belief that the Scots are 'the chosen people'. In the decades which followed, Scotland embarked on Covenanting wars where people martyred themselves for their beliefs and for the great noble vision of 'Heaven on earth'. Anyone standing in the way of this vision was mercilessly killed in the name of God. But by 1690 it was clear to the Scots reformers that the Godly Commonwealth, the theocracy to which they aspired, had not been and could not be established.

Religious toleration was forced on Scotland, following the Act of Union. Magistrates were forbidden from supporting the edicts of Kirk sessions and this meant that excommunication and other church discipline lost much of its power. Inevitably, the Church's control on the populace at large began to wane.

Over three hundred years have elapsed since then. Few Scots regularly attend church, yet that chapter in Scottish history lives on in Scottish life and still shapes deep Scottish attitudes. It is for this reason that Wallace Notestein, in his historical survey of the Scottish character, argues that 'What differentiated the modern Scot in character from other peoples more than anything else was the Reformation. He may be an Episcopalian or a Glasgow Marxist, but he is in some degree a product of the Presbyterian movement'.[4]

The Scottish Dream

One of the enduring legacies of the Reformation is that many Scots, almost unconsciously, uphold the idea that we should still be striving for perfection. In a fascinating article on Scottish novels in the 1950s and 60s Glenda Norquay examines the work of four Scottish writers: James Kennaway, Alan Sharp, George Friel and Robin Jenkins. Ultimately she concludes that the central characters in these novels all feel dissatisfied with the judgmental, restrictive nature of Scottish culture and that 'the escape they envisage is not simply into an alternative world but into a world which offers perfection: flight must lead them into Eden'.[5]

In their book, *Ten Modern Scottish Novels*, Isobel Murray and Bob Tait do not employ the same terminology as Glenda Norquay but nonetheless they still present us with the idea that Scottish writers long for Eden. 'It is possible to discern in many of them a yearning for a pre-industrial, pastoral Scotland,' they argue, adding, 'we are struck by a yearning for solidarity, for the very possibility of a sense of common purposes and values which would be life-giving rather than life-destroying'.[6]

A similar yearning can be found in the works of writers like Edwin Muir and Lewis Grassic Gibbon. In English literature there is a longing for Arcadia but this is the desire for a pre-industrial, green landscape where the English village reigns supreme. Jeremy Paxman argues that the 'English dream is privacy without loneliness' so it is a far cry from the longing for the communitarian paradise that dominates Scottish thought.

In Scotland, our Calvinist legacy has predisposed us to the need for redemption. It is a need which fuses the sense of a fallen, corrupted world, with the desire for salvation. As Scotland is no longer a culture dominated by God, nowadays redemption mainly takes a secular form. So the dream is of a world where flaws have been replaced by perfection. In America 'the American Dream' is the result of a fusion of strong Protestant impulses with migrants' ambitions to find a better life. It is primarily a dream of *individual* salvation via hard work and material success – a dream supposedly made possible by a land of opportunity and equality. By contrast, the Scottish dream rarely assumes a materialistic form. It sometimes takes an individual form, as is the case in some of the novels Glenda Norquay analyses. But the Scottish dream is mainly a dream of *collective* redemption and salvation; it is about us once again building the New Jerusalem.

According to Alan Sharp, one of the writers analysed by Norquay, the need for collective salvation is even apparent on the football terraces:

> Scotland lives in the grip of dream. The original dream was of a Kingdom of Heaven on earth, a serious attempt to produce a total theocracy. The failure of that attempt, it's my conviction, has left a

psychic fault in the Scottish character. They're prone, at the drop of a whisky bottle, to commit themselves to perfection, to Eden in a way, an Eden that they've never inhabited. At football they believe, as they stand there on the terracing, that they're going to see football played of the purest essence, that the game's suddenly going to be irreducibly perfect. They remain dissatisfied with anything less than this, and they remain hopelessly, endlessly optimistic that it will happen the next day.[7]

Stuart Cosgrove has also argued that for Scots fans, football is 'a dream that relates to the nation and its progress'. In recent years the performance of the Scottish football team has been so bad it has led to nightmares not dreams, but there is widespread agreement that Scots football fans for many decades lived in a world of fantasy and possibility – a world which bore little relation to what the Scottish team was likely to achieve on the pitch.

Scots often talk as if current social problems could suddenly be wiped out because people have a conversion as dramatic as Paul's on the road to Damascus – a conversion which turns good Scots folk from materialism towards wholesome pursuits and values. The Scottish-born journalist Ian Jack, in an article on his father, describes how he inherited this longing for a 'golden age' and day-dreamed about a time when people would see the light. 'The people . . . would be filled with goodness. They would abandon Freemasonry and flee the public houses,' writes Jack. '. . . and board tramcars for evenings organised by the Independent Labour Party. They would flood out of football grounds . . . and cycle off with tents, to the Highlands.'[8]

Of course, Ian Jack is being ironical and is all too aware of the naiveté of his daydreams but these are the types of dreams many Scots cherish. One of the most influential Scottish books of the 1980s was *A Search for Scotland* by the liberal educator R.F. Mackenzie. It is a beautifully written book about Scotland which is seductively idealistic and it is not difficult to see why it was hailed as a masterpiece by Scottish figures on both the left and right of the political spectrum. Near the end of the book Mackenzie writes: 'Self-interest and material comfort plays a larger part in the lives of most of us than we confess to,' [9] yet his vision for Scotland is one where people have eschewed urban life and wealth. According to Mackenzie 'rural life' holds 'the prospect of happiness if we have enough food in our bellies and are free from back-breaking toil, so that we feel free to enjoy the sight of the dew-pearled hillside and the snail on the thorn.' [10]

Describing the effect of an outward-bound trip to Rannoch on a group of teenagers in Fife, Mackenzie writes: 'As they fitted comfortably into their natural habitat, we began to get glimpses of how a Scottish cultural revolution might be set in motion. It would begin in the country places.' [11] As the Scottish dream is for the nation as a whole, the dreamer must assume, as Mackenzie does, that it is capable of animating all Scottish people. So an essential feature of the Scottish dream is that it is blind to individual differences. In the Mackenzie example we will all come to love snails or countryside, once the scales of materialism have fallen from our eyes.

It is in politics, however, that we are most likely to see the Scottish dream in action – particularly the type of left-wing politics which have dominated the Scottish political landscape for decades. Jimmy Reid alluded to the dream in one of his newspaper columns when he wrote: 'My dad wept with joy when Labour won in 1945. He was dreaming of a New Jerusalem. John Smith would have understood, but not Blair and Mandelson. Their souls were never seared by the vision splendid.'[12]

'The Vision Splendid'

Almost all socialist creeds have idealistic or moral underpinnings but, paraphrasing George Orwell, some are more idealistic and moral than others. Marxist-Leninist thought is based on 'dialectical materialism' and sees itself as 'scientific'. As a result it has little time for socialist movements which are simply based on the idea that a socialist society would be morally better or more humane than capitalism. Within the Labour Movement which thrived in Britain in the early decades of the twentieth century, there was a huge range of opinion and again some of the parties and sects were more idealistic and moral in their views than others. What is clear is that socialists from Scotland, almost irrespective of grouping or party, had a strong ethical and idealistic base to their beliefs. Indeed many writers on socialism in Scotland point out how religion played a greater part in the movement's ideology than Marxism. For example, Keir Hardie, the man credited with founding the Labour Party, was from Lanarkshire and the influences on him were mainly religious. An ILP colleague said of Hardie: 'So far as he was influenced towards Socialism by the ideas of others it was . . . by the Bible, the songs of Burns, the writings of Carlyle, Ruskin and Mill, and the democratic traditions in working class homes in Scotland in his early days.'[13]

Some of the great Scottish socialist politicians of this time – Hardie, Maclean and Maxton – passionately tried to improve the living conditions of ordinary people and their campaigns to raise men, women and children out of squalid poverty and inhumane working conditions cannot be seen as idealistic. But inevitably, as Scottish religious thought and history played such a large part in the creation of Scottish Labour ideology, these political reformers were not desiring to win mere palliative, economic measures; they were in their own way also attempting to create the Kingdom of Heaven on Earth. As one Scottish Labour Party pamphlet of the time argued, the change they were pursuing did not simply amount to capitalism being replaced by communism 'but also the greater transition from the semi-human to the wholly human. . . Socialism is the only gospel of earth that makes for the spiritual emancipation of the human race.'[14]

For men like James Maxton, these socialist ideals became entwined with his aspirations for Scotland and the Scottish people. His was a huge vision not just of a Scottish Parliament but a 'Scottish Socialist Commonwealth'. At a rally in the St Andrew's Hall in Glasgow in 1924 Maxton declared:

> Give us our Parliament in Scotland. Set it up next year. We will start with no traditions. We will start with ideals. We will start with purpose and courage. We will start with the aim and object that there will be 134 men and women, pledged to 134 Scottish constituencies, to spend their whole energy, their whole brain power, their whole courage, and their whole soul, in making Scotland into a country in which we can take people from all nations of the earth and say: This is our land, this is our Scotland, these are our people, these are our men, our works, our women and children: can you beat it? [15]

Party Politics and Fallen Dreams

I am not suggesting that the creation of a socialist Utopia ever gripped the whole Scottish nation, let alone the whole of Clydeside, in the 1920s. Even in those elections where old-style Labour did exceptionally well, they never won an outright majority of votes in Scotland. And even when their vote was high, many Scots voted Labour because they liked aspects of the socialists' programme not because they shared the whole vision. But the Scottish socialists' vision of Utopia owed so much to Knox and the Covenanters that it became entwined with the Scottish dream of collective redemption and still plays a huge part in the psychology of the nation.

This does not mean that a majority of Scots consciously buy in to the notion of collective redemption or live with a sense of Utopia. (Sadly many people in contemporary Scotland live in such bleak circumstances that they have little hope or optimism for their own lives, let alone an aspiration for communal perfection.) But what it does mean is that when people feel involved in politics in Scotland they are often animated by the Scottish dream. Lindsay Paterson argues that it is Utopian attitudes and ultimately the Scots' 'fallen dreams' which partly account for the disappointment many Scots felt shortly after the Scottish Parliament was set up.[16]

Even when Scots do not uphold notions of a full-blown Utopia – a perfect society where people all live happily together – a watered-down version of such thought processes persists. And the label we could give to this dilution is 'panacea politics'. Scottish politics is literally awash with examples of people claiming their schemes, notions and ideas could at a stroke cure many, if not all, of Scotland's ills.

The early days of the National Party for Scotland, the fore-runner of the SNP, were blighted by the political equivalent of such snake oil salesmen, all claiming that their idea, if adopted, would revitalise Scotland. A state of affairs which led party officials such as Lewis Spence to despair:

> I am all for the new nationalism, but at the moment it presents to me a maelstrom boiling and bubbling with the cross-currents of rival and frequently fantastic theories, schemes and notions . . . Some hark back to the hope of a sixteenth-century Scotland regained, others suggest a national approchement (*sic*) with France, still others a Jacobite restoration. A certain group sees in the expulsion of all the English and Irish in Scotland the country's only chance of survival . . . We are informed by one school of critics that only if Scotland returns to the Catholic fold shall she be able to rekindle the fires of her art, by another, equally absurd, that the Presbyterian faith alone is the true guiding star of Scottish artistic effort.[17]

In his book on Scottish nationalism, the New Zealand academic, Harry Hanham, maintained that even in the late 1960s SNP policy was essentially a weird mixture of notions from 'Douglas Social Credit' (a political scheme much loved by Scottish literary figures such as Hugh MacDiarmid and Leslie Mitchell), 'Christian Socialism, anarchism and political Radicalism'. 'Everything,' Hanham caustically adds, 'except a frank acceptance of the modern state and of modern bureaucratised industrial, political, trade union, and commercial empires.'[18]

In more recent times, Isobel Lindsay, a politics lecturer and former member of the SNP, argued that the Party's belief that Scotland's salvation lies in independence in Europe was 'an escape into a Utopia' for, she maintained, the Party exaggerated the extent to which Scotland would be able to influence decision making in European institutions.[19] Indeed many nationalists' commitment to independence appears to be so strong simply because they believe that breaking away from England will at a stroke solve many of Scotland's problems. Before the Scottish Parliament was in full swing, many pro-devolutionists argued that this simple transfer of power could remedy many of Scotland's ills. Months after the Parliament had been established, Gerry Hassan devoted a section of one of his articles to 'Caledonia Dreaming: The Vision Thing and Scottish Politics' and in it he wrote:

> The dream of Scottish home rule was always about more than a Parliament on the Mound – our Camelot on the hill. The early labour movement pioneers and idealists who set up and maintained the nationalist movement through difficult times were inspired by more than that. Their vision was of a Scotland which challenged the old vested interests of clubland and corporate Scotland and established a self-government beyond the political realm in the economic, social and cultural. That is a genuine clarion call for modernisers in any or no political party to unite behind today. We have achieved constitutional change our predecessors could only dream of; it is time to bring the political change and the new Scotland into being.[19]

Twelve years on from the establishment of the Parliament it is hard not to see Hassan's words, and the countless others written in this vein, as little more than idle fantasy. It is a fantasy which I shared in earlier, halcyon days but which frankly looks rather daft in the cold light of devolution Scotland. I am not saying that none of this vision could ultimately be achieved, but like much in Scottish politics there is a strongly Utopian ('the lion will lie down with the lamb') quality about our aspirations and visions. After all, if we return to Hassan's vision, how realistic is it to expect people across the political spectrum to unite for anything (other than national security issues)? How realistic is it to expect the Scots, who have a long history of being disputatious, to pull together in the way he envisages?

The tendency to panacea politics has been evident in the way some Scottish Government ministers have presented some of their policies. For example, when Henry McLeish was First Minister he passionately claimed that 'dignity' for elderly Scots would be achieved with the introduction of free personal care. In fact this initiative, although expensive to the public purse, does not mean any additional spending on the care of elderly people as it is a scheme designed mainly to reimburse the personal care costs of those elderly Scots who are already footing the bill out of their private income. It is, in effect, an expensive scheme which has contributed little to the lives of many elderly people who are lonely and struggle to cope because of inadequate pensions, the scarcity of residential care homes and sheltered housing, and a lack of home helps. But despite the limitations of the measure Henry McLeish presented it as a scheme which would, at a stroke, improve the day-to-day lives of older people living in Scotland.

Interestingly, Kate Fox in *Watching the English* never represents her compatriots as having Utopian leanings. Indeed the opposite is true. Fox argues that England's grounded empiricism, pragmatism and 'matter-of-factness' are summed up in what she sees as a major English slogan – 'Oh, come off it! – which is used routinely to squash pretentious or abstract ideas.[21] Of course, Scottish scepticism and logic can also lead to criticism of people for being airy-fairy. Nonetheless, for the reasons I've set out here, there is a much greater tolerance in Scotland, than England, for Utopian dreams and panaceas.

Of course, thanks to personality differences, idealists, Utopians and dreamers can be found in all cultures – even England. The issue here is whether these longings are encouraged or discouraged by the prevailing culture. In Scotland, ideals and dreams do not simply emanate from individuals, or a few small-scale religious or political groups; they are woven into the fabric of Scottish life and we can trace these Utopian threads right into the heart of Scottish culture and politics.

Having a strong Utopian disposition myself I have no desire to knock this tendency in other Scots. I still believe it is noble for human beings to aspire to a world based on social justice, where poverty has been abolished. Indeed I would go further and say that this penchant to envision an idealised future where everyone is spiritually and culturally better off is a positive feature of many Scots and is much needed in a world where even the concept of continual social progress is struggling to stay alive.

But like our commitment to egalitarianism, the tendency to Utopian ideas is double-edged. By encouraging us to dream of perfection it drains our energy and makes us cynical. Our Utopian longing can also increase our frustration with ourselves and our culture and catapult us into feelings of worthlessness and self-criticism. Such feelings simply do not help us grapple with the very real problems which confront Scotland. Of course we need some inspiring visions but we also need pragmatic, realistic and achievable proposals which command widespread support and help us create a Scotland which may not be perfectly just and fair, but is significantly better than the one we currently inhabit.

Notes

1 T.C. Smout *A History of the Scottish People 1560-1830* (Collins: London, 1969), p.72

2 Campbell Mclean 'Who is Their God' in Alastair M. Dunnett (ed.), *Alistair MacLean Introduces Scotland* (Andre Deutsch: London, 1972), p.201

3 Quoted in Magnus Magnusson *Scotland: The Story of a Nation* (HarperCollins: London, 2000) p.424

4 Wallace Notestein *The Scot in History: A Study of the Interplay of Character and History* (Yale University Press: United States, 1947), p.103

5 Glenda Norquay 'Four Novelists of the 1950s and 1960s' in Cairns Craig (ed.), *The History of Scottish Literature: Volume 4* (Aberdeen University Press: Aberdeen, 1989), p.275

6 Isobel Murray & Bob Tait *Ten Modern Scottish Novels* (Aberdeen University Press: Aberdeen, 1984), p.3

7 Douglas Dunn *Scotland: An Anthology* (HarperCollins: London, 1991), p. 34

8 Ian Jack *Before the Oil Ran Out* (Flamingo: London, 1988), p.6

9 R.F. MacKenzie *A Search for Scotland* (Fontana Paperbacks: London, 1991), p.261

10 Ibid., p.34

11 Ibid., p.172

12 Jimmy Reid *Power without Principles* (B&W Publishing: Edinburgh, 1999), p.26

13 Quoted in T.C. Smout *A Century of the Scottish People 1830-1950* (Collins: London, 1986), p.256

14 Ibid., p.263

15 Quoted in Gordon Brown *Maxton* (Mainstream Publishing: Edinburgh, 1986), p.160

16 Lindsay Paterson 'Scottish Democracy and Scottish Utopias: The First Year of the Scottish Parliament' in *Scottish Affairs*, Autumn 2000

17 Quoted in H.J. Hanham *Scottish Nationalism* (Faber and Faber: London, 1969), p.154
18 H.J. Hanham *Scottish Nationalism*, p.175
19 Quoted in Andrew Marr *The Battle for Scotland* (Penguin Books: London, 1992), p.192
20 Gerry Hassan 'Modernising Scotland: New Narratives, New Possibilities' in Gerry Hassan and Chris Warhurst (eds) *A Different Future: A Modernisers' Guide to Scotland* (The Centre for Scottish Public Policy/The Big Issue: Glasgow, 1999, pp.26-7
21 Kate Fox *Watching the English* (Hodder: London, 2004), p.405

10. Holier Than Thou

Yer sins go doon beside yer name
in the Book o No Rubbin Oot
                    Bill Duncan, *Wee Book of Calvin*

By all accounts, before the Reformation the Scots were a merry, pleasure-loving people who lived for the moment. But this new reformed religion was all about logic, reasoning and understanding. It was a cerebral religion which not only downplayed the importance of spiritual experience, aesthetic sense and beauty, but eventually demonised enjoyment of any kind. So the Kingdom of Heaven the Scots pursued was no paradise where people lazed about in beautiful palaces, thinking spiritual thoughts, being artistic, having fun, copulating or eating fruit; it was a world where everyone worked hard, led serious, frugal lives in accordance with the Bible and worshipped the Lord.

For all that John Knox is seen as the kill-joy who turned the Scots into a guilt ridden people, he was not opposed to all forms of enjoyment. Nor was he particularly a promoter of Sabbatarianism. Such Puritanical edicts were a later development in Scotland's Reformation. And when they came they gripped the nation with a vengeance – doing anything on a Sunday, other than worshipping the Lord, was forbidden. So was celebrating

Christmas or other traditional holidays. 'Gorgeous and vaine apparel' was criticised and people were exhorted to dress in sober colours. 'Hodden grey' was the Kirk's choice. Any form of enjoyment, such as card playing, gluttony, drinking, festive burials or weddings was also attacked. In 1649 the General Assembly of the Church of Scotland passed an act decreeing an end to 'promiscuous dancing'. Sex, the most natural of all human activities, was seen as vile by the Church authorities and any type of sexual activity outside the strict confines of the marriage bed deemed a serious breach of Church discipline. The elders even quizzed married couples on their sexual relationship.

At the height of its power, the Church was able to exert its authority over most people living in Lowland Scotland and much of the Highlands. Only the nobility and vagrants managed to escape its discipline. Yet despite the obvious power of the Kirk, its ministers never managed fully to eradicate the Scots' liking for pleasure, and many Scots disregarded the Church's teachings in their personal lives. By the mid eighteenth century the power of the Kirk had waned so much that Robert Burns was not only able to reject its teachings but also to satirise its views. In his own life, Burns pursued pleasure, enjoyment, and romance and had the illegitimate children to prove it. He poked fun at 'the holy Willies' and celebrated love, sex and pleasure in his poems and songs. Burns was not a lone transgressor. Many historians comment that even at the height of Kirk authority in Scotland, fornication and drunkenness were commonplace and huge numbers of children were born out of wedlock.

Guilt-edged

But while the Kirk failed to regulate the behaviour of all Scots, and transgressions against its strict puritanical code were fairly common, it did manage to do one thing – inveigle its way into everyone's consciousness so that they believed they *should* behave in accordance with the Kirk's teachings. Inevitably this meant that when individuals transgressed they felt an over-whelming sense of guilt. And alongside football, guilt is still a national pastime. Those who are most sensitive to its powerful, but often invisible, presence are Scots exiles.

Alastair Reid is a poet and writer who, like many fellow Scots, has travelled the world. Born in Whithorn in 1926, he has lived in many places round the world including the United States, France, Greece, Spain and Central and Southern America. Reid is a gifted writer – a skill he used for many years as a columnist for the *New Yorker* – and this talent, coupled with his astute observations as both an insider and an outsider, mean he has written some of the most perceptive articles on contemporary Scotland. In his book *Whereabouts: Notes on Being a Foreigner*, he explains why he chose to leave his native Scotland behind:

> The spirit of Calvin, far from dead, stalked the countryside, ever present in a pinched wariness, a wringing of the hands. We were taught to expect the worst – miserable sinners, we could not expect more. A rueful doom ruffles the Scottish spirit. It takes various spoken forms. . . a man in Edinburgh said to me, 'See you tomorrow, if we're spared,' bringing me to a horrified standstill. 'Could be worse' is a regular verbal accolade; and that impassioned cry from the Scottish spirit 'It's no right!' declares drastically that nothing is right, *nothing* will ever be right – a cry of doom. . . The

> wariness is deep-rooted. I prize the encounter I
> once had with a local woman on the edge of St
> Andrews on a heady spring day. I exclaimed my
> pleasure in the day, at which she darkened and
> muttered, 'We'll pay for it, we'll pay for it. . .'[1]

Columnist Anne Smith calls the complex blend of Scottish feelings of guilt 'the Knoxplex' and maintains that 'the victim . . . is convinced that he is only truly alive if he is suffering, or working (one and the same thing usually)'.[2] Many Scots are also aware that they often feel guilty if they catch themselves having a good time or feeling happy. Andy Dougan, of the *Evening Times*, puts it down to 'that Calvinist thing that whatever good things happen to you they are all hideously undeserved.' Dougan adds that this means you 'are bound to . . . be visited with some catastrophe in the near future in compensation.'[3] Many commentators on Scotland have observed how many Scots go through life seeing it as something to be endured rather than enjoyed.

Another prevailing belief is that enjoyment or even happiness is not only unimportant but potentially dangerous as such 'inessentials' divert your attention from life's true purpose. As a result of the Kirk's traditional teaching most Scots in earlier centuries saw 'real' life as being about hard work which should be undertaken, not so much for your own personal benefit, but for the benefit of God and others. This work ethic may have dimmed over time and with the advent of a more hedonistic society but it is still there. Indeed it is why Scotland was a favoured site for inward investment for many years – the Scots are known to have very positive attitudes to work.

Many Scots, even today, uphold the essentially Calvinist idea that a person's life should be 'a pilgrimage towards an objective'.

Just simply living your life unthinkingly is not good enough. To be meaningful, life has to be imbued with a sense of purpose. Andrew Carnegie, the Scottish self-made millionaire, would regularly remind young people, 'we've not been put in this world just to enjoy ourselves'.

Even when the power of the Kirk began to wane in Scotland, some individuals still continued to channel their sense of mission into religious activities and over the years many Scots became missionaries both at home and abroad. As religion declined in significance, people redirected their need for a purposeful life into other activities. One obvious conduit for such a sense of purpose is the quest for knowledge and educational attainment. Many scholars in Scotland have pursued their studies with a quasi-religious zeal, often exhausting themselves in the process. Scots also commonly try to satisfy their need for meaning by entering occupations where they can be of service to others. This is surely why medicine and teaching have held such great attraction for the Scots. Indeed the idea of public service is particularly appealing, given the Calvinist legacy.

And then there is politics. Politics, particularly radical politics, has also been an important avenue for the Scots to fulfil their sense of mission. According to one of his biographers, Keir Hardie, founding father of the Labour Party, was a man with a strong 'Covenanting temperament' and 'missionary style'.[4] In more recent times, John Smith, the Scottish MP and leader of the Labour Party until his untimely death in 1994, was one man for whom politics was a 'calling'. In a book about Smith's life and politics, Gordon Brown asserted that the more Smith progressed in his political life the more he felt his actions closely bound up with his Christian beliefs – the desire to help others, to strive for a better and more just society, to seek to improve people's lives and opportunities through the power of the community.[5]

The SNP too has had its share of purposeful Scots; men like Dr Robert McIntyre, who was an important figure in the Party's reconstruction in the 1940s. McIntyre was the son of a United Free Minister and a specialist in tuberculosis working mainly with the poor before he dedicated his life to Scottish politics. He won a parliamentary by-election for the SNP in Motherwell in 1945 and was the first SNP MP at Westminster (though the seat was lost in the general election a few months later).

It is important to realise that the importance of mission and purpose may be a Calvinist legacy but it is so much part of Scottish culture that it has the capacity to affect all Scots, including those who are atheists or Catholics. Robert Crawford, who was Chief Executive of Scottish Enterprise, is a good example. Crawford was brought up a Catholic and attended a Catholic school but, as he himself admits, he is a 'driven' man, a 'secular Calvinist'.

Thinking in Black and White

As we have already seen already in previous chapters, the Scots have a tendency to see everything as black or white. Things, people, events are either/or, good or bad. This tendency to polarise is characteristic of all Christian cultures and derives its power from the Christian belief that God is a single being who is all that is good and pure while the Devil incarnates all that is evil. The ancient Greeks did not worship one God but believed there were numerous gods, each with different personalities and manifesting different aspects of good and evil. Some Eastern religions do not split good and evil in this way. Instead they see the world as an interplay of two forces, such as yin and yang. Indeed God in some Eastern religions has many faces and characteristics and has both a good and bad side.

In Scotland, the influence of Calvinism may have increased the tendency to polarise even further. So too has the predominance in Scottish cultural life of the mental function Jung defines as thinking. Indeed as extraverted thinking itself can easily lead to fairly simplistic either/or categories, we can see why black and white thinking should be so prevalent in Scotland. For example, the Scots tend to see people in terms of good or bad; clever or stupid; generous or selfish; talented or hopeless. The old Scottish proverb 'Ye're either aa dirt or aa butter' sums up such a view of people.[6] Sydney and Olive Checkland, in their book on Victorian Scotland, argued that the Scots' tendency to Manichean thought polarised issues and 'left little room for the middle ground upon which real debate about human behaviour could take place, and where most of life resided'.[7]

Another of the problems underlying Scottish thinking is that we make little distinction between good and bad faith. Acting in good faith includes those occasions when we make mistakes, not out of malevolence or from questionable values, but because we haven't thought things through properly or are forced to act in some ways because of external circumstances such as the pressure of time. Essentially we make mistakes or make questionable judgements in good faith because we are human. But when we act in bad faith we know that what we are doing is wrong and we still choose this course of action because it suits our own very narrow interests and we simply do not care about the wider repercussions. But in Scotland the prevailing mindset is that each individual is personally responsible, and culpable, for any mistake or questionable judgement that he or she makes. It is as if the Scots think that bad faith is the norm, not the exception. This means that in Scotland a common, if unconscious fear, is that at any moment you might be held to account for your actions by your peers and that no excuses, or mitigating circumstances, will be allowed.

Moray McLaren. in his edited collection called *The Wisdom of the Scots*, is so anxious about being denounced for the work that he prefaces the book with a six-page 'apologia'. Essentially it is an elaborate attempt to get his defence in first. It wasn't his fault, he tells us, he refused first time round, the publisher and his friends twisted his arm. McLaren even recounts the scene:

> Fighting a rearguard action, I then put it to my
> friend that I hadn't the temerity to place my name
> on an anthology impartially representing 'the
> wisdom of the Scots'. 'It would be all very well,' I
> added, 'just putting forward my on own view. I can
> stand up to the knocks against them. But when it
> comes to what other people said and . . . ' [8]

I know exactly the type of thought processes which led McLaren to get in his defence in first, as every hour I have spent on this book I have also wrestled with these same Scottish demons. Apart from the fear of making mistakes and being denounced and reprimanded further down the line I have been plagued by a recurring question: 'Will so and so be offended and annoyed at me even questioning one of Scotland's holy cows let alone trying to slay it?' Indeed while on the subject perhaps I could squeeze in my own apology and say I know that I will have got some of my facts wrong but I am not an academic and I don't have ready access to a university library or colleagues to keep me right. . . And I'm sorry if I have offended anyone I didn't mean to and please believe me my intentions are good – I just want to normalise some of the debate about Scotland and make Scotland a better place to live for everybody . . . Honestly!

You Tak the Low Ground, and I'll Tak the High Ground

The Scots desire to see things in terms of black and white, right or wrong can easily lead to moral absolutism – the belief that your viewpoint is not only right but morally superior to others. Surveying Scottish history you can regularly see such a mindset in action. Of course, we can expect it in spades from religious figures, like John Knox or Andrew Melville, who believed with utter conviction that they were acting as God's emissaries and whose refusal to compromise was legendary. Leaving aside some of the Enlightenment geniuses such as Hume and Smith, who were open-minded, tolerant thinkers who wanted to learn from others, a strong sense of moral authority was evident in the attitudes and writings of many of Scotland's 'great men'. Thomas Carlyle is a brilliant example of this as is Hugh MacDiarmid. MacDiarmid may have been an atheist but in many of his journalistic writings he adopts the same tone to castigate others for their beliefs or shortcomings as many a minister denouncing sinners from the pulpit. In our own time, Jimmy Reid and other left-wing commentators, for all that they may have been atheists, used religious imagery to attack opponents and argue that they are damned:

> Jesus went into the Temple and banjoed the money
> changers. Kicked over the tables. Told the greedy
> that they had only a snowball in hell's chance of ever
> getting through the portals of Heaven. His Heaven
> was obviously a Tory-free zone which effectively puts
> the bar up on the Blairites as well. [9]

One of the devices which is common in the writings of socialists like Jimmy Reid, William McIlvanney and Tommy Sheridan is to characterise an argument in totally black and white terms. 'Which side are you on?' they'll ask, and effectively this means, my side or the wrong side. Even when Scottish writers are not avowedly political there is still a tendency to characterise other people's motives and actions in simplistic terms. You are either out for number one or you are for the common good. No grey areas are recognised, let alone allowed. Any whiff of advantage or self-interest and that is you damned for ever.

Another device Scottish political or literary figures commonly use is to define Scottishness, not as something conferred by birth or residency, but by belief. In the past century these core Scottish beliefs have been delineated most clearly by those who are left of centre – by men like Hugh MacDiarmid with his notion of the 'true Scot', or by modern-day socialists like McIlvanney or Reid. The hegemony of left-wing views in Scotland undermines the political culture for it means that people cannot even question, let alone attack, key Scottish beliefs without feeling they are on the back foot – arguing from a defensive position.

Iain McLean, one of Keir Hardie's biographers, remarks: 'For Hardie the boundary was too vague between rightness and righteousness, and between righteousness and self-righteousness'.[10] Hardie, like many other Scots created in this mould, was only too ready to make personal attacks on political opponents who disagreed with him. The irony is that many of these thinkers stress the importance of co-operation and harmony yet, in reality, they are determined for their views to prevail.

Edward Caird, in an article on Carlyle argued that he was 'quite incapable of the "give and take" of social life, or, indeed, of doing anything in regard to others, except simply to insist on his own will and his own opinions'.[11] And this assessment would fit a number of Scottish political thinkers. I must stress, however, that such thinkers' political ideology is rarely authoritarian in content and we can only use the term 'authoritarian' to describe their personal style and interactions with people.

My Way

Scotland's Calvinist past has bequeathed to contemporary Scots two potentially contradictory attitudes to authority and they lead inevitably to tension. The first flows from the central Calvinist tenet of God's magnificence and humankind's abject state. This means that in comparison with the majesty of God even our noblest achievements are worthless. Calvinism thus taught the Scots to feel humble and submissive and to obey unquestioningly their spiritual Lord and master. But alongside this essentially master/servant relationship, the Scots were also encouraged to see themselves as equal to others in the eyes of God. As we have already seen, the Scottish Kirk is built on democratic foundations – in place of religious aristocracy, the Scots have elected bodies. What's more, to ensure that the Scottish people would never again be 'hoodwinked' by priests or clerics, the reformers ensured that the Scottish people, even the poor, were taught to read and understand the Bible for themselves. The Scots were thus encouraged to be somewhat sceptical and independent-minded. And this spiritual independence of the individual parishioner is further encouraged by Presbyterianism's complete opposition to a priestly figure who acts as an intermediary between an individual and God. To this extent, every individual is equally in charge of his or her spiritual destiny.

So we can see how submissiveness to divine authority coupled with a belief in fundamental human equality means that the Scots are rather perplexed and confused by authority. The Victorian Scot Thomas Carlyle illustrated some of this Scottish ambivalence. Carlyle believed passionately in the importance of heroes and urged others to seek out and obey heroes. He wrote screeds on some of his own heroes – Napoleon and Oliver Cromwell, for example – but he was incapable of paying homage, let alone giving due respect, to any of his own contemporaries.

With the rise of atheism in Scottish society it is easy to see why the historian Christopher Harvie named one of his books on modern Scotland *No Gods and Precious Few Heroes* – lines borrowed from the Scottish poet Hamish Henderson. Or why some argue that a 'Scottish guru' is a contradiction in terms.

Individual Scots clearly vary in their attitude to authority. Some are prepared to accept authority and will eagerly toe the line. Others find it much more difficult to respect someone as a leader. But no matter what the outer behaviour is, I believe that most Scots deep down hanker after authority – that they are searching for an omnipotent God who knows all the answers and never makes mistakes. A perfect being. But, ironically, even God would find it difficult to convince many Scots of His perfection for, as Alexander Scott sardonically explains:

Scotch God
Kent His
Faither[12]

Notes

1 Alastair Reid *Whereabouts: Notes on Being a Foreigner* (Canongate: Edinburgh, 1987), pp.24-25

2 Quoted in Iain Finlayson *The Scots* (Oxford University Press: Oxford, 1988), pp.44-45

3 Andy Dougan *Evening Times*, 6 October 2000

4 Iain MacLean *Keir Hardie* (Penguin Books: London, 1975)

5 Gordon Brown 'John Smith's Socialism: His Writings and Speeches' in Gordon Brown, James Naughtie & Elizabeth Smith *John Smith: Life and Soul of the Party* (Mainstream Publishing: Edinburgh, 1994), p.67

6 David Murison *Scots Saw* (James Thin: Edinburgh, 1981), p.34

7 Sydney & Olive Checkland *Industry and Ethos: Scotland 1832-1914* (Edward Arnold: London, 1984), p.133

8 Moray McLaren *The Wisdom of the Scots* (Michael Joseph: London, 1961), p.15

9 Jimmy Reid *Power without Principles* (B&W Publishing: Edinburgh, 1999), pp.247-8

10 Iain MacLean *Keir Hardie*, p.162.

11 'Edward Caird on Carlyle' in A. M. D. Hughes *Thomas Carlyle Selections* (Oxford University Press: London, 1957), p.XXV

12 *The Collected Poems of Alexander Scott*, David S. Robb (ed.) (Mercat Press: Edinburgh, 1994) p.144

11. The Enterprise Problem

If we learn anything from the history of economic
development, it is that culture makes all the difference.
David Landes, *The Wealth and Poverty of Nations*

In his celebrated study of economic history, Professor David
Landes informs us that there is a joke in Russia that 'the peasant
Ivan is jealous of neighbour Boris, because Boris has a goat. A
fairy comes along and offers Ivan a single wish. What does he
wish for? That Boris's goat should drop dead.'[1]

It is fairly easy to understand why Russians, brought up in a
collectivist state, should be rather envious of others' success
and lack motivation and ambition for themselves. But research
published in 2000 by Jonathan Levie and Laura Steele at the
Hunter Centre for Entrepreneurship shows that at least one in
four Scots share Ivan's views and that the Scots are more jealous
of other people's success than the citizens of any other small
nation. This study also shows that three quarters of Scots believe
that everyone should have the same standard of living regardless
of effort, skill or risk.[2] It is these types of attitudes which may
well underlie Scotland's low business birth rate.

Dr Jonathan Levie collects data annually for the Global Entrepreneurship Monitor (GEM) which allows researchers to make international comparisons in entrepreneurial activity. And GEM repeatedly shows that while the prevailing business climate in Scotland should be 'reasonably good' for starting a business, Scotland's entrepreneurial performance is poor.

At the time of writing the first edition of this book Tom Hunter, in his introduction to the 2001 GEM, states that Scotland is 'a Division Three player and our ratios of opportunity entrepreneurship are at half the levels of other small nations.' Almost a decade on, despite various initiatives to boost entrepreneurial activity in Scotland, Hunter is effectively making the same point by saying 'we didn't make it to the World Cup'.[3]

Following a conversation I had with Dr Jonathan Levie on various reasons for Scotland's poor results, he went back and aggregated the UK GEM survey data for 2002 to 2009 (a total sample size of over 180,0000). What he wanted to see was whether Scots who left Scotland for other parts of the UK were more entrepreneurial. The results were startling: not only did this prove to be the case but depressingly those born in Scotland and living in Scotland had the lowest TEA (Total Enterprise Activity) rate than any other group. Those born outside the UK had a 9.4 per cent TEA rate in Scotland; the English in Scotland's rate was even higher at 12.7 per cent whereas the indigenous Scots' rate was a mere 3.9 per cent.[4] These are highly significant figures as it shows that it is not the prevailing environment or economic conditions which are suppressing Scotland's enterprise rate: the problem must be cultural.

Part of the problem seems to be 'fear of failure'. The 2000 GEM report highlighted the fact that more Scots than the inhabitants of any equivalent nation reported this as one of the biggest obstacles to starting a business. This finding has been less stark in recent years but certainly, in comparison with the English, more Scots (an additional 19 per cent) explain their fear of failure as due to 'the embarrassment' they would experience if their business failed.[5]

It is not difficult to see why the cultural pressures I have outlined in previous chapters would lead to these types of fears and inhibit enterprise. In this chapter I shall elaborate these points and look in more depth for the possible origins of Scotland's 'dependency culture'.

A Capitalist Cradle

Before beginning my brief survey of history, it is worth pointing up that what is surprising about Scotland's low level of entrepreneurship is that eighteenth-century Scotland furnished many of the ideas necessary for the Industrial Age to take off and for capitalism to become the dominant economic system. Lord Kames argued that private property was central to industrial development and without it societies do not develop beyond savagery. David Hume argued that it is the need to preserve property rights that gives rise to government and laws. Adam Smith produced the Bible of capitalist economics – *The Wealth of Nations*. Smith not only coined the phrase 'the division of labour' but also showed how important it was in the creation of wealth.

The Scottish contribution to the revolution in economic production in the eighteenth century was not confined to intellectual ideas. It was James Watt from Greenock who perfected the steam engine which literally powered the industrial revolution. One of the consequences of Watt's invention is that factories could be footloose – they no longer had to be sited near swift running rivers or close to sources of coal.

The ideas for Smith's theory in *The Wealth of Nations* came from his observations of Glasgow merchants, particularly tobacco lords, when he was Professor of Moral Philosophy at Glasgow University in the mid eighteenth century. Glasgow was one of the first cities to capitalise on trade with the American colonies. The money from such activities, the natural resources and geography of the Clyde, the enduring Scottish interest in science and engineering as well as the determination and seriousness of purpose encouraged by Presbyterianism, all contributed to the explosion in industrial activity in the west of Scotland. Men who had made a comfortable living running small businesses now invested time and money developing the new industries. By the nineteenth century Scotland was a world producer of ships, coal, steel, iron, cotton and other textiles.

Nowadays Scotland is not only a country with a poor business birth rate but also has lower economic growth than the UK as a whole and low productivity. Scottish productivity is significantly lower than the figures for the United States, France and Ireland. Scotland has also acquired the reputation as a country with a dependency culture. The Scots are seen by outsiders as a people who expect the state to house them and give them dole money when the economy is in the doldrums. So, what has occurred in the past century or so to put a spoke in the wheel of this once great engine of enterprise?

The Loss of Entrepreneurial Attitudes

One plausible explanation for Scotland's loss of entrepreneurial spirit is that successful Scots became enthralled by English values. The American history professor, Arthur Herman, takes this view and argues that at the end of the nineteenth century:

> . . . Scotland's upper and middle classes were losing that hard-driving entrepreneurial edge which had been a part of their cultural heritage. They increasingly settled into the ideal of the English gentleman. The values of Eton, Cambridge and Oxford, of the Reform and Athenaeum clubs, and of Lord's Cricket Ground steadily replaced those of a grittier homegrown variety.[6]

The Tennant family personifies such Anglicising tendencies. Originally a poor family from Ayrshire, the Tennants lifted themselves out of poverty through basic enterprise and education. Charles Tennant, a gifted scientist, refined the process of chemical bleaching in the eighteenth century and founded the St Rollox work in Glasgow which ultimately became a huge industrial empire. A vastly wealthy family, they later established a family seat in Peeblesshire. By the 1880s the Tennant boys were educated at Eton and the girls came out in London society. A baronetcy followed as did intermarriage with some of the English aristocracy. In our own time, most people know of the family only as a result of the socialite Colin Tennant's association with Princess Margaret and his life on the island of Mustique. He was just one in a long line of family members who had no interest in making money but only in spending it.[7]

Undoubtedly there is some truth in Herman's explanation of the loss of Scottish entrepreneurial spirit, but there is nothing uniquely Scottish in this phenomenon. Countless commercial dynasties in England, America and elsewhere have likewise become enfeebled following the death of the self-made man who founded the enterprise, and his replacement by sons who do not share their father's drive or values. Herman also argues that the middle class Scot became obsessed with respectability and that this further undermined and 'distorted' the Scottish entrepreneurial spirit. He specifically claims that it 'blocked innovation and creativity in ways that could be stifling, even dangerous'.[8]

It is certainly true that successful entrepreneurs need to follow their hunches and be creative and that usually means careering along oblivious to the dictates of conventional life. A society with very prescriptive rules of how people *should* behave will probably find it difficult to sustain high levels of entrepreneurship. It is not uncommon for nationalist commentators to argue that the Scots' obsession with respectability is simply further proof of the imposition of bourgeois English values. But it is easy to find indigenous Scottish reasons for the importance of respectability in Scotland.

Herman links the 'need to conform to social norms' and 'the emphasis on conformity' to Enlightenment ideals. Ideals which confirm the importance of others in both social and moral terms. But Herman does not probe far enough to find that the taproots nourishing the importance of respectability in Scotland run deep into the nation's cultural life: the combination of the cultural preference for the outer, extravert world, the supremacy of collectivist values and the rigid social control once exerted by Kirk sessions mean that in Scotland other people's opinions assume enormous importance in an individual's life. So conforming to established notions of 'respectable' behaviour is very important to the Scots. But this poses an important question: why did business activity in Scotland become separated from what people deemed to be respectable? Are we simply to blame this on the English as well or is there another answer?

The Scottish Experience of Industrialisation

After reading various historians' accounts of Scotland's social and economic past I am convinced of one thing: the vast majority of working class Scots from the early nineteenth century on did not feel positive about capitalist wealth creation for the simple reason that they were either direct casualties of it or their families had suffered acutely from its effects in the past. In the nineteenth century Scotland was the second most urbanised country in the world. And perhaps it was the speed of this urbanisation and the predominance of heavy industry which explain why industrialisation wore such a particularly harsh and brutal face in Scotland. In industrial areas the vast majority of inhabitants lived in tenements. In late nineteenth-century Glasgow this was as high as 85 per cent of city dwellers. The tenements were often warm and dry, and so in some ways preferable to the black houses or damp cottages many had left in rural Scotland or Ireland, but the conditions were often appalling. In 1890 more than half of families lived in one room – called 'single-ends'. Sanitation was inadequate and often shared. Many buildings were infested with vermin and suffered from an acute lack of ventilation and light. No wonder visitors to Edinburgh, Glasgow and Dundee were appalled at some of the living conditions they witnessed. A nineteenth-century reporter for the West of Scotland Handloom Weavers Commission asserted that he had 'seen human degradation in some of its worst phases, both in England and abroad' but it was not until he visited Glasgow's wynds that he believed 'that so large an amount of filth, crime, misery and disease existed in one spot in any civilised country'.[9]

There were many reasons for Scotland's atrocious housing conditions but one is worth highlighting here. The Scots like to think of themselves as more compassionate to the poor than their southern neighbours when in fact throughout the nineteenth century the English were much more generous to those in need. Professor Tom Devine reports that even in the early twentieth century 'the annual cost of relieving paupers per head of population in Scotland was a full 50 per cent lower than in England.'[10] The Scottish Kirk was responsible for poor relief and firmly believed that people would not work if they were given money for nothing. They also believed the poor were generally responsible for their own predicament. This is why the Checklands write: 'In a sense it is fair to regard Scottish welfare provision in the nineteenth century as being, even more than that of the English, mean, grudging and censorious.' [11]

This lack of entitlement to adequate poor relief in Scotland, during periods of unemployment or sickness, meant that workers felt very vulnerable. Many Scottish jobs were heavily dependent on world markets and so were precarious. So the prudent Scottish worker, forced to accept an annual lease on a tenement house, would play safe and commit himself and his family only to the most basic accommodation just in case he fell on bad times. As tenements were the principal type of housing in the urban areas, workers who did manage to accumulate some savings were less likely to become owner occupiers than their counterparts in England because tenements, involving a system of factors and common repairs, were not such attractive propositions for home ownership.

In 1917 the Government appointed a Royal Commission on Housing in Scotland which reported an 'almost unbelievable density'. The Commission pulled no punches: the free market and private landlords – many of them employers and churchmen – had completely failed to provide adequate housing for Scotland's working class. The Royal Commission believed a radical solution was necessary and proposed that 'the State must at once take steps to make good the housing shortage and to improve housing conditions, and that this can only be done by or through the machinery of the public authorities'.[12]

Over the following decades massive programmes of munic-ipal housing took place in Scotland. Given the scale of the problem the provision of decent housing for everyone in Scotland was a huge task. Even in 1951, decades after the launch of countless slum clearance projects, 15.5 per cent of Scots lived in overcrowded accommodation compared with 2.1 per cent of English people. Nowadays, it is easy to look at some of the huge council schemes (or 'deserts wi windaes' to use Billy Connolly's phrase) that were created in places like Pilton, Craigmillar, Easterhouse or Drumchapel and ask why on earth they were ever built. But when you read about the scale of Scotland's housing problems over centuries it becomes clear that desperate solutions were needed. The tragedy is that within decades of these brave new council housing programmes, thousands of new Scottish slums had been created.

But to return to our quest to unearth the reasons why a strong Scottish spirit of enterprise did not survive the nineteenth century. From even a cursory inspection of Scottish housing and poor relief we can see that the Scottish working classes' experience in previous times bred two attitudes which do not help the creation of an enterprise culture. Trapped in atrocious living conditions where there was little prospect of improvement, the Scots often developed a strong dislike, hatred even, of an economic system whereby more fortunate individuals make money out of the less fortunate. The second attitude, which the experience of bad housing and meagre poor relief has bred, is an overwhelming desire for financial security and an unwillingness to take risks. A wrong decision could mean the difference between a life which, although poor and miserable, had some semblance of dignity and respectability, and the most wretched existence in an infamous slum.

In 2001 Thomas Stanley and William Danko published a booked called *The Millionaire Next Door* which examined the background of American millionaires and shows how, generations later, Scots still display this intense fear of falling on hard times. The authors' research shows that while people of Scots ancestry make up about 1.7 per cent of all US households, they account for 9.3 per cent of the millionaires. (Scots were three times more likely to be millionaires than those of English descent.)[13] However, Stanley and Danko also show that the Scots are the least entrepreneurial of all the successful ethnic groups and have usually accumulated money through saving and prudent investment. In other words, even centuries after the actual experience of life in poverty-stricken Scotland, Scots are still unprepared to take financial risks.

The Autocrats

The Scottish working classes' experience of private enterprise was not confined to housing; most worked in Scotland's industrial enterprises. Apart from the scandalous conditions which endured throughout the industrial world at that time – the employment of children, long working hours and the lack of basic health and safety measures, for example – Scottish workers had other reasons to feel aggrieved. In the late nineteenth century wages in Scotland were significantly lower than in England. Although they improved considerably in the early twentieth century, even as late as 1924 Scottish incomes were 8 per cent lower than in the rest of Britain. More important for our understanding of why the Scots were no great admirers of private enterprise, is the fact that many of Scotland's workers were employed in capital-intensive industries dominated largely by autocrats. Sydney and Olive Checkland argue that in the nineteenth century at least, these autocrats were very much moulded in the Presbyterian image:

> They included such names as Colville, Baird, Yarrow, Tennant, Lorimer, Elder, Pearce, Neilson and Beardmore. . . They were autocrats, their decisions were made, conveyed, and not discussed. They had a strong desire to keep everything in their own hands. A man like Beardmore, perhaps the greatest of them, took his own authority over the concern to be absolute and rightful: he and his peers were not given to self-doubt and self-questioning . . . though the business might be slipping away or heading into a crisis, it would be a courageous junior who would raise his voice. . . The magnates of the Scottish basic industries at the end of century may perhaps be taken as a distillation of the Victorian ethic. It centred upon the dominant male of middle age or

over, brooking no interference, speaking only with his equals so far as there was any conferring at all, keeping under authority not only his labour force but also his wives and daughters. Even his sons could be kept under tutelage until old age or death broke the grip.[14]

Unsurprisingly, the Checklands argue that these men believed that workers were there just to obey orders – 'to be tell't'. In the mid nineteenth century there had been some consultation with the workers in Scottish enterprises but, according to the Checklands, this had disappeared by 1900 and they were given little information about the company. 'Labour had become in large measure merely a hired input,' they write, 'with an underlying fear of dismissal.'[15] No wonder labour relations were terrible in many Scottish industries and that many became heavily unionised. So the owners of Scotland's great industries may have been grudgingly respected by fellow Scots but they were feared, intimidating demigods rather than attractive, enterprising role models.

An Alien Culture

In the Highlands too people continued to view capitalist business as alien. After the failure of the 1745 Jacobite rebellion the Government in Westminster attempted to eradicate the threat posed by the Highlands by brutally eliminating its distinctive culture. Highland dress and music were proscribed. The speaking of Gaelic was forbidden. The authorities confiscated estates which had been held by Jacobite rebels and various schemes were introduced to stimulate the economy and introduce industry. The people were to be encouraged to be entrepreneurial and industrious. The Highland threat was reduced by such means but economic development did not happen in the way London envisaged. There were various reasons for this including lack of capital, the lack of a middle class and the sheer number of people, arguably the most entrepreneurial, who emigrated. But, according to Graham Watson, the bigger obstacle to business development was that Highland culture was based on kinship and communal values and stressed the importance of helping one another. It also frowned on risk-taking and encouraged conformity to group norms and so inhibited the development of entrepreneurship.[16]

For a variety of reasons then, many ordinary people in Scotland had very little reason to feel positive about capitalism. As realists, however, once they won the right to vote, many supported the Liberal or Conservative Parties, both of which espoused the virtues of capitalism. But, as Highlanders or members of the Scottish working class they often had very little reason to embrace the capitalist business ethic as their own. Of course, similar attitudes could be found in industrial areas of England, but the difference is that such anti-capitalist attitudes fitted more neatly with the Scots' view of the world. Throughout Scotland people were inclined to collectivist, not just individualist values and inevitably found it more difficult to embrace an economic system which resulted in a few becoming exceedingly rich while the vast majority lived in poverty. The Utopian nature of Scottish religious beliefs also predisposed the Scots to the idea that everyone should be working towards some kind of collective redemption.

So in Scotland, ordinary people who wanted their sons to get on encouraged them to acquire jobs as draughtsmen or clerks, for example. Indeed any 'collar and tie' job in a safe, secure establishment was respectable. Better still was going to university and then entering a profession such as teaching, medicine, law, accountancy or the ministry. For girls, an office job was respectable as was entry into an acknowledged female profession such as primary school teaching or nursing. And, judging from Scotland's low business birth rate, these attitudes are still very much in force.

The Influence of Thomas Chalmers

So much for the working classes. Let us move on to look at the attitude of the middle class and the Church to wealth creation. If you read about the early days of Scotland's industrial revolution it is easy to picture these entrepreneurs as men with a Bible in one hand and a ledger in the other: men who saw no tension between the two sets of philosophies – God and Mammon. But by the nineteenth century the huge social costs of industrialisation in Scotland were so appalling they were impossible to ignore and the Kirk in Scotland became dominated by attempts to find solutions. One of the leading figures in this movement was Thomas Chalmers. He was an influential figure and the fact that an estimated 100,000 people attended his funeral in Edinburgh in 1847 testifies to his importance and popularity. Chalmers was an evangelical within the Scottish Kirk and was particularly concerned about the spiritual and physical condition of Scotland's poor city-dwellers. He was a constitutional radical (and led the Great Disruption in the Church of Scotland) but his views were politically conservative:

> He stressed the correctness of the laws of political economy, the futility of trade unionism and

democracy, the divine origins of a hierarchy where
rich and poor had their obligations and their place,
and the prime responsibility of the individual for
his own material and spiritual health.[17]

Chalmers believed that the solution lay in creating a 'Godly
commonwealth' made up of parish communities. Chalmers's
views were complex. Although he believed that the poor were
often responsible for their own suffering, and rejected the
notion of compulsory poor relief and state intervention, he also
believed passionately in community and that the rich had social
obligations:

> The other part of his message, that the possession of
> wealth and power was ignoble without equivalent
> philanthropy and a sense of personal responsibility,
> was the inspiration to generations of soul-searching
> men to give generously of their money and time to
> the community. That Victorian Scotland was as
> world-famous for serious philanthropists – like
> William Collins of the temperance movement and
> William Quarrier of the children's homes – as it was
> for drunkenness and bad housing was due in no
> small degree to Thomas Chalmers.[18]

As a result of Chalmers's evangelical zeal, the nineteenth
and early twentieth century in Scotland was a time of 'aggressive
Christianity'. Sunday schools were set up and temperance
societies and missions of all kinds appeared. Chalmers himself
attempted to show in a couple of experimental projects how
the ethos of a rural parish could be transplanted to the city.
One such experiment was in the Tron parish in Glasgow. Poor
relief was suspended in the area and money was gathered from
voluntary donations. Only the poor who passed a character test

were awarded any monetary benefits. This and other similar projects initiated by Chalmers were finally judged to be failures. Quite simply the scale of Scotland's social problems were too huge for such palliative measures to have any real effect.

Professor Tom Devine argues that Chalmers's belief that poverty was the fault of the poor and their immoral ways held sway in the Scottish Kirk until the 1870s and only began to crumble in the last quarter of the nineteenth century as a result of the 'impact of intellectual and social forces in the secular world'.[19] Research and reports from social pioneers like Charles Booth and Seebohm Rowntree showed how poverty was more the result of social factors than individual moral character. At the same time a more liberal theology was gaining ground both within the Church of Scotland and the Free Church. By the end of the nineteenth century the notion of 'the elect' had disappeared altogether from the beliefs they espoused. A number of ministers even began to adopt radical political views. Although members of the established Scottish Kirk varied enormously in their attitudes to trade unionism or Christian socialism, for example, it is fair to say that it was no longer intent on blaming the poor themselves for their misfortunes. By the same token, it also stopped portraying the rich as spiritually favoured. The rich were not often condemned as such – after all their money was needed by the Church itself – but those who had money were in a sense stripped of the Kirk's explicit blessing.

So it is not difficult to see why Scotland's middle classes increasingly preferred, and still prefer, their offspring to go into respectable and secure professional careers rather than get their hands morally dirty in real capitalist enterprise. Indeed, as it became abundantly clear in nineteenth-century Scotland that the country's growing wealth and economic success would not automatically, as many religious and Enlightenment figures once believed, raise the masses' living standards to tolerable levels, the enthusiasm of the Scottish middle and upper classes for the prevailing economic system appears to have weakened.

Throughout this book I have argued that Presbyterianism has had a huge impact on Scottish culture and character. I have also argued that Presbyterianism has both an individualistic strand – the individual's personal relationship with God – and a collectivist strand expressed in the idea that we are responsible to and for one another. But by the late nineteenth century, due to the ultimate failure of men like Thomas Chalmers to make a dent on Scotland's endemic social problems, the collectivist strand won, if not the upper hand, a strong grip on Scottish culture. The significance of this is best seen if we compare Scotland with the United States – a country which places a great emphasis on the individual.

America, America

In his book *American Exceptionalism*, Seymour Martin Lipset maintains that Americans see the world in substantially different ways from Europeans and that to understand this you have to understand the American creed. At the heart of this creed is a belief that the powers of the state should be curtailed and that state intervention should be kept to a minimum. In America, Protestant sects have had a huge impact on shaping the nation's mentality but their core beliefs are somewhat different from the original ideology which influenced Knox and his supporters. As the economic historian David Landes points out, it was later versions of the 'Protestant ethic which degenerated into a set of maxims for material success and smug, smarmy sermons on the virtues of wealth.'[20] Under the influence of such ideology, Americans believe that the moral person *should* work hard and strive to make money. Indeed survey evidence shows that 88 per cent of Americans say they admire people who have become rich through hard work.[21] For Americans, therefore, there is nothing contradictory in a religious person being rich.

America is the wealthiest country in the world but is also the country with some of the largest disparities in income. The very rich and the very poor do not quite live side by side (the rich ensure this is not the case as they often live in developments surrounded by security fences) but they inhabit the same cities, albeit on different sides of the track. To the European mind these huge inequalities are outrageous, particularly in a society which claims to be religious, but the American mind sees no contradictions. In fact many Americans would attribute the poverty that exists to government welfare programmes. A staggering 85 per cent of the American population believe that even in the land of minimal welfare provision and health care, 'Poor people have become too dependent on government assistance programs'.[22]

Lipset subtitles his book on American exceptionalism, 'a double-edged sword', as he argues the country's ideology has both positive and negative aspects:

> . . . it fosters a high sense of personal responsibility, independent initiative, and voluntarism even as it also encourages self-serving behaviour, atomism, and a disregard for the communal good. More specifically, its emphasis on individualism threatens traditional forms of community morality, and thus

has historically promoted a particularly virulent strain of greedy behaviour.[23]

So Lipset associates with the American creed various unfortunate developments within that society – the high divorce rate, crime rate, drug taking and litigiousness. He does not mention, though it is obviously linked to the protection of individual rights, the gun culture and the deaths caused by firearms. America's reluctance to sign up to international protocols to limit climate change can also be seen as part of this individualistic philosophy.

We can also find an explanation for the high crime rate in the USA – a rate Lipset shows is three times higher than most other developed countries – in the emphasis American society places on personal success. Individuals are not simply encouraged to stand on their own two feet, they should also be 'winners'. 'The moral mandate to achieve success,' argues the famous American sociologist Robert Merton, 'thus exerts pressure to succeed by fair means, if possible and by foul means if necessary.' [24] No doubt this is one of the reasons why there has also been such a prevalence in America of lawlessness, risky business ventures, 'rackets', bootlegging and so on, as people will take large risks or resort to illegal means if necessary to make money. In fact some American analysts believe this is the inevitable outcome of a society which places a high value on material success.

Scotland's Economic Salvation

I have devoted time to summarising some of the key aspects of American beliefs not because I think these are the attitudes we should import, but simply to show how different they are from the contemporary Scottish view of the world. Andrew Carnegie once famously proclaimed that 'the United States was Scotland realised beyond the seas'.[25] But he was mistaken. Even if Chalmers and the evangelicals had won the battle for Scotland's heart and mind in the nineteenth century the country was unlikely to have developed along American lines because the notion of community and the sense of being responsible for other people are deeply held Scottish values. Ultimately Scotland found the solution to her pressing social and economic problems in collectivism, not individualism and thus Scotland followed a decidedly un-American path.

By the mid to late nineteenth century, many of those who had wealth and power in Scottish society were increasingly won round to the importance of municipal or state action to solve mounting social problems. Even many of Scotland's great entrepreneurs became advocates of state planning and intervention. As many of the industries these men, or their families, had created were dependent on world markets and vulnerable to foreign competition, by the end of the nineteenth century much of Scotland's industry was built on an increasingly shaky foundation. A major problem was that Scotland was too dependent on heavy industry and had too few growth industries. Compared with England it also had too little indigenous demand for service jobs and consumer durables since wages had traditionally been lower in Scotland than England. This problem was exacerbated further by the fact that Scotland had a smaller professional or middle class as a result of centralisation of such jobs in the south of England. So by the early twentieth century it was clear that more economic diversity was needed in Scotland.

In 1931 a group of leading industrialists, led by the influential Clyde shipbuilder Sir James Lithgow, set up a Development Council which aimed to attract new industries north of the border and counter Scotland's reputation for shop-floor militancy. But, partly as a result of the activities of Tom Johnston, the Labour MP who was Secretary of State in Churchill's coalition Government from 1941 to 1945, they soon became passionate corporatists. The Development Council quickly became a strong advocate of the kind of powerful central government planning of the economy that was to become such a feature of post-war Labour government strategy. Johnston then went on to create various organisations which finally became what is still known as the Scottish Council for Development and Industry (SCDI). Following its creation, post-war Scotland benefited from a number of significant inward investment projects from the rest of the UK and from the United States. By 1951, Ferranti, NCR, Honeywell and IBM had all set up in Scottish locations. Scotland also took state-led corporate planning to its heart with the Toothill Report on the Scottish Economy, the creation of the first new towns and the establishment of the Highlands and Islands Development Board. When the HIDB was launched in 1964 it was estimated that the SCDI had been instrumental in bringing more than 250,000 new jobs to Scotland.[26]

Private enterprise and the free market had, historically, failed the Scottish people. As is clear from looking at the west end of many of Scotland's towns and cities, some Scots became incredibly rich as a result of industrialisation but the vast majority lived mean, deprived lives in the midst of industrial squalor, yet often alongside wealth and grandeur. This is why T.C. Smout says at the end of his book on Scotland from 1830 to 1950 that 'what was shocking to contemporaries, and is shocking to us, is how little one of the top two or three richest countries in the world did for its citizens until well into the twentieth century'.[27]

It was the machinery of state which did much to improve the lives of most ordinary Scots. It was the government or local councils which cleared the slums, built decent houses, introduced sickness benefits and old age pensions and provided free health care. It was the government which forced employers to operate within a regulatory framework which guaranteed fair treatment for workers. And it was also central government, through its regional policies, which managed to attract some foreign investment, and hence jobs, into Scotland from the 1950s on. The benefits of such policies were not just felt in the urbanised Lowlands but the Highlands and Islands as well. This is exactly the point former Chair of Highland and Islands Enterprise, James Hunter makes in his book *The Last of the Free* when he writes: '(growing up) . . . in the Highlands and Islands in the 1950s and 1960s was to have access to opportunities of a sort never before on offer to the area's population.'[28]

The Makings of the Dependency Culture

The state certainly did much to improve life for thousands of ordinary Scots, but inevitably this approach also created many of the problems of contemporary Scotland. Just as Lipset refers to America's creed being a 'double edged sword', with positive and negative outcomes, the creed that Scotland adopted similarly has had good and bad effects. Government solutions did improve living conditions for many Scots but it ushered in a culture where decisions are made by committees of experts or government departments far removed from the lives of the people affected by them. In other words, it is a system completely at odds with the philosophy of self-help and self-determination advanced by socialist radicals of the past.

For me one of the finest moments in Scottish history was when socialist radicals, like Jimmy Maxton, inspired poor working class people to love learning and to hanker after a society which would create the circumstances which would allow them to maximise their potential. Nowadays people may be better housed, clothed and fed, but poverty still remains in whole tracts of Scotland. The poverty I'm referring to is not just material deprivation but the lack of desire and ambition to make something of yourself and your life. In Scotland the combination of strong collectivist values and our version of egalitarianism encourages people to know their place. It encourages us all to toe the line and conform. When we add to these attitudes the dependency which welfare policies and corporatism can encourage, it is easy to see why we have some significant economic problems in Scotland – low productivity, low business birth rate, and many impoverished communities where people seem to be devoid of motivation and ambition for themselves or their families.

Often it is outsiders who are most able to pick up on attitudes which we take for granted so it is interesting to read what the New Zealand academic H.J. Hanham writes about this aspect of Scottish life in his book on Scottish nationalism:

> The ordinary Scot since the 1930s has simply sat back and waited until the good things from the south have at least reached Scotland – new shops, new social security benefits, new industries, new towns. There has been a clamour when they have not come soon enough to please him. But there

has been little disposition to do anything positive to help, or appreciation of the invaluable work done in Scotland by . . . bodies devoted to the fostering of Scottish industry. The ordinary Scot has been prepared to accept that his more enterprising fellows will emigrate as a matter of course and that Scotland will become a pensioner dependent on England.[29]

The Safety Valve

Hanham is right to raise emigration in this context. One of the pressing questions which arises from the analysis which I have set out in this chapter is this: why did the Scots who once had the reputation for being a lively, active, intelligent and inventive people become subdued and somewhat dependent? The answer lies partly in emigration, for it acted as a safety value, allowing those who were not prepared to accept the limited life on offer to escape. In *The Scottish Nation 1700–2000*, Professor Tom Devine explains that the period from 1821 to 1915 saw a huge amount of emigration from Europe, particularly to North America and Australasia. Throughout this period three countries topped the list for emigration – Norway, Scotland and Ireland. For most decades it was the Irish who came top but for four of the great surges of emigration (in the 1850s, 1870s, the early 1900s and the inter-war years) Scotland was the country producing most emigrants. Between 1841 and 1911 over 600,000 Scots emigrated to England, and Devine argues that if this migration is included in Scotland's figures 'Scotland then emerges clearly as the emigration capital of Europe for most of the period'.[30]

The Museum of Scotland houses a famous Scottish painting

'The Last of the Clans' by Tom Faed. Painted in 1865 it depicts the tragic plight of Highlanders forced to pack up and leave their native land. But throughout the nineteenth century and into the twentieth many more Highlanders *chose* to leave than were actually forced to go. In the words of Marjorie Harper, a Scottish emigration specialist, 'the Highland diaspora . . . owed as much to persuasion as persecution'.[31] In their introduction to *The New Penguin History of Scotland*, the editors argue that the enforced clearances of the Highlands have dominated the debate about emigration from the area. Effectively they argue that Highlanders were traumatised by the experience and that 'such bitter memories' have become 'embedded in its oral culture'. And they explain that a possible answer for such deeply held feelings may lie in the traditional Highland attitude to land:

> One answer may be the existence of a widely held
> belief that land was a communal entity within a
> moral economy . . . Those doing the evicting were
> held to have a moral responsibility towards those
> under them, including obligations based on real or
> notional kinship. Associated with this is the fact
> that the Gaels were subject to a cultural displace-
> ment that was more severe than for Lowlanders,
> who were more used to cities and commercialism
> . . . The dissolving forces of political and cultural
> change which . . . turned landowners from chiefs
> into landlords during the eighteenth century had a
> profound impact on Gaelic society, also turning
> kinsmen into crofters.[32]

There are many reasons why emigrants choose to leave their homeland. Experts refer to them as 'push/pull' factors. The Scots were, as we know from the clearances, often pushed by land-lords who wanted to do something else with their estates. They were also pushed to leave Scotland by unemployment, poverty and atrocious living conditions. But often it was not those suffering the poorest conditions who left. Many emigrated because they were pulled by the opportunities and the possibilities of life in a new country. This was also true in the Highlands and the Lowlands. In 1906 the Board of Agriculture, concerned about the declining rural population, reviewed the reasons and reported that particularly in Scotland 'many of the best men have been attracted to the colonies, where their energies may find wider scope and where the road to independence and a competency is broader and more easy to access'.[33]

Emigration siphoned off the Scots who wanted to make something different of their lives. It helped to remove those who were the most curious, the most opportunist, the most restless and the most ambitious. There's little doubt that the constant removal of such enterprising types from the country must have had some lingering effect on Scottish culture and attitudes.

Some regard emigrants as Scotland's major export, but exports bring benefits to a country. In Scotland's case emigration was, and still is, a brain drain. It is a route out of Scotland for those who are not content with the limited world on offer to them or who simply want to leave Scotland's constricting attitudes so that they can spread their wings.

Scotland's future

Indigenous business development, as opposed to inward investment, has been part of the UK government's economic agenda since the 1970s. The SNP Government in Holyrood from

2007-2011 made 'sustainable economic growth' its number one 'Purpose'. Critical to this was fostering 'a self-sustaining and ambitious climate for entrepreneurs.' Yet little has really been achieved given that GEM is still showing Scotland performing poorly in comparison with equivalent countries.

Much of the difficulty the Scots have with setting up in business appears to emanate from the type of personal issues I highlight in this book – a general lack of confidence, a fear of failure, a fear of success, an ambivalence about money, and an over-concern with others' views. But just as important is the fact that Scottish culture as a whole is ambivalent about wealth creation. This attitude has been there for over a century but sharpened in the 1980s as a result of Margaret Thatcher's occupation of Number 10 Downing Street. Many Scots have simply taken the view that being Scottish means playing down the importance of money-making and a pro-business agenda.

My political leanings have always been to the left and I understand the basis of these views. Nonetheless I believe that a wholehearted attempt to grow indigenous small businesses and social enterprises is the best option for Scotland. It is certainly more attractive than inward investment, for example, as the jobs this creates are often low-paid and precarious. The only other alternative is dependence on the state for employment or benefits – a state which is destined to shrink as a result of public sector cuts.

If we want to change Scottish culture to make it more positive about wealth creation we must separate it from an excessively Thatcherite ideology which encourages greed and argues that there is no such thing as society. We must also refuse to accept that being more positive about wealth creation means embracing and importing American ideology and values. We have to find our own way – a way that removes the specific Scottish blockages to entrepreneurship and business development; a way that respects, not negates or denies, Scottish history and culture.

One of the best actions that Scottish agencies could take to stimulate more interest in business development is to promote business not just as something which you can do to improve your own life but as something which has positive social benefits for the community. Building a business creates jobs. Spending money also creates jobs and puts money in other people's pockets. Making money also gives people the opportunity to spend some of it for the collective good.

Businesses can also be set up as social enterprises where they are run, not for profit, but in pursuit a wider social goal. These initiatives need to be more widely known. The more difficult part will be emphasising the importance of entrepreneurship and the collective good while at the same time trying to free up individuals so that they feel enabled to be more creative and independent; less worried about what other people think of them and whether they are going to fail.

Given Scotland's history I believe we can only become more entrepreneurial if we do not become too ideological about it. We must show that it is possible to have more positive views of entrepreneurship and still be in favour of public spending and a fairer distribution of wealth. I also think it is a mistake to argue that Scotland will only become more entrepreneurial if the country embarks on substantial deregulation or slashes corporation tax. As Tom Hunter once pointed out, entrepreneurs do not decide to set up in business because the tax rate is favourable, they do so because they feel inspired and motivated. And such feelings are largely encouraged by an individual's prevailing environment. It is that we have to change if we want Scotland to have a more enterprising culture – a culture where we cherish our own dreams rather than wish the demise of our neighbour's goat.

Notes

1 David Landes *The Wealth and Poverty of Nations* (Abacus: London, 1999), p.518

2 Jonathan Levie and Laura Steele *Global Entrepreneurship Monitor, Scotland 2000* , University of Strathclyde

3 Tom Hunter in Jonathan Levie and Laura Steele *Global Entrepreneurship Monitor, Scotland 2001,* University of Strathclyde, p.3

4 Private correspondence with Jonathan Levie

5 Jonathan Levie *Global Entrepreneurship Monitor,*2009 p.3

6 Arthur Herman *The Scottish Enlightenment: The Scots' Invention of the Modern World* (Fourth Estate: London, 2002), p.349

7 For a history of the Tennant family see Simon Blow *Broken Blood* (Faber and Faber: London, 1987)

8 Arthur Herman *The Scottish Enlightenment*, p.353

9 Quoted in T.M. Devine *The Scottish Nation 1700-2000* (Penguin Books: London, 1999), p.334

10 T.M. Devine *The Scottish Nation*, p.343.

11 Sydney & Olive Checkland *Industry and Ethos: Scotland 1832-1914* (Edward Arnold: London, 1984), p.99

12 Quoted in T.M. Devine *The Scottish Nation*, p.346

13 Thomas Stanley and William Danko *The Millionaire Next Door* (Simon and Schuster: USA, 2000)

14 Sydney & Olive Checkland *Industry and Ethos: Scotland 1832-1914* (Edward Arnold: London, 1984), p.178

15 Ibid., p.178

16 Graham Watson ' "Nothing New Under the Sun": Are there Lessons to be Learned Today from Government Support for Businesses in the Highlands after the Uprising of 1745?',

    M.Sc. Thesis in Entrepreneurial Studies, University of Stirling, 1993

17 T.C. Smout *A History of the Scottish People 1560-1830* (Collins: London, 1969), p.186

18 Ibid., p.186

19 T.M. Devine *The Scottish Nation*, p.380

20 David Landes *The Wealth and Poverty of Nations*, p.176

21 Seymour Martin Lipset *American Exceptionalism: A Double-edged Sword* (W. W. Norton & Company: London, 1997)

22 Ibid., p.287

23 Ibid., p.268

24 Quoted in Seymour Martin Lipset *American Exceptionalism*, p.47

25 Quoted in Arthur Herman *The Scottish Enlightenment*, p.328

26 For further information see Alf Young 'The Scottish Establishment: Old and New Elites' in Gerry Hassan and Chris Warhurst (eds.) *Tomorrow's Scotland* (Lawrence and Wishart: London 2002), pp.157-9

27 T.C. Smout *A Century of the Scottish People 1830-1950* (Collins: London, 1986), p.275

28 James Hunter *Last of the Free: A Millennial History of the Highlands and Islands of Scotland* (Mainstream Publishing: Edinburgh, 1999), p.347

29 H.J. Hanham *Scottish Nationalism* (Faber and Faber: London, 1969), p.47

30 T.M. Devine *The Scottish Nation*, p.468

31 Marjorie Harper in Michael Lynch *The Oxford Companion to Scottish History* (Oxford University Press: Oxford, 2001), p.232

32 R.A. Houston & W. W. J. Knox *The New Penguin History of Scotland: From the Earliest Times to the Present Day* (Penguin Books Ltd: London, 2001), p.xxxiii

33 Quoted in T.M. Devine *The Scottish Nation*, p.484

12. Complex Inferiority

What is Scotland? A nation, a province, a lost
kingdom; a culture, a history, a body of tradition; a
bundle of sentiments, a state of mind; North
Britain or Caledonia? Such are the questions which
Scots have been asking themselves, implicitly or
openly, ever since 1707 . . .

Janet Adam Smith, quoted above, is right to point out how since the Union of the Parliaments the Scots have been obsessed by issues of Scottishness and Scottish identity.[1] Over the years, countless Scottish writers have prodded the subject with their pens to check that it is still breathing; many have pronounced that Scotland and her people are not in good health. G.M. Thomson in his 1920s book, *Caledonia*, asserted that 'the Scots are a dying people'.[2] George Scott Moncrieff described Edinburgh as 'dead' and the whole of Scotland as 'an abortive carcass rotting somewhere to the North of England.'[3] Edwin Muir's journey round Scotland in the mid 1930s convinced him that although 'Scotland has not been a nation for some time, it has possessed a distinctly marked style of life; and that is now falling to pieces, for there is no visible and effective power to hold it together.'[4] And a decade or so before devolution, the nationalist writer Paul Scott warned that various developments 'threaten the survival of the national identity'.[5] In recent times Cairns Craig has argued that 'Scottish culture has . . . always lived under the shadow of its possible annihilation.'[6]

In Chapter 2, I argued that cultural analysts in Scotland often portray Scottish identity and consciousness itself as problematic. The Scottish literature professor Douglas Gifford even writes about 'the schizophrenic Act of Union in 1707' and claims it 'contained the seeds of Scotland's nineteenth century crises of identity'.[7] But while literary specialists and political theorists such as Tom Nairn may claim that in the past there was something double and divided about the Scots' sense of themselves, historians are much more circumspect. In *The New Penguin History of Scotland*, for example, Graeme Morton and R.J. Morris argue that in the nineteenth century 'Scotland had a remarkably confident national identity'[8] – that just as Scots today can have complex political identities, combining a sense of Britishness with Scottishness, so too did our forebears. In short, these historians believe there was nothing strange or pathological about the Scots' sense of themselves in the nineteenth century.

Over the years the Scots have fretted about the health of Scotland and Scottish identity yet, paradoxically, a sense of Scottishness has been robust and fairly impervious to Anglicisation. Even when the Empire and feelings of Britishness were at their height Scottish identity was strong enough to see off the nineteenth-century attempt for Scotland to become simply 'North Britain'. In the twentieth century it was in such good health it became an effective springboard for varying degrees of political nationalism. The rise of the SNP and the popularity of various devolution campaigns would not have been possible without a strong Scottish identity. Now a Scottish Parliament once again sits in Edinburgh, after almost three hundred years of suspension, and survey evidence shows that a growing number of Scots say they feel much more Scottish than British.

Brown, McCrone and Paterson in *Politics and Society in Scotland* show how, since survey data became available in 1986, 'it is clear that people living in Scotland give priority to being Scottish' rather than British. Indeed they add 'between six and nine times more people stress their Scottishness than their Britishness. This is a remarkable and consistent finding.'[9]

So why has Scottish identity been so resilient? I believe there are four simple explanations.

A Negatively Defined Identity

First, Scottish identity is so strong because it can be reduced to a few simple words – *The Scots are not English*. Few countries can distil their identity into a soundbite and, like it or not, in the modern world soundbites are often more powerful than complex, sophisticated arguments. So the simple fact of not being English has afforded the Scots a strong, albeit negatively defined, identity. Many Scots analysts and commentators remark on this feature of Scots identity but they usually label it as wholly negative – a sign of rampant insecurity which gives rise to petty anti-English feeling. There is little doubt that the Scots' negatively defined identity displays itself in all sorts of unwanted ways and is a manifestation of a previous power battle which Scotland lost. But despite its weaknesses it has considerable strengths; it has been a constant star in the firmament. No matter what happens it is still there. And the very fact that it is always there has helped the Scots resist some of the pressures of continual Anglicisation and assimilation, and ensured the continuation of a strong *Scottish* sense of self. So if we are trying to chart why Scottish identity since 1707 has been robust and resilient, the sense of 'not being English' is our first port of call.

Distinctive Scottish Institutions

The second reason why Scottish identity has remained so strong following the Union is the terms of the Act of Union itself. There was no popular will in favour of the Union and rioting broke out in the streets in the days leading up to it. As there was no stomach in Scotland for an incorporating Union with England, the Scottish Parliament, thanks to the tenacity of men like Andrew Fletcher of Saltoun, did its best to ensure that Scottish identity and institutions would survive the Union of the Parliaments. So Scotland lost political sovereignty in 1707 but retained her separate Church, legal system and schools. Religion had played an important part in the formation of Scottishness as we know it and the Church's continuing influence was not threatened by the Union. What's more the Act allowed the Scots to administer and determine policy in education and poor relief – services which had most impact on the lives of ordinary people in the days and centuries which followed.

So the Scots may have been bribed and browbeaten into the Union but they still managed to secure terms that permitted a distinctive sense of Scottishness to remain following the joining of the Parliaments.

A Storehouse of National Symbols

A third explanation for the resilience of Scottish identity is the wealth of Scottish 'iconography'. National identity is inevitably abstract and difficult to define. So a country's identity must not only be able to persist over time it must also be capable of transmission from one generation to the next. This means it needs to attach itself to easily understood symbols or icons. As various commentators, such as David McCrone, have pointed out, Scotland is knee-deep in national symbolism:

> . . . if anything, it is overwhelming. It appears in
> films, novels, poems, paintings, photographs, as
> well as on shortbread tins.
> . . . tartan; kilts; heather; haggis; misty landscapes;
> couthy (and slightly weird) natives; Jekyll and
> Hyde; Scottish soldiers; Take the High Road; MQS
> (Mary Queen of Scots); BPS (Bonnie Prince
> Charlie); Balmorality; Harry Lauder. . . [10]

Not only are these symbols strong and enduring they are
quite different from the symbols associated with England. For
example, among the English symbols Paxman lists in his book
on England are 'village cricket and Elgar, Do-It-Yourself, punk,
street fashion, irony, vigorous politics, brass bands, Shakespeare,
Cumberland sausages, double-decker buses, Vaughan Williams,
Donne and Dickens, twitching net curtains. . .' [11] And so the list
goes on. A lot of the items on Paxman's list, like 'fish and chips,
curry and bad hotels' apply to the whole United Kingdom not
just England. Many of them are not that distinct. None of these
symbols has the immediately recognisable quality of tartan or
pipe bands, for example. This is why Charles Jennings writes:
'Englishness, unlike Scottishness, is baffling, diffuse.' A few
sentences on he asks: 'What common culture do we, the English,
hold dear?' [12]

A striking feature of any list of Scottish icons is that it is
dominated by Highland symbolism. There's little doubt that
Scotland's fascination with tartan is attributable to Sir Walter
Scott. He was made a Baronet in 1820 and two years later was
responsible for stage managing George IV's state visit to Scotland
in which the King wore a kilt (and pink tights) and the entourage
were similarly decked out in tartan. The Westminster Govern-

ment banned the wearing of Highland dress in 1747 and it is Scott who was responsible for its reappearance as elite costume. And this was just the beginning of royalty's love affair with the Highlands. Queen Victoria bought the Balmoral estate in 1848, opening yet another Scottish tourist trail. So for all these reasons Scott is credited with, or more accurately blamed for, giving Scotland an anachronistic and bogus national identity. Thanks to him, and James Macpherson of Ossian fame, Lowland Scotland literally stole the clothes off Highlanders they had previously despised. Condemnation of tartanry and use of Highland symbolism by some critics has fuelled a great deal of negative comment on Scotland and the Scots yet as the celebrated historian William Ferguson points out:

> In the ethnic or cultural sense the words Highland and Lowland now have little relevance. Most Scots of the old ethnic stock nowadays are of mixed Lowland and Highland forebears – and the word 'most' here is used advisedly. This can be proved by a glance at the telephone directory of any major urban community in Scotland. There will be found a plethora of Highland names, in Glasgow or Edinburgh, Aberdeen or Dundee. Where have all those Gaelic names come from . . .?[13]

Whatever view you take on the appropriateness of Scottish iconography one thing is clear – it has made a huge contribution to the continuation and strength of Scottish identity.

Scottish Beliefs and Preferences

Our fourth port of call in this quest for the strength of Scottish identity is that many Scots feel that the mindset they are encouraged to adopt is distinctly different from their neighbours'. However, as I argued earlier, most Scots are not aware of the forces in Scottish culture which shape their mindset. In previous chapters, I have outlined what these forces are and for brevity I have summarised the main points in Table 1 overleaf. For comparison, the table includes a similar list for England. In reading this table it is important to bear in mind that this summary is trying to capture the essence or spirit of Scotland and England. Of course, it does not describe every individual in each country. So it has to be read as the characteristics and values which the culture of each country encourages.

Over the years some of these Scottish characteristics have been watered down as a result of pressure from England. This is most true of Scotland's desire for generalism in education and the love of speculation and reasoning from first principles. These were features of Scotland's traditional approach to education but in the nineteenth and early twentieth centuries Scottish universities were forced to model themselves along English lines. But it is also true that English culture has been moderated as a result of Scottish preferences. It is impossible to read the history of Britain in the nineteenth and twentieth centuries and not be struck by how often it was the Scots who provided progressive thinking within the United Kingdom. In the nineteenth century much of the progressive thought behind the Liberal Party and the ruling class's openness to demands for the extension of the suffrage came from Scots such as Lord Brougham and Lord Macaulay within the Westminster Parliament.[14] The Labour movement too was heavily influenced by Scots like Keir Hardie or James Maxton who were animated by their Presbyterian background. Labour Governments have had a number of Scots in key Cabinet positions.

So even though Scotland lost her sovereign Parliament, her distinctive language and many traditional ways of life, her strong preferences and unifying belief system means that the Scots have retained to this day a distinctive set of attitudes and beliefs. In other words, despite all the fears of Scottish soothe-sayers, who have predicted the demise of Scotland as a separate cultural entity over the years, Scottish identity, consciousness and preferences have more than just survived. They have remained remarkably strong and resilient. And I think it speaks volumes for Scottish tenacity and strength of character that it has endured in the way it has. As the historian J.M. Reid once remarked: 'For centuries the Scots had to fight bitterly and almost continuously for the mere chance to remain Scottish'. Reid is also right to say that as the Scots 'were poor, few and remote from the great centres of European life' they have every right to feel proud that 'in spite of everything, they had contrived to remain themselves.' [15]

Complex Inferiority

My argument that Scottish identity has always been robust despite the fear that it would fade away is not the same as arguing that Scotland's relationship with England has not been psychologically damaging for the Scots. The relationship has undermined Scottish confidence and sense of self-worth and the problem may well have predated the Union. The American historian Wallace Notestein, in his book *The Scot in History – a Study of the Interplay of Character and History*, argues that early records show the Scots were well-known to be 'proud' and 'boastful' and that these traits seemed due in part to their insecurity. Notestein writes:

> The sensitiveness of the Scots to what was said
> about them was not unrelated to their habit of
> boasting about themselves. The chronicles furnish
> abundant proof that the Scots were peculiarly
> sensitive to what the English thought about them
> and any criticism of their courage or military
> prowess met with instant notice and reply.[16]

In other words, the Scots may well have had a hang-up about the English long before the Union. So what is this 'sensitivity' or lack of confidence all about? There are various ways to characterise and analyse the relationship between Scotland and England. We could liken the two countries to siblings and look at the rivalry between them and its psychological effects on the junior partner. We could follow the example of Beveridge and Turnbull and show how the Scots were repeatedly told they had been civilised by the Union and so developed an 'inferiorist' mentality similar to that of colonial peoples. But the conceptual tool which I think best helps us to understand the psychological relationship between Scotland and England can be found in the famous work of the great French intellectual, Simone de Beauvoir – *The Second Sex*.

De Beauvoir's Concept of 'The Other'

De Beauvoir argues that in the natural relationship between two human beings both see themselves as sovereign beings – the One – and – 'the Other'. This 'fundamental hostility' between individuals and groups is not usually a problem as the Other 'sets up a reciprocal claim'.[17] Foreigners abroad, for example, view the inhabitants as 'Others' but they must come to see that they too are defined as abnormal and alien. For de Beauvoir

Table 1 Comparison of Scottish and English cultures

Scotland	England
Active, energetic	Reflective
Outward looking	Insular
Emphasis on speech (even in literature)	Love of the written word
Sociable	Private – emphasis on 'home'
Collectivist	Individualistic
Group rights (e.g. focus on Scottish freedom)	Individual rights (e.g. against the state)
Belief that what a person does affects others	Emphasis on the importance of privacy ('an Englishman's home is his castle')
Preference for generalism in education; breadth	Emphasis on specialism in education; depth
Principles	Pragmatism
Opinionated, passionate, committed	Open-minded
Judgmental (pronounced sense of right and wrong)	Tolerant; live and let live
Drawn to abstract thought and ideas	Prefers concrete information and facts
Speculative	Cautious, guided by experience
Forward looking	Backward looking
Drawn to vision and possibilities	Traditional

Table 1 continued

Scotland	England
Initiate change or are at least open to the idea of change if it seems logical	Conservative; hark back to the past
Motivated by Utopian dream of collective redemption for all Scots – a perfect community	Dream of 'privacy without loneliness'; drawn to a green, isolated landscape
Emphasis on individual mission to improve the world for others	It is up to the individual to choose his or her own life
Emphasis on plainness and simplicity	'Manners maketh the man'; like refinement
Equality important	Fair play important
No disgrace to be born poor	Snobbery
Prone to sentimentality	Prone to cultivate cranks and eccentrics
Sense of under confidence and seesawing from feelings of inferiority to superiority	Sense of superiority

the tragedy of woman's experience is that historically she has given up her own claims to sovereignty and accepted man's definition of her as the 'inessential Other'. Man is the neutral sex – the norm – whereas woman is defined with reference to him. This notion helps us to understand that while there are countless books on women's condition, men do not need to write specific books on their experience or interests as they constitute the 'mainstream'. It is the so-called 'ordinary' books on history, philosophy, religion, literature and so on which represent men's perspective on the world. Unconvinced? Then how about the fact that in the English language the word 'man' is used interchangeably to mean homo sapiens and to describe an individual male. Many men fail to understand why modern women can make an issue of nomenclature, and seem blissfully unaware that language is symbolically important as it under-scores women's marginality from 'mainstream' culture – from the norm.

For brevity, I have charted the parallels between women's growing consciousness and Scots consciousness in Table 2 overleaf. As you will see, women's experience of marginaisation is similar to the daily experience of many Scots. This helps to explain the Scots' great sensitivity about terminology on the BBC or other English-dominated media. When 'England' is used instead of 'Britain' many Scots intuitively know it symbolises Scotland's marginal status; her role as 'inessential Other'. Their sensitivity on such apparently trivial issues can then make Scots look like paranoid, nit pickers – even to fellow Scots.

Isobel Lindsay illustrates the way Scots culture is marginal-ised in other ways. She writes that 'the Scots as a nation', both middle and working class, 'have experienced something akin to what the lower classes experience as a sub-group in the larger society. Our language or dialect was rejected as inferior and the centres of power and influence increasingly moved outwith the country.'[18] Following the Union, the definition of good manners, pronunciation and correct usage of the English language emanating from the English ruling class led the Scots to question their speech and manners. No doubt the lure of English patronage ensured that many an ambitious Scot paid attention to what the English defined as 'proper speech'. This comes across clearly in accounts of the Scottish Enlightenment when even these intellectual giants, in the wake of criticism from the south, were embarrassed by their Scottishness and became obsessed by expunging 'Scotticisms' from their speech and writing. Many even participated in elocution lessons run by the poet James Beattie. David Hume's lack of confidence in his native language led one wag to remark that the atheist Hume 'died confessing, not his sins, but his Scotticisms'. Hume himself wrote:

> Is it not strange that, at a time when we have lost our Princes, our Parliaments, our independent Government, even the Presence of our chief Nobility, we are unhappy, in our Accent & Pronunciation, speak a very corrupt Dialect of the Tongue which we make use of; is it not strange, I say, that, in these Circumstances we shou'd really be the People most distinguish'd for Literature in Europe? [19]

As the stronger and more dominant partner in the Union, the English were able to arrogate to themselves the notion that they were right – the defining point, the barometer – and were able to judge anything different from them as inferior. Even Sir Walter Scott, a committed Unionist, believed this to be the case. 'The English act on the principle that everything English is right,'

Table 2 Comparison of women's and the Scots' view of themselves and reactions to their inferior position

Women	Scots
Women perceive themselves as different from men.	The Scots perceive themselves as different from 'the English'.
Women know they are judged by men as 'inferior' both because they are the 'Other' – a marginal afterthought – and because men have power over them (money, status, legal rights).	The Scots fear they are seen as inferior because the English – as the larger, stronger, richer partner – use their experience and views to define, for example, a good education, good manners, proper pronunciation. Also the English have more political and economic power.
Women feel themselves to be inferior (because they are socialised in a society which accepts male dominance) and therefore they lack self-confidence.	Scots believe that Scotland was a barbaric, uncivilised place before the Union. They feel they couldn't do without the English to keep them civilised and well-governed. They may talk confidently (Wha's like us?) but secretly fret about being inferior.
Women may begin to resent the way their marginalisation is symbolised in language so they become hypersensitive to terms such as 'chairman'.	The Scots become very touchy about language, e.g. letters to the BBC's *Points of View* programme about sports commentators' use of British and English.
As women's consciousness of subordination grows, men are often portrayed as inferior or inadequate in some way. Gross generalisations abound (e.g. 'all men are bastards').	The Scots often stereotype the English as arrogant people who talk loudly in restaurants. They tend to blame the English and their own lack of political power for anything which goes wrong.
As women's collective confidence grows and they become more financially independent of men, what would be denounced as 'sexism' in the past sometimes gets ignored or is deemed irrelevant.	As the Scots' confidence grows and they have their own Parliament, and so more ability to control their own affairs, there is less reason to pay attention to the English let alone blame them for all their ills.
The increasing empowerment of women leads men to question the meaning of masculinity. Males begin to suffer an identity crisis. They start to write books on the topic.	As the Scots, and others, grow in confidence and in power, the English start to worry about their identity. Jeremy Paxman and others write books on the subject.

he wrote, 'and that anything in Scotland which is not English must therefore be wrong.' [20] A sentiment echoed centuries later when the former Historiographer Royal in Scotland, Gordon Donaldson, claimed that 'in English eyes anything that is not English is peculiar; worse than that, it is backward if not actually barbarous.' [21]

De Beauvoir's theory is founded on the notion that rightness and selfhood are at the heart of any notion of sovereignty and that this plays its part in the relationship between two individuals (the master and slave, for example) and in the relationship between groups or nations. According to this theory, there is nothing unusual in the English defining themselves as the One, the norm, for that is the nature of sovereignty. The tragedy for Scotland is that, for both physical and economic reasons the English were able to impose their sense of superiority on 'the Other'.

The Relationship with England

So the sense of being if not exactly 'wrong', then 'not right' – a marginal Other – is, I believe, a key aspect of Scottish consciousness and it has been around for a long time. I am not arguing that the Scots over the generations have simply accepted the superiority of the English or their status as inferior, wrong 'Other'. If you read Scotland's history after 1707 it is clear that sometimes it suited the Scots to play second fiddle to England's 'superior' performance. And if that meant accepting the 'rightness' of the English approach, or emulating what Scots have sometimes described as their 'more mature' neighbour, then so be it. On other occasions the Scots have balked at the very idea of playing second fiddle and have been fiercely opposed to their own distinctly Scottish tunes being drowned out by English ways. Indeed there have been times when the Scots believed that if they took up the inferior fiddle and played England's tune, Scottish identity itself may disappear.

The historian N.T. Phillipson has shown how throughout the eighteenth and nineteenth centuries the Scots vacillated in their attitude to assimilation and subordination. The Scots demonstrated most opposition to assimilation when the English attempted to abolish small Scottish banknotes in 1826. It was during the time of this perceived threat to Scottish identity when Sir Walter Scott, a great believer in the benefits of the Union, took up his pen and lambasted the English for always thinking they were right. Phillipson argues that this is an important incident in Scottish history as it highlighted an on-going dilemma for Scots: how to maintain a Union which did 'boast advantages', while asserting their independent identity as Scots. Phillipson argues that they needed 'a passive ideology' and the formula was provided by Sir Walter Scott himself. He claims that Scott

> . . . showed Scotsmen how to express their nationalism by focusing their confused national emotions upon inessentials, like the few sinecures and offices of state . . . like the use of the word 'Scotch', the phrase 'north Britain', or the present queen's monogram on letterboxes; like the campaign to prevent the disbanding of the Argylls. By validating the making of a fuss about nothing, Scott gave to middle class Scotsmen and to Scottish nationalism an ideology – an ideology of noisy inaction.[22]

But this is much too rational and mechanistic an argument for the Scots' sensitivity to so-called 'inessentials'. Life is not as simple as Nick Phillipson makes out. Phillipson's notion takes little account of how people's identity is formed or maintained, whereas the idea of the Scot as marginal Other leads to a much fuller, more human, understanding of the importance of these types of symbolic issues and the protests which ensued. The Scots did not need to be taught the importance of symbolism by Sir Walter Scott; they would have felt sensitive to marginalisation anyway because they were able to decode the significance of this symbolism and to see how it posed a *real* long-term threat to Scottish identity and self-worth. Indeed some of the things which Phillipson cites as 'inessentials' are very pertinent. As any psychologist will tell you, what we call ourselves, and what names others use to refer to us, are major elements in our identity and sense of self. Using the term 'North Britain' instead of Scotland is a denial of the Scots' history and sense of distinctive culture. No wonder most objected and the term gradually disappeared from view – living on for many years only on hotel fronts.

Phillipson may dismiss such protests as 'noisy inaction' but, as Lindsay Paterson points out, they were often successful. England did withdraw her proposal to abolish Scottish banknotes and the same formula worked on other occasions for the Scots. Paterson writes:

> . . . the English had no particular interest in imposing on Scotland . . . The worst that could be said was usually that the English acted in ignorance of Scotland and were willing to rescind a policy only when the Scots complained loudly enough and with enough of a consensus.[23]

In truth, England has always featured heavily in Scottish identity. Pre-Union the dominance of England, and the threat she posed to Scotland, affected how Scotland behaved. William Ferguson asserts, for example, that even in medieval times Scottish historians attempted to give weight to the distinctiveness of the Scottish Church to create a 'bulwark' against York and Canterbury's 'jurisdictional claims' over the Church in Scotland.'[24] Post-Union, Scotland's relationship with England, and the Scots' views of the English, have been complex and have varied enormously. Sometimes the Scottish elite and the Scottish people as a whole have believed they were working in partnership with the English – a feeling which guaranteed the Scots were energetic partners in the building of the British Empire or in fighting alongside the English in battle. In the nineteenth century there were even those, such as the great literary figure, Thomas Carlyle, who strongly supported the idea of Scotland simply becoming North Britain. But they were in the minority and by the late twentieth century it was evident that British identity had weakened with the loss of Empire and the decades of peace.[25]

Even when the Scots feel most in step with England, and in partnership with them, they still succumb from time to time to paranoia, imagining all kinds of slights and plots where all that may really exist is English insensitivity or even indifference. In this mode the Scots can become bitterly anti-English. But on occasions these negative views are justified as England is indeed seeking to encroach on Scotland's jealously guarded territory. Margaret Thatcher's poll tax was just such an encroachment. But it is also possible to move to the opposite end of the spectrum and see that there are occasions when the Scots believe that the English are in some ways superior. However, this is not a position which any self-respecting Scot can hold for long and so there is a tendency to seesaw back and forth between dislike and admiration for England and her ways.

So the Scots' views of England and the English are complex and vary enormously. The range of views testifies to one important fact about the Scots – England matters very much to them. Yet Scotland barely registers on the English horizon. A fact that prompted Alastair Reid to observe that 'of all the grievances nursed by the Scots, none is greater than the fact that the English apparently do not bother to hate back.'[26]

Many commentators on Scotland simply blame the English for the Scots' lack of self-confidence. 'It was towards the middle of the eighteenth century that the intrepid Englishman discovered Scotland,' writes George Scott Moncrieff. 'He found a great deal for horror, ridicule, and pious defamation, and succeeded in leaving Scotland with an inferiority complex to this day.'[27] It is not uncommon for Scots to attribute any Scottish problem you can name to 'the auld enemy'. If anything, the 'blame the English' mentality in Scotland has grown in recent years and is becoming irritating even to committed Scottish nationalists. They see the Scots' attempt to attribute everything they do not like about Scotland to the Union with England as part of the problem which must be solved. In other words, such nationalists know that blaming the English is a manifestation of Scotland's political and cultural immaturity and must stop if the Scots are to build their confidence and start solving the myriad of problems they face.

I have argued in this chapter that there are various reasons why the Scots' relationship with England undermined, and continues to undermine, Scotland's confidence and feelings of self-worth. However, it is a mistake to believe that the Union and the relationship with England is the sole cause of Scotland's feelings of inferiority. Indeed rather than seeing Scotland as a country with an inferiority complex it is better to see Scotland as suffering from *complex inferiority*. In other words, the reasons for the Scots' lack of confidence are many and varied. Politics is one important strand in this confidence crisis but it is interwoven with many other threads.

So if Scotland were able to take more charge of her own affairs, as a result of independence or more devolved powers, Scotland's national self-confidence would undoubtedly grow. However, I do not believe that such a change would dismantle the barriers to confidence for Scots as they are not confined to the political sphere and also emerge from our upbringing and personal lives. As the title of the next chapter suggests it is all to easy for Scots to feel that they are 'never good enough' and much of this has nothing to do with our relationship with England.

Notes

1 Janet Adam Smith 'Some Eighteenth-Century Ideas on Scotland and the Scots' in N.T. Phillipson & Rosalind Mitchison (eds) *Scotland in the Age of Improvement* (Edinburgh University Press: Edinburgh, 1970), p.107

2 G.M. Thomson *Caledonia: Or The Future of the Scots* (Kegan Paul, Trench, Trubner: London), p.10

3 George Scott Moncrieff 'Balmorality' in David Cleghorn Thomson *Scotland in Quest of her Youth* (Oliver & Boyd: Edinburgh, 1932), p.83

4 Edwin Muir *Scottish Journey* (Victor Gollancz Ltd: London, 1935), p.25

5 P.H. Scott *1707: The Union of Scotland and England* (Chambers: Edinburgh, 1979)

6 Cairns Craig 'The Fatricidial Twins' in Edward J. Cowan & Douglas Gifford *The Polar Twins* (John Donald: Edinburgh, 1999), p.27

7 Douglas Gifford 'Introduction' in D. Gifford (ed.) *The History of Scottish Literature: Volume 3* (Aberdeen University Press: Aberdeen, 1989), pp.5-6

8 Graeme Morton and R. J. Morris 'Civil Society, Governance and Nation' in R.A. Houston & W.W. J. Knox *The New Penguin History of Scotland: From the Earliest Times to the Present Day* (Penguin Books: London, 2001), p.410

9 Alice Brown, David McCrone & Lindsay Paterson *Politics and Society in Scotland* (MacMillan Press: Hampshire, 1998), p.208

10 David McCrone, Angela Morris & Richard Kiely *Scotland – the Brand: The Making of Scottish Heritage* (Polygon: Edinburgh, 1999), pp.49-50

11 Jeremy Paxman *The English: A Portrait of a People* (Penguin Books: London, 1999), pp.22-23

12 Charles Jennings *Faintheart: An Englishman Ventures North of the Border* (Abacus: London, 2001), p.88

13 William Ferguson *The Identity of the Scottish Nation – An Historic Quest* (Edinburgh University Press: Edinburgh 1998), p.315

14 See Arthur Herman *The Scottish Enlightenment: The Scots' Invention of the Modern World* (Fourth Estate: London, 2002), Chapter 10

15 J.M. Reid *Scotland's Progress: The Survival of a Nation* (Eyre & Spottiswoode: London, 1971), p.9

16 Wallace Notestein *The Scot in History: A Study of the Interplay of Character and History* (Yale University Press: Yale, US, 1947), p.95

17 Simone de Beauvoir *The Second Sex* (Penguin: Harmondsworth, 1972), p.17 For a full exposition of de Beauvoir's concept of 'the Other' see Carol Craig, 'Simone de Beauvoir's "The Second Sex" in the light of the Hegelian Master-Slave Dialectic and Sartrian Existentialism', PhD Thesis, University of Edinburgh, 1979

18 Isobel Lindsay 'Nationalism, Community and Democracy' in Gavin Kennedy (ed.) *The Radical Approach: Papers on an Independent Scotland* (Palingenesis Press: Edinburgh, 1976), p.23

19 *Letters of David Hume* edited by J.Y.T. Grieg (Oxford, 1932), 1, p.255

20 Quoted in Paul Henderson Scott *The Boasted Advantages – The Consequences of the Union of 1707* (The Saltire Society: Edinburgh, 1999), p.5

21 Quoted in Paul Henderson Scott, *The Boasted Advantages*, p.1

22 N.T. Phillipson 'Nationalism and Ideology' in J.N. Wolfe (ed.) *Government and Nationalism in Scotland* (Edinburgh University Press: Edinburgh, 1969), p.186 My emphasis.

23 Lindsay Paterson *The Autonomy of Modern Scotland* (Edinburgh University Press: Edinburgh, 1994), p.63

24 William Ferguson *The Identity of the Scottish Nation – An Historic Quest* (Edinburgh University Press: Edinburgh, 1998)

25 For an interesting account of the creation of British identity see Linda Colley *Britons: Forging the Nation 1707 – 1837* (Vintage: London, 1996)

26 Quoted in Douglas Dunn *Scotland: An Anthology* (HarperCollins: London, 1991), p.25

27 George Scott Moncrieff 'Balmorality', p.73

13. Never Good Enough

When I did well, I heard it never;
when I did ill, I heard it ever.
                                Scots Proverb

My parents attended the 'Towards A Confident Scotland' conference I helped organise after the publication of the first edition of this book. As elderly, working-class folk with limited education and no experience of attending such events they were intimidated. We had decided to ask everyone who attended to put a hope or aspiration for Scotland on a card and stick it up on the wall. They were paralysed and unable to participate. My sister worked out why. 'There isn't a right answer,' she assured them, adding, 'and no-one is going to judge which one is best.' Only once these fears were allayed were they able to stop worrying that someone, in an authoritative, teachery voice, would boom 'who wrote that?' and give the culprit a shirrackin.

In the Glasgow housing estate of Drumchapel recently I ran a workshop where I talked with participants about what stopped them going back to education and doing new things in life. Many recounted how much they were put down when they were at school. A woman recalled that one teacher repeatedly told her that she was 'only fit for cleaning toilets'. This was an extreme example of what I've regularly heard over the years. Because I ran so many courses in Scotland related to confidence I have listened to thousands of Scots recount stories about how they were harshly put down by teachers, and often by parents.

I am not suggesting that the above examples are exclusive to Scotland. In the past many people experienced harsh, authoritarian parenting and teaching styles as this was in tune with the values and beliefs of an earlier age. What's more, as the French sociologist Pierre Bourdieu argued convincingly – class and status distinctions mean that when people from low status groups are out of their class 'habitus' they often lack confidence and are unable to function.[1] So I accept and recognise how common it has been for teachers in various education authorities to demean their pupils; for parents to be authoritarian; and for working people and the poor to feel inadequate in a range of social situations outwith their daily lives. Nonetheless I contend that there are inherent beliefs and practices at work in Scottish culture which mean that Scots, not just from low status background, are often unduly fearful and that this fear inhibits their confidence.

The picture which emerges from earlier chapters shows that deep within Scottish culture is the great pressure to achieve and show that you are worthy but, at the same time, another set of values weakens the pursuit of that achievement for fear that you might get above yourself. Neither set of values is great for our confidence, sense of agency or self-determination. The fact that these pressures conflict with one another simply makes matters worse. Being pushed forward and held back at the same time leads to inertia, frustration and feelings of powerlessness.

Of course, there is more to the problem of confidence in Scotland than this. Again I have outlined some of this in earlier chapters and aim to build on the psychological dimension in what follows.

A Fundamental Fear

In 2005 I wrote an article for an English journal about some of the work I had undertaken in Scottish schools. At one point I wrote 'overly fearful of getting it wrong, teachers. . .' The woman editor got in touch to say that she didn't understand what I meant by 'getting it wrong' and could I elaborate? I was dumb struck. How could she fail to understand this? Surely it was obvious that it meant doing something in a manner that was different from the tried and tested way to do things and could easily land you into trouble? This started me thinking: was this a difference between the two cultures? So I started my own research. For the next few years when I gave talks I would ask the audience 'is the term "getting it wrong" meaningful or does it require elaboration?' Almost every Scot knew exactly what it meant. Some people from other cultures – including England – would understand while others did not. In short, the desire to 'get it right' and avoid 'getting it wrong' is so deeply ingrained in Scottish culture that it is part of our socialisation process whereas in other countries it appears to be more linked to personality, family upbringing, or other unidentified factors. On numerous occasions English people in the audience would say – either publicly or privately to me afterwards – that something had just clicked with them. They could never understand why their Scottish spouse would hang back and not try new things; why they were so fearful of the consequences. Now they had a better understanding of their partners' fears.

I think the 'getting it wrong' fear emanates from various historical factors I've already outlined in this book – the prying and spying which was so dominant in Scottish life; the church discipline; the deep inequality in land ownership and the actions of authoritarian bosses. But there are other reasons as well such as the character of Scottish schools.

There are many reasons why Scotland can take pride in her education system which historically produced the most literate nation in the world. But some have argued that even in its heyday it was too obsessed with teaching facts, with tests and with examination results. One 1920s critic summed this up when he described the Scottish education system as 'the gospel according to marks'. Mary Rose Liverani writes humorously of her experience of Glasgow schools in the 1940s:

> Play was never simply play, nor learning simply learning. You were always being tested. Tested in the morning for tables and whack with the pointer if you were too slow. Tested for the names of capital cities and dead kings, tested for writing, up light and down heavy so that your fingers clawed in cramp from the strain of controlling your pen, tested for spelling, tested for the dozen rule, tested for the score rule, tested every Friday so that your fingers trembled independently in anticipation when you sat down at your desk.[2]

Schools, like the Kirk and those that held power over folks' lives, reinforced the idea that there is always a 'right' answer or way to complete tasks. This was a characteristic of traditional Scottish schools admirably summed up by Alexander Scott in his poetic gem:

> **Scotch education**
> I tell't ye
> I tell't ye.[3]

The fear of getting 'it' wrong has at its core another assumption – that we are all the same and should be thinking and acting in the same way. A decade or so ago I did some work with the management team of a small, international company in Dumfries. The CEO was American and had worked round the world. In fact he was something of an expert on how countries' business cultures varied. His observations on Scotland were at one with what I'm presenting here. However, for him the most remarkable factor about Scotland, which he said he had never encountered anywhere in the world, is that Scots have no concept that 'there is more than one way to skin a cat'. 'Everyone thinks there is one right way to do something and judges and criticises others for not doing it the right way,' he remarked. In such an environment those with the most power, or those who are the most bullying or critical, intimidate and undermine quieter, or less confident types.

Generally people are at their most confident when they are carrying out tasks in their preferred way. Trying to do something by someone else's formula will generally be more stressful and undermine confidence. Listen carefully to Scottish train guards making passenger announcements and you'll hear exactly what I mean. They would be much less stilted, and easier to listen to, if they could forget about making mistakes or being judged and speak more naturally.

Scotland is not a country which understands or celebrates difference and this can be observed in a variety of different contexts. In equality issues, for example, Scottish organisations have never pursued, or even understood, 'managing diversity' preferring instead a more traditional, group-based 'equal opportunities approach'. The lack of appreciation of difference can even be seen in 'the best small country in the world' slogan that used to greet foreign visitors when they arrived at Scottish airports. To my mind this slogan immediately poses the question 'best for what'? Weather, food, service, education, landscape? Even if it's landscape surely there is a world of a difference between a south sea beach and the mountains and glens of Scotland. There is no such thing as 'best' in this context – best is in the eye of the beholder. All of this escaped the sloganeers and the politicians who supported the campaign. They may want to appear aspirational but this slogan simply reveals the Scots' inability to understand and respect difference.

The Risk of Failure

Of course, the fear of 'getting it wrong' does not thrive simply because there is too strong a sense of the right way to do things and a lack of appreciation of difference in Scotland. The fear is so powerful for if we do indeed 'get it wrong' and fail or make a mistake then we shall visibly prove to the world that we are truly worthless.

Confirmation of these underlying fears has come from some of the most unexpected quarters in Scotland. The famous Glasgow-born comedian Stanley Baxter recounts that on his first day at primary school the pupils were all given paper and crayons and encouraged to draw anything they liked but he was 'petrified' as he was 'sure to get it wrong!'[4] He also says that this fear of failure dogged him for the rest of his career. He puts this down to a pushy, overbearing mother, and no doubt this played a part but he was also brought up in a culture which encourages such fear. In a recent interview Stanley Baxter explained that the more successful he became the more his anxiety and fear of failure mounted. As a result he turned down spectacular opportunities such as starring in a Broadway production and a Harry

Potter film. Stanley Baxter is unequivocal about the grip such fears had on his life: 'the reality was I was afraid of not being good enough,' he tells us.

Stanley Baxter is not alone. Scots will often avoid doing anything where they may make a mistake or not do well. In the words of an old Scots' saying: 'Better sit still than rise up and fa'.'[5] This is partly why performing or speaking in public can be such an ordeal for many Scots. It is also why many adult Scots are extremely inhibited about trying their hand at anything artistic or creative. Overly concerned about 'getting it right', they simply cannot get into the mindset which encourages their creative juices to flow. The trouble with this approach to life is that it prevents people from growing and developing, for learning new skills or trying out anything new inevitably means making mistakes. Pamela Stephenson reports that her husband Billy Connolly has a fear he 'won't master' things and that 'Any time when there's a fear that he won't be able to do something . . . then he will slip back into that "You're stupid, you'll never amount to anything" stuff.'[6] Indeed, for all his international success, Billy Connolly exemplifies a common Scottish fear of being worthless.

As we saw in an earlier chapter Scotland has a critical culture that likes to put people in their place and many people internalise a very critical, judgmental voice. Pamela Stephenson is a psychotherapist and in her biography of her husband she reports that he started drinking, and ultimately required therapy, to help him cope with the general feelings of worthlessness engendered by his Glasgow boyhood:

> On the surface, Billy's life was quite jolly, but
> inside he was lost. When he made public

appearances, he arrived to great fanfare. He would
open shops and cut ribbons while pipe bands
played. A little voice inside, however, kept nagging
him. It sounded a bit like Mona (his aunt). 'Who
do you think you are? You don't deserve this.'[7]

The power of that great Glasgow novel *The Dear Green Place*
is that its author, Archie Hind, so brilliantly conveys how Mat,
the protagonist, has internalised extremely negative ideas about
himself from his culture and that this continually gets in the
way of his aspiration to be a writer. For example, Mat repeatedly
refers to his own writing as 'guff'. His existential crisis at the
end of the novel takes the form of his inner 'Glesca keelie voice'
berating him and his realisation that he is 'divided against
himself': 'Ye're nut on, laddie. Ye're on tae nothin'. . . Ye're nut
quoted,' the inner voice tells Mat. [8]

Another way the feeling of worthlessness commonly
manifests itself is in the fear of being 'found out'. I was the first
person in my family to attend university and I spent the first
few months fearing that I would be ejected from the lecture
theatre because there had been some mistake. Other Scots tell
similar stories. Pamela Stephenson maintains that Billy Connolly,
for all that he was exceptionally good at what he did, 'still felt
like a fraud sometimes, a welder who hadn't been found out'.[9]
Sometimes this type of fear relates specifically to how well a
person can do things, or how clever they are. But often it is
about whether they are a 'good' or 'worthwhile' person.

For many Scots being criticised is another horror. One of
the great paradoxes is that Scotland has an extremely critical
culture yet your average Scot loathes being criticised and is
terrified by it. Even being looked at the wrong way can provoke

some Scots to aggression. Indeed many Scots become quite aggressive in conversation if they feel they are being slighted and over the years this has led to the common English observation that the Scots are 'chippy' – aggressively defensive if they have any reason to feel they are being put down. And it is not uncommon in Scotland for a person who is criticised to go immediately on the defensive ('well you are a fine one to talk, let me tell you. . .') rather than listening to what is being said, deciding if it is of value and learning from it.

Nowadays management consultants talk about a 'blame culture' existing in some organisations and such a culture certainly flourishes throughout Scottish life, as is well illustrated by the following extract from Douglas Fraser's contribution to *Being Scottish*:

> Something or somebody else must be to blame. The boss. The rich. The poor. The central belt. Lairds. Edinburgh lawyers. Subsidy junkies. Catholics. Protestants. The poll tax. The current Scotland football manager. Men. Wummin. Lanarkshire politicians. People who blame other people.[10]

If anything goes wrong the Scots are not likely to analyse the problem, learn from it and ensure that it does not happen again. Instead the hunt is on to find the 'eejit' who has made the mistake and rub his or her nose in it. In such an environment people are not likely to admit their mistakes and will often try to deflect the blame by saying 'it wasnae me'. In Scotland an unedifying stand-off inevitably follows when someone somewhere has messed up. Such punitive views of people's misdemeanours may even account for the fact that the Scots lock up a higher percentage of criminals than most European countries.

Proving Ourselves Better than Others

It is almost inevitable that in a country where people are so intent on having to prove their worth that 'winning' and beating others can become so important. Of course, we'll find this in business and sports, where the stakes are high and competition is often the name of the game. But in Scotland excessive competitiveness often manifests itself in everyday life, particularly humour. Routinely people make jokes at others' expense and put them in their place. Indeed it is common in Scotland, in both young and old, for people to command respect or gain kudos in their peer group simply from their ability to put others down. Most foreigners in Scotland report being shocked by Scottish humour because it is so rude. I have heard psychologists working with young people talk about Scotland having a 'killer culture'. There is nothing new about this. James Boswell, the eighteenth-century literary figure, detested 'the Scots strength of sarcasm which is peculiar to the North of Britain'.[11]

It can be shocking to see such competitiveness displayed in families. A few years ago I overheard a conversation while picking raspberries in Stirlingshire which showed such attitudes are alive and well. A father was picking with his eight year old daughter. He just couldn't resist telling her how much better he was at it than she was and showing her his basket. After a while he then said, 'Och you're quite good at picking really. You're good at picking your nose'. And then if that wasn't insulting enough he added, 'ye've picked a right beauty there' and then had a good laugh at his own joke.

Glebe Street

Many of the aspects of Scottish life and culture I have addressed so far in this chapter, and elsewhere in the book, are clearly displayed in the chronicles of Scotland's most famous and 'happy family' – *The Broons* – a comic strip produced weekly in the *Sunday Post* newspaper and produced as an annual.[12] I chose a year at random (1997) and analysed the content of its stories. By far the most common storyline (thirty-eight stories out of ninety-seven) was about embarrassment. This was usually caused by someone trying to do something different or getting above themselves and then being caught out. The last picture usually shows the culprit 'black affronted' or with a right red face. Examples of such behaviour include Daphne (the fat, ugly daughter) having the cheek to think she could become a model, go cycling or sign up for a blind date. Hen gets his comeuppance for taking up bird watching, of all things, and trying to do his own car repairs. In many cases the story is simple: the character in question overestimates his or her ability to do something and ends up making a right mess of it, much to the amusement of the rest of the family. Sometimes a family member is supported by the others but more often they become the butt of jokes. When Paw sees Hen, Joe and Daphne dancing he says 'call that dancing? I thocht ye had midges in yer vests'. When Joe tries lifting weights even Maw puts him down by saying 'my washin' pooder's stronger'.

I am not arguing that this type of humour is all there is in *The Broons* and that there are no moments of support or tenderness; no times when the family comes together to help one another or be loving – in their fashion at least. But the laughing at one another and putting each other down, particularly for doing anything different, is much stronger.

It's Got to Be Perfect

So let's just summarise where the quest to prove yourself worthwhile often leads for Scots. As it is not acceptable to stand out from the crowd individuality and ambition are restricted. This then reduces the quest to prove yourself worthwhile to not 'getting it wrong', not making mistakes and not being criticised by others. However, while this looks like a low-key, unambitious agenda paradoxically it means we are setting ourselves up to be perfect. Only a perfect being would never fail, make mistakes or do things to attract others' critical judgement.

'Too many people take second best but I won't take anything less. It's got to be perfect.' So says Scottish pop group 'Fairground Attraction' in their hit single 'Perfect'. And the quest for perfection is a recurrent theme, not only in Scottish culture, but also in the lives of individual Scots – a theme admirably summed up on a tee shirt I came across in Nova Scotia, Canada, which read: 'Not only am I perfect. I am Scottish too'. Individual Scots through their fear of failure are often unconsciously aiming for perfection and when they do not attain it they are projected to the other end of the scale and they feel worthless. Perfect or worthless, or saved or damned according to the belief system of earlier generations, is the seesaw most individual Scots are on and it is not a comfortable way to live your life.

As rational beings, conscious of their own failings, the Scots do not seriously think they are perfect, but they think they *should* be and they do not like the feeling of worthlessness which descends upon them when they have to cope with the harsh realities of their own imperfections. This is why criticism must be avoided at all costs. If it happens, the criticism should be deflected as quickly as possible or denied. Whatever happens the criticism must not stick, as that will only provide unwanted testimony of their imperfections. It is one thing for a Scot to feel worthless and aware of personal faults. It is quite another for him or her to let others know these imperfections. It is imperative to maintain the pretence of perfection at all costs.

The Fixed Mindset

Since the first edition of the book I have learned a great deal about the work of an American psychologist, Professor Carol Dweck and I now think that her 'self-theories' can help us understand aspects of what I've been arguing in the previous pages.[13]

Dweck argues from her empirical research that there are two basic mindsets about achievement and people in general. The 'fixed' mindset upholds the idea that people's ability is fairly fixed and not open to change. According to such a view, people are either intelligent, sporty, arty, good at maths and so forth or they aren't. This mindset also labels people according to personal characteristics. So people are either good or bad, caring or selfish etc. The growth mindset has a different starting point. It sees people as essentially malleable. In other words, they aren't fixed but have huge potential for growth and development.

It is important to note that Dweck is not disputing the fact that some people find some types of activities or learning easier than others. What she disputes is that others can't change or learn:

Just because some people can do something with

little or no training, doesn't mean that others can't do it (and sometimes do it better), with training. This is so important, because many, many people with the fixed mindset think that someone's early performance tells you all you need to know about their talent and their future.[14]

This simple theory of different views of people has enormous implications for learning, achievement and relationships.

Effect of growth and fixed mindsets

For people who have a fixed mindset, success is exceptionally important as it is a way to validate yourself and show how intelligent and talented you are. It is also a way to prove you are better than others who lack these fixed qualities. Conversely, failure is toxic for those with fixed mindsets as it proves that you aren't talented or clever. This means that failure, and mistakes, have to be avoided at all costs. Indeed Dweck argues that for people with fixed mindsets, 'the loss of oneself to failure can be a permanent and haunting trauma.'[15] By extension, it also means that fixed mindset people feel they must be careful with anything that might be challenging and risky as it increases the risk of failure and thus showing their lack of ability. It is best, according to this view, to harbour thoughts about 'what you could have been' rather than risk failure. Psychologists often refer to such strategies as 'self-worth protection'.

This viewpoint also leads people to be very touchy about any critical feedback as it suggests an innate lack of ability. People with a fixed mindset also view tests as a valuation, not of a specific set of skills, but of how innately clever or capable a person is.

Fixed Mindset	Growth Mindset
• Ability and personal characteristics fixed by nature.	• Ability and personal characteristics are malleable.
• Failure, mistakes and criticism must be avoided at all costs as they reveal bad things about you.	• Failure, mistakes and criticism can be helpful as they help you learn and get better.
• It is riskier to try and fail than not try at all.	• People improve through effort and hard work.
• If you have to work hard it shows that you are not a 'natural'.	• It is not competition with others which is the most important thing – it is about self-improvement.
• We must compete with others to *prove* that we are intelligent and have good qualities.	
• Confidence is fragile and so has to be protected.	

From an educational point of view what is particularly worrying about the fixed mindset is how it sees effort as reprehensible in some way. According to this perspective, people who are naturally clever and gifted don't have to practise and try too hard. In other words, people who need to put effort into something are showing their deficiencies.

People with a growth mindset have a completely different view of success and failure. Of course, they are motivated by success and want to achieve it, but for them success shows that you have mastered something, been stretched and learned new skills: doing well is not a demonstration of intelligence or talent. This then frees up growth mindset people to see failure, not as a negative, undermining judgement on them as people, but as something they need to learn from so they can succeed in the future. A natural extension of this mindset is to relish, and seek out challenges, rather than avoid them as it is through being challenged that people grow and develop. Failure can often be a painful challenge to growth mindset people but it is still seen as something to learn from rather than something which defines you as an individual.

In the eyes of those with a growth mindset, tests do not measure your basic intelligence or potential (no test can do that); tests can only give a snapshot of how capable you are at something now. What's more, criticism, particularly from someone you respect and you can learn from, is a gift – a way to accelerate learning – and not something to be feared.

Finally, for people with a growth mindset, learning and development is all about one thing – *effort*. The more you put in the more you will accelerate your learning. What's more, growth mindset people value learning for its own sake, irrespective of the outcome.

A Labelling Culture

Leaving aside the fact that Scotland has traditionally been a culture which extolled the virtues and importance of hard work and effort, in all other respects much of my argument in this chapter indicates that we are a country which very much upholds the idea of the 'fixed mindset'.[16] Using Dweck's perspective we can see that part of the problem is that we have too firm a notion of human beings as fixed, unchangeable entities – they are either stupid or clever, worthwhile or worthless. This is indeed the Scotland that Bill Duncan, a Scottish teacher and novelist, presents in his book, *The Wee Book of Calvin*. Indeed the most striking feature of Duncan's humorous distillation of the Scottish Calvinist mentality is the way that individuals – often children – are judged and labelled. Needless to say the labels are mainly damning and suggest worthlessness. One telling example from Duncan's books reads: 'Ye can tell the criminal from the face in the crib'.[17]

Historically Scottish education was so intent on testing and discriminating between those who were clever and those who weren't, that it was likened to a 'giant sieve'. In 1921 The Scottish Education Department declared:

> There is no denying the fact that in every country only a relatively small percentage of the population will be endowed by nature with the mental equipment which they must possess if they are to profit by Secondary School or University study. A frank recognition of this truth is essential, if a proper organization is to be established.' [18]

This was the start of the notorious 'qualifying examination' which reigned supreme in Scotland until the 1960s. Youngsters' basic intelligence was judged on the basis of tests. Indeed Scotland was the first country in the world to test the intelligence of its entire school population in the 1932 and 1947 Scottish Mental Surveys. The impetus from the 1932 survey was to ascertain 'the incidence of mental deficiency in Scotland.' [19]

A leading English expert on intelligence, Professor John White, has written extensively on the fact that those thinkers with most influence on original theories of intelligence have all come from a 'similar thought-world', namely a puritan, Calvinist, dissenting or Presbyterian heritage – or what Max Weber referred to as 'ascetic protestantism'.[20] This religious perspective, often influenced by the notion of predestination, led to a particular idea of intelligence and distinct educational practices. In his book *Intelligence, Destiny and Education* White does not devote too much time to Scotland but his observations on the influence of this type of religious inheritance is very telling as it sums up many of the strongest criticisms of Scottish education over the years.[21] For example, White argues that it leads to a definition of intelligence confined to the ability to apply logic or handle abstract concepts, rather than something more practical. It leads to a polarising concept of intelligence similar to the idea of the 'saved and the damned'. Thus intelligence is seen as something which is fixed and limited – not grown and developed. These ideas lead to an obsession with the two ends of the spectrum – the intelligent and gifted at one end and the feeble minded, mentally deficient at the other. The vast majority who inhabit the middle in such a concept of intelligence are largely ignored. Finally, this fixed notion of intelligence leads to a great deal of testing and grading so that the bright children can be separated from the dull and appropriate labels attached – labels with a huge influence on that child's future trajectory in education and life. Of course, the Scottish education system is in the process of major changes but this encapsulates the ideology which reigned supreme for years and which still inhabits our consciousness.

As I know from my extensive training experience in Scotland where I often discussed the topic, negative, personal labelling of children by teachers was also extremely common. Youngsters were often repeatedly denounced as 'sleekit', 'useless', 'a dunce' 'dross', 'as thick as mince', 'a big stiffy', 'a waste of space'. One man recalled in one of my sessions that one of his teachers continually called him 'a wee flyman'.

However, what's interesting about Dweck's work is that it isn't just critical labels which undermine and de-motivate – positive ones have that effect as well. For example, Dweck's research shows that telling youngsters that they are 'intelligent' after a test can undermine their motivation to take a harder test in case they fail and prove a disappointment. In other words, they are worried that they reveal that they aren't as intelligent as adults want them to be. So the problem here is labelling of any kind – not just criticism. Indeed Dweck has worked with a number of adults who were labelled 'gifted and talented' when they were young and reports that this has had a very negative effect on many of them: the label often leads to a profound sense of disappointment when (as is usually the case) they do not continually live up to the sobriquet. It also commonly leads to a persisting fear of failure in exactly the way that Stanley Baxter described.

John White also argues that protestant asceticism has led to a particular theory of intelligence which is simply unsupported by fact: people can improve their IQ with training. The 'growth mindset' – the notion that we develop our intelligence and other skills – has had a welcome shot in the arm in recent years from neurological research. The Canadian psychiatrist and researcher, Dr Norman Doidge, argues forcibly in his book *The Brain that Changes Itself* that the most important new knowledge to be gained from recent research into the workings of the brain is that it is 'plastic'.[22] The idea that we are given an allotment of IQ or natural ability at birth is wrong – we literally grow our brains as well as our intelligence and skills through learning and practice. Quite simply, the brain is not fixed but malleable; it is changed by experience.

The Impact on Parenting, Personal Relationships and the Workplace

I have concentrated here on achievement and intelligence but as I indicated earlier, the labelling of people, the division into worthwhile and worthless, saved and damned has huge implications for parenting. One of the most compelling aspects of Dweck's work is that it shows how damaging it is to continually judge children – not just at school but in the home. In the past parents doled out lots of negative labels – selfish, greedy, spoiled, stupid, clumsy. . . When you think about it there is a world of a difference between a parent saying to a child 'that was a stupid thing to do' and 'you are stupid'. These days many parents do not want to repeat the experience they had as children and have gone to the opposite end of the scale and lavish praise on their children. They are now 'the cleverest girl in the class', 'the brightest boy in the school', 'the fastest runner', 'the best dancer', 'the most beautiful'. . . But paradoxically this often leads to insecurity – will my parents still love me if I don't win the race or other girls are prettier?

Listen to parents' conversations and you will see how they are always comparing their children with one another: this one is bright, the other is not. One is sporty and the other is not. . . These judgements lead children to feel that they are continually being measured and assessed. As children are capable of picking up subtle messages, they know that what is really at stake is their worth as human beings. This is why Dweck argues that youngsters with fixed mindset parents know that their concern with poor grades is not so much about their failure to learn a specific thing but that the poor mark shows that the child is not clever. Often these young people feel that they never quite live up to their parents' ideal. Surely it is best to let our children know that we love them simply for being themselves and for being our offspring – unconditional love shorn of any judgement or comparison?

Seeing people as fixed, unchanging entities also has profound repercussions for personal relationships. For example, I can denounce and berate my sister as 'selfish' because of something she has done or I can look for extenuating circumstances for this behaviour and concentrate on the fact that she does not always behave that way. I can criticise my partner harshly for being lazy or crabbit or explain his behaviour by saying that he is tired and stressed.

As a workplace manager I can write people off because I have decided they aren't able to do things and so I don't even give them the opportunity for training or promotion. I can set up 'talent management' schemes to find and invest in the most talented employees. If I take this course of action then I discard the majority and continue the notion that ability is fixed and innate rather than grown and developed through training, experience and hard work.

In recent years in workplaces there has been a growth in what Malcolm Gladwell calls 'the talent myth' – the idea that there is only a small number of gifted individuals to run organisations.[23] Indeed it is this notion that has led to huge salary increases and big bonuses which have become rife in recent years. Professor Danny Dorling argues convincingly that the idea of IQ and innate talent are needed to rationalise the favourable treatment of an elite and the resulting inequality – inequality which has got much worse in recent years in the UK and the USA.[24]

As the above shows the notion of an intelligent, talented elite is not limited to Scotland and is very responsive to economic conditions. However, my argument mirrors John White's argument: our religious inheritance has particularly predisposed Scottish culture to black and white, polarising judgements about people's personal worth, intelligence and capabilities.

Personal Development and Self-Awareness

The idea that people are essentially fixed at birth renders personal development irrelevant – we cannot change no matter how many gurus or personal development books tell us otherwise. If personal development or change is irrelevant then so too is self-awareness.

It was the Greek philosopher Socrates who issued the injunction 'know thyself' and Aristotle who brilliantly elaborated the challenge: 'Anyone can become angry – that is easy. . . but to be angry with the right person, to the right degree, at the right time, for the right purpose, and in the right way – this is not easy'.[25] Self-awareness may be important for these philosophers' idea of 'the good life' but in Scotland since change is not feasible it is basically self-indulgent to spend time analysing yourself in any way.

The generalised lack of self-awareness means that we have little chance of understanding what makes other people tick. Alastair Reid, the Scottish-born poet, translator and essayist has lived most of his life in foreign lands and is a keen observer of Scottish life. According to Reid, in an essay on growing up in the Borders, the Scots, in comparison with other peoples he has known, do not appear to have much inner emotional life and they display little understanding of other people:

Ask who someone is, and you will be given a catalogue in reply, of family connection, of employment, of memorable feats, of external idiosyncrasies, but nothing more – nothing which might come from insight or observation or personal judgement. It is as though all the human characteristics we associate with 'personality' and an inner life just did not exist. In short, what perplexes me about the Scots as a vague generality, and about the Borders in overwhelming particularity, is the almost complete absence of the analytical dimension, the capacity to see into oneself and other people.[26]

This lack of insight may be one of the reasons why we continue to live with an outmoded belief system which easily undermines not only our lives as individuals Scots but also our collective endeavours.

Explaining Some of Scotland's current problems

Scotland is a country which manifests some serious health and social problems and it is no exaggeration to say that well-being is compromised for many Scots. For example:

- Scotland is 6th in the world in the use of illegal drugs (after Afghanistan, Iran, Mauritius, Costa Rica and Russia) and 8th in the world in the use of alcohol. (England is 14th) [27]

- In 2007 UNICEF presented research which showed that children in the UK have the worst well-being in wealthy, developed countries.[28] Scottish figures suggest that our children would be at the bottom of the UK table – the bottom of the bottom.[29]

- Scottish life expectancy is lower than England's. In some deprived areas of Glasgow men's life expectancy is 55 – the lowest in the developed world and lower than in some third world countries.[30]

- In 2005, the World Health Organisation revealed that Scotland had one of the highest rates of violent crime in Europe and murders with a knife were three times higher than in England and Wales. Thanks to creative policing particularly in Glasgow gang violence has fallen dramatically but violence is still a major challenge for Scotland. [31]

- In 2009/10 10.4 per cent of the Scottish population aged 15 to 90 were on daily anti-depressants. [32]

- In 2008 the Scottish male suicide rate was 24.1 per 100,000 population, compared to 12.6 in England and Wales.[33]

I think that much of what I've covered in this chapter helps us to explain some of these figures. Of course, structural factors such as employment, income inequality and so forth play a vital part but psychological and cultural factors also make an important contribution to what we could term Scotland's 'ill-being'.

Self-determination theory is a highly influential perspective on well-being. These ideas, first outlined by Richard Ryan and Edward Deci, draw on extensive empirical research undertaken internationally on what human beings require for psychological well-being. These psychologists present evidence to show that there are three fundamental psychological needs or 'nutriments' – the need for *competence, autonomy and relatedness*.[34] In this context autonomy does not mean independence from others. Rather it is about being able to take decisions for yourself that allow for self-organisation and self-regulation.

Deci and Ryan argue that human beings are naturally inclined to fulfill these needs and when they do they confer 'considerable adaptive advantage' both for the individual and the group. Self-determination theorists argue that we do not have to explain motivation – people are naturally motivated – and that people are programmed to 'seek out novelty and challenges, to extend and exercise [their] capacities, to explore, and to learn'.[35]

However, the prevailing environment and surrounding culture can undermine individuals' natural motivation to grow and develop. Indeed research repeatedly shows that external rewards, threats, pressures and directives, can undermine individuals' natural motivation. Passivity, alienation and apathy can also result when basic needs for autonomy, competence and relatedness are thwarted. I believe that it is the thwarting of these basic drives which creates many of the problems in Scotland. People who are overly fearful of failing, making mistakes, being criticised, 'getting it wrong' and proving themselves worthless do not continue to grow and develop – they become stuck. Routes to individual fulfillment, growth and development become blocked. Frustration, alienation and apathy are not good relationship builders so the need for relatedness also suffers.

I contend from the argument I've set out in this chapter and elsewhere in the book that in Scotland the path leading to the fulfillment of fundamental psychological nutriments has become more blocked and less navigable than it is in equivalent societies. No doubt it has led to millions of Scots leaving Scotland to find fulfillment of their psychological needs in distant lands. Many that remain manage to find satisfactory ways to navigate the blockage and fulfill their needs but many do not: they drink excessively or take drugs, they lash out violently at others, they neglect their children's welfare, they take anti-depressants, and they become physically ill. In some tragic cases they take their own lives.

Of course the factors I've outlined here are not the whole story but they are important constituent parts – they are the cultural factors with which we need to grapple if we are to find ways to remove the blockages which unwittingly prevent many Scots from never feeling 'good enough' and from living flourishing lives.

Notes

1 P. Bordieu *Distinction: A Social Critique of the Judgement of Taste* (Routledge: London, 1984)

2 Mary Rose Liverani *Winter Sparrows: Growing Up in Scotland and Australia* (Nelson: London, 2000), pp.88-9

3 *The Collected Poems of Alexander Scott* David S. Robb (ed.) (Mercat Press: Edinburgh, 1994), p.144

4 Brian Beacon 'Stanley Baxter: a dame of two halves in *The Herald Magazine* 23 May 2011

5 Quoted in W. Gordon Smith *This is My Country: A Personal Blend of the Purest Scotch* (Souvenir Press: London, 1976), p.223

6 Interview with Pamela Stevenson *Sunday Herald Magazine*, 7 October 2001

7 Pamela Stevenson *Billy* (HarperCollins: London, 2001), p.155

8 Archie Hind *The Dear Green Place* (Hutchison: London, 1966), p.228

9 Pamela Stevenson *Billy,* p.175

10 Douglas Fraser in Tom Devine and Paddy Logue *Being Scottish* (Polygon: Edinburgh, 2002), p.77

11 Quoted in Janet Adam Smith 'Some Eighteenth Century Ideas on Scotland and the Scots' in N.T. Phillipson & Rosalind Mitchison (eds) *Scotland in the Age of Improvement* (Edinburgh University Press: Edinburgh, 1970), p.113

12 *The Broons* (D.C. Thomson, Dundee)

13 See Carol S. Dweck *Self-Theories: Their Role in Motivation, Personality and Development* (Taylor S Francis: Philadelphia, 1999)

14 Carol S. Dweck *Mindset: The New Psychology of Success* (Ballantyne Books: New York, 2007), p.70

15 Carol S. Dweck *Mindset*, p.34

16 For a discussion of the role of effort and hard work in traditional theories of intelligence, see John White *Intelligence, Education and Destiny* (Routledge: Oxford, 2006)

17 Bill Duncan *The Wee Book of Calvin: Air-Kissing in the North East* (Penguin: London, 2004)

18 Quoted in Robert Anderson 'Education aned Society in Modern Scotland' in *History and Education Quarterly* Vol.25, No.4 Winter 1985), p.474

19 See Martin Lawn 'The Institute as Network: The Scottish Council for Education Research as a network and international phenomenon in the 1930s' in *Paedagogica Historica* Vol.40 Nos.5&6, October 2004

20 John White *Intelligence, Education and Destiny*, p.6

21 For a summary of these arguments see Carol Craig *The Tears that Made the Clyde* (Argyll Publishing: Glendaruel 2010), pp.226-242

22 Norman Doidge *The Brain that Changes Itself* (Penguin: London, 2007)

23 Malcolm Gladwell *What the Dog Saw and Other Adventures* (Little Brown: New York, 2009), pp. 357-75

24 Daniel Dorling *Injustice: Why Social Inequality Persists* (The Policy Press: Bristol, 2010)

25 Aristotle *Nicomachean Ethics* (Oxford University Press: Oxford, 1998)

26 Alasdair Reid 'Borderlines' in Karl Miller (ed) *Memoirs of a Modern Scotland* (Faber and Faber: London, 1970) p.160

27 'Melting the Iceberg on Scotland's Drug and Alcohol Problem': Report of the Independent Enquiry (October, 2010), p.7

28 Unicef 'An Overview of Child Well-Being in Rich Countries' (Report from Unicef Innocenti Research Centre, Report Card 7, 2007)

29 See John McLaren 'Index of Well-being for Children in Scotland' (Barnardo's Scotland, July 2007)

30 See Carol Craig *The Tears that Made the Clyde*, pp.27-36

31 'Scotland tops the list of most violent countries' *The Times* 19 September 2005

32 See information retrieved from
    http://www.scotland.gov.uk/Topics/Statistics/Browse/Health/
    TrendMentalHealth

33 See information retrieved from
    http://www.isdscotland.org/Health-Topics/Public-Health/
    Publications/2011-08-05/2011-08-05-Suicides-
    Summary.pdf?26157778502

34 For an introduction to Self-Determination Theory's concept
    of human needs see Edward L. Deci and Richard M. Ryan
    'The "What" and "Why" of Goal Pursuits: Human needs and
    the self determination of behaviour' in *Psychological
    Inquiry* Vol.11, No.4, 2000, pps 227-268

35 E.L. Deci and R.M. Ryan (eds) *Handbook of Self-
    Determination Research* (University of Rochester Press:
    Rochester NY, 2002), p.70

14. 'Nae Gless':
Pessimism in Scotland

Failure is not the killer; we are used to that. It is
the hope that gets you every time.
> Owen Campbell, in *Being Scottish*

'Dour' is a word that is commonly used to describe the Scots individually or collectively. The stereotypical Scot is sullen or at best expressionless and there's certainly some truth in this portrayal. In 1995 the traditional musician Jimmy Shand's 'Bluebell Polka' unexpectedly made it into the music charts. A journalist asked the Scottish iconic figure if he was elated and he replied: 'Elated? I have never been elated in my life. But I am quite pleased.'[1] I've heard repeatedly about Scots managers abroad distressing their staff by their negativity: the most positive comment they can muster is to tell people that their work is 'not bad'. Even modern day Scots commonly see people who are upbeat and positive as gushy and superficial.

In short, when it comes to emotions we prefer to be on the negative as opposed to the positive side. This is partly a reflection of the strength of scepticism within the culture. George Davie in *The Democratic Intellect* recounts that in the nineteenth century Scottish philosophers found optimistic theories 'distasteful in the extreme' as they implied 'a superficial view of life through rose-coloured spectacles'. Indeed Davie proceeds to quote a passage from David Masson contrasting Scottish and English thinking styles:

A Scotchman, when he thinks, cannot so easily and
comfortably as the Englishman repose on an upper
level of propositions co-ordinated for him by
tradition, sweet feeling, and pleasant circumstance
. . . No, his walk, as a thinker, is not by the
meadows and wheatfields, and the green lanes,
and the ivy-clad parish churches, where all is
gentle and antique and fertile, but by the bleak sea-
shore which parts the certain from the limitless
where there is doubt in the sea-mews' shriek, and
where it is well if in the advancing tide, he can find
a footing on a rock.[2]

If we fast-forward more than a hundred and fifty years to
the present we'll see that the Scots not only continue to pay
attention to the sea mews' shriek but also to defend this view
of the world. In the nineteenth century Scottish thinkers had to
defend their philosophical tradition against Anglicisation; in
recent times the threat has come from Americanisation, particularly the 'little book' culture. I am thinking here about Bill
Duncan's sophisticated and ironical retort to such a view of the
world in his *Wee Book of Calvin: Air-kissing in the north east*.
Duncan devised this as an antidote to the racks of bland, smarmy
American books advancing a superficial, candy-floss view of the
world. 'Let the Wee Book be your companion,' he writes. 'Let it
fall open at any page and its contents will envelop you like the
sudden chill greyness of a North Sea haar, leaving you silent,
sullen, cold and glowering, even in the face of the most
potentially heart-warming moments.'[3]

Of course, this is humour but the success of the book is in
part, that it sets out two competing views of the world – one
positive, the other negative – and to be true to ourselves as
Scots we've got to affirm the negative no matter how tough and

unattractive this is. This is who we are, like it or not. Rather Bill Duncan's aphorism 'self-pity never biled a haddock'[4] than any amount of 'chicken soup for the soul' – a series of so-called 'inspirational' books by Jack Cranfield.[5]

I am certainly no fan of an American happy clappy approach to life. But I think we need to be careful. Positive emotions *do* matter and denying this fact may account for some continuing Scottish problems – 'Shettleston Man' dying years before his time or doing so badly at football that we never make it to the World Cup

The Negative Brain

> . . . with nothing to do, the mind is unable to prevent negative thoughts from elbowing their way to center stage. . . Worries about one's love life, health, investments, family, and job are always hovering at the periphery of attention, waiting until there is nothing pressing that demands concentration. As soon as the mind is ready to relax, zap! the potential problems that were waiting in the wings take over.[6]

Ironical though it may sound both leaders of the new positive psychology movement – Mihaly Csikszentmihalyi (quoted above) and Martin Seligman – argue that the brain tends to prioritise negative information. Indeed Seligman argues that the brain is 'hard-wired' for negativity. Drawing on the work of evolutionary psychologists he argues that our ancestors needed to be alert to danger to survive and that it is their genes we have inherited – not their happy-go-lucky relatives as they were more likely to have been eaten or drowned in a flood.[7]

From a simple survival point of view, then, it makes sense for our brains to prioritise negative rather than positive information. This helps to account for the fact that people, throughout the world, pay more attention to criticism than praise and to the bad things that happen in life rather than the good. In short, negative emotion always has the ability, as Seligman describes it, 'to trump' positive emotion. This is why Seligman, Csikszentmihalyi and others argue that we have to 'learn' to keep negative emotion in check and amplify positive feelings. Indeed they quote research which shows that negative emotions are so powerful that we need at least three positives to every negative in human interaction for the prevailing atmosphere to be positive. In some contexts this ratio rises to seven positives to every negative.[8]

The Importance of Positive Emotions

Until the advent of positive psychology, most empirical psychologists had little interest in positive emotion. In fact, they often only paid attention to feelings of positive emotion, such as joy or happiness, as an indicator that an individual wasn't suffering from depression! While it was easy for psychologists to understand the role of negative feelings they found it very difficult to account for positive emotions such as joy, contentment, pride and so forth.[9]

Ground-breaking work by Professor Barbara Fredrickson has now provided an explanation. Her work is known as 'the broaden and build theory of positive emotion'.[10] On the basis of her empirical research, Fredrickson argues that negative emotions narrow people's perspective and keep them focused on the specific problem in hand (originally, flight or fight) whereas positive emotions 'broaden' people's likely thoughts and actions as well as their behaviour. According to such a perspective it is when we are experiencing positive emotions that we foster relationships and grow and develop our capacities. These personal resources have lasting benefit to us and hence help us cope better with adversity. Studies also show that positive emotions are good for our health, while negative emotions, if sustained, undermine it. Indeed Fredrickson argues from her research that being in a positive frame of mind is the essential ingredient in 'human flourishing'.[11]

It is worth mentioning in passing that there are some learning activities or mental tasks which are easier to perform when in a neutral or even slightly negative state as they require focus. Interestingly these are activities, such as applying logic or undertaking precise accountancy tasks, for which Scots were once renowned!

Returning to the general point, there is something of a paradox here: the brain finds it very easy to be negative but it is very important for human beings to experience positive emotions as it is in this emotional state that we nurture and develop our health, our relationships, and our intellectual and psychological reserves.

Such a paradox leads ultimately to the conclusion that it is crucially important for human beings to learn how to side-step the natural negativity of the brain and to experience more positive emotion. Traditionally it has been the prevailing culture, particularly religious ideas and practices, which teach people how to keep the negative brain in check and amplify good feelings. In early societies this was often the point of cleansing practices such as the use of sweat lodges. Buddhists by contrast teach acceptance and meditation techniques. New Testament Christianity preaches forgiveness, love and gratitude – an approach to life which does enhance well-being according to recent positive psychology research.[12] One reason why well-being has not increased in advanced Western societies in line with wealth is that religious practices and spirituality have been replaced by the values of consumer capitalism which encourage us to focus on what we don't have in our lives.[13]

And what of Scotland? Could it be the case that one of the problems for us is that Scottish culture has never been very good at encouraging us to deal with the natural negativity of the human brain? Indeed rather than encouraging us to learn how to experience positive emotions has Scottish culture, at least from the Reformation on, encouraged us to amplify negative feelings? This is not wholly true: Scottish Calvinism valued effort and hard work and encouraged people to participate in meaningful activities, arguing that 'the devil makes work for idle hands'. Indeed as Mihaly Csikszentmihalyi points out, in the quote above, negativity and worry can easily result from an idle brain if not idle hands. So the Scots' emphasis on activity, learning skills and finding a sense of mission were important ways to avoid negativity and promote a sense of personal satisfaction, through engagement or what Csikszentmihalyi calls 'flow'.[14]

However, in other respects Scottish culture seems to have encouraged negative feelings. Much of the argument in earlier chapters on Scotland's traditional religious views is of a country ruled by an Old Testament God who thunders 'thou shallt not' and punishes the human race for 'original sin' rather than a country which paid attention to the loving God of the New

Testament. Equally, the material in the last chapter, illustrating how strong and pervasive the fear of failure is in Scotland, along with other negative attitudes towards the self, suggests that our culture has stoked everyday fear rather than taught people how to allay it. As Scots we are encouraged to pay particular attention to the critical, negative inner voice rather than find ways to counteract it.

All this has produced not only Scots dourness but pessimism – negative emotions about the future – and may help us to account for some problems in Scottish life. As the words confidence and optimism are commonly used interchangeably in everyday life, this new material is a useful addition to our study of confidence in Scotland.

A Pessimistic Culture

In 2005 I attended a talk given by the distinguished British architect who was at that time Edinburgh's City Design Champion – Sir Terry Farrell. Over a hundred attended from a variety of different professions. Following the lecture almost everyone who spoke was extremely negative. For example, one said, 'Do you not often wonder, Sir Terry, what kind of city you've got involved with? – look at the waste paper bins and lighting in Princes Street. We can't even get the street architecture right.' Another said, 'When you walk round this city and look at buildings like the St James's Centre you have to ask yourself what kind of culture would put up stuff like this and ruin its heritage?' Others criticised the Parliament building where we were meeting. There were so many comments in this vein that Sir Terry eventually said that he had read *The Scots' Crisis of Confidence* and it was like one of the chapters coming to life.

To my mind, Sir Terry's response to these criticisms was a model of realistic optimism. He acknowledged the problems but did not see them as insurmountable: yes the street architecture was poor; yes there were a lot of horrible, modern buildings; but the same could be said about every city in Europe. Edinburgh was not noticeably worse than lots of different places in this respect but perhaps the city's failings stood out more because it had so many beautiful old buildings. However, Sir Terry did go on to say that he thought there was a particular (though by no means unique) issue in the city about people being unduly negative and not pulling together but this didn't mean that it always had to be like that. Change was always possible.

I recount this incident here as a reminder of how easy it is in Scotland for us to get into a really negative discourse and focus almost exclusively on what's wrong and what we don't like. Alexander Scott satirised this well in two of his poems: [15]

Scotch Optimism
Through a gless,
Darkly.

Scotch Pessimism
Nae
Gless.

The type of negativity on display at the Farrell lecture is often referred to as pessimism as it is about focusing on the downside of life – it is about seeing the glass as half empty, not half full. Optimists by contrast look on 'the bright side', a viewpoint which psychologists call 'dispositional optimism'.[16] But some psychologists, most notably Martin Seligman, have a different way of defining optimism and pessimism and it provides a useful insight into Scotland's thinking style.

Explanatory Style

For Seligman, 'The basis of optimism does not lie in positive phrases or images of victory, but in the way you think about causes.'[17] Indeed he argues that each of us has an 'explanatory style', a way of thinking about the causes of things that happen in life. According to Seligman, we develop our explanatory style during childhood and, unless we take deliberate steps to change, it will last for the whole of our lives, acting as a prism through which we explain to ourselves why things, both good or bad, happen.

Seligman argues that there are three central dimensions which we use to interpret events in our lives. He refers to these dimensions as *permanence, pervasiveness* and *personalisation*. Permanence simply means believing that when something goes wrong, then it will *always* go wrong. In short, pessimists are folk that believe that bad fortune lasts. Pervasiveness refers to the belief that misfortune is not simply confined to one domain but pervades *everything*. For example, a pessimist who fails an examination will tend to believe that everything is going wrong with his/her life. In short, when things go wrong for pessimists, they tend to 'catastrophise'. Personalisation involves the attribution of responsibility when things go wrong. Pessimists usually blame themselves; so for the pessimist the problem is *me*.

An optimistic thinker by contrast is someone who when a problem arises believes that it is temporary, restricted to this one thing and emanates from specific circumstances that aren't necessarily about what he or she has done.

Examples of a pessimistic explanatory style are common in Scottish life. Read the press, listen to people's conversations on politics or look back through some of the quotes in this book and you'll see how common it is for us to see problems as

322

permanent and intractable, worse than they actually are and somehow our own fault – often due to some deep psychological or genetic fault. Scottish stereotypes often evoke this way of seeing the world – just think of Private Fraser in *Dad's Army* and his catchphrase 'We're a' doomed, I say. Doomed.'

Explanatory style is not just relevant to how people look at bad events but also to how a person interprets good things as well. And this is where Seligman's work becomes really interesting when applied to Scottish culture. To understand optimism and pessimism in the face of good events, we need to reverse the pattern outlined above. Optimists see good fortune, such as passing a maths exam with flying colours as permanent (I'm going to keep doing well in maths), pervasive (I'm going to keep doing well at school) and something about them (I really worked hard/I'm good at maths). Whereas pessimists are more likely to see something good as temporary (the work will get harder next year), specific (it was just this one subject) and something they aren't responsible for (it was an easy exam, I was lucky).

From my experience I can see that the Scots are often pessimistic in the face of bad events but, unexpectedly, are even more likely to be pessimistic in the face of good events. Here's an unlikely example. I did some work for a couple of American companies in Scotland and they were totally unnerved by the pessimism of their workforce; when they announced a big investment in the companies, their Scottish workforce were not pleased – they were looking for the catch. 'Where are you going to cut back?' they asked.

Another telling example is Scottish football, particularly our bids to qualify for the World Cup finals. In October 2007 I was at Hampden for the Scotland v Ukraine match. Scotland had 21 points from the games they had played so far and across the seven groups only two countries – Germany and Croatia had better scores. Scotland had also beaten World Cup finalists France twice in the last year – and one of these victories was still ringing in our ears. As I went into the stadium I stopped to chat to a man I know who works in public relations. He is generally an upbeat, positive man – a far cry from the dour Scot who goes round talking about doom and gloom. Nonetheless he stood on the steps telling me he feared Scotland was going to lose. 'I just feel pessimistic. I don't think we can do it,' he said. I asked why and all he could do was mutter about how we were 'fated to lose'.

Now I can well understand why there is a fear in Scotland about becoming super-confident. The spectre of the 1978 World Cup in Argentina still hangs over the nation. All that stuff about Ally's army and Scotland winning the World Cup was so embarrassing given our subsequent performance. That's why many still believe that, for our dignity, it's much better to keep aspirations in check and when we lose we'll have the comfort of saying: 'We were right. We knew we would get beat.'

But I think there is more to it than this. Pessimists believe that good fortune does not happen as a result of your own actions. For them success is more of a fluke, a miracle or magic. And the whole point about miracles and magic is that they don't happen everyday and they certainly are not under your control. If the Scotland team wins against strong opponents then it is simply a fluke and not because Scotland has played well.

Despite a great deal of pessimism, Scotland did win against Ukraine. The following game was against then World Champions

Italy. The day before the match I was asked to write a short piece for a national paper on how the Scots should prepare themselves for defeat. It was easy to see the psychology at work here: Let's assume we'll lose and then we'll avoid being on an emotional roller-coaster – high and positive one minute and down in the dumps the next. If we're negative and we win then it'll be a great bonus.

Rugby suffers from similar thinking. I was at a pre-match event at Murrayfield in March 2008 for a Scotland v England match. Former Scotland rugby captain David Sole and ex-England rugby internationalist Jason Leonard went up to the podium to talk about the forthcoming match. Sole, like other speakers before him was extremely negative about Scotland's chances. These ex-captains put on a regular bet on the Calcutta Cup. Leonard, understandably, bet on England winning. Sole told the audience he was going to let his 'heart rule his head' and go for a narrow Scottish victory. In other words, he was hoping Scotland would win but really thought otherwise.

In the end Scotland won 15 to 9. After the game, Leonard and Sole returned to the podium to give their comments. As Sole took his £20 winnings from Leonard he said, 'No doubt I'll be giving you it back next year' – a text-book example of pessimism in the face of good events. Rather than seeing Scotland's success as something which could be sustained it was no more than luck, a one-off, something we can't count on. Of course, we can't but that's because pessimism is a self-fulfilling prophesy.

The Pay-back Factor

In Scotland, at a very simple level we appear to think that we must always prepare ourselves for the worst. If something goes well, we see it as a stroke of good fortune, rather than the beginning of something positive. As we've not been brought up to congratulate ourselves, we rarely see good fortune as something we have brought about ourselves; rather it is a fluke. Either way there is the sense of good events as temporary.

But there's an added twist here which we could call 'the pay-back factor'. Life is not meant to be easy; we are all miserable sinners therefore if life is going well some compensatory mechanism will soon be at work to ensure that we'll have to pay for this good fortune. I regularly catch myself having such thoughts. This is another point I have discussed with thousands of Scots and I know I am not alone.

Optimism and pessimism can be measured so it is worth asking if there is any empirical evidence of Scottish pessimism. At the centre I run we know of a few small studies which suggest low levels of optimism in Scotland in comparison with equivalent groups in the USA and Italy.[18] However, these studies measured dispositional optimism, not explanatory style and do not cover the pessimism in the face of good events which I think is particularly strong in Scotland. Nonetheless, one 2009 study in Wellhouse, a housing scheme in Easterhouse, Glasgow showed exceptionally low levels of optimism in the participants who took part —the lowest group mean that we have ever encountered.[19]

How Optimism Develops

Optimism and pessimism, according to Seligman, is partly genetic but also the consequence of the attitudes we observe in parents, particularly our mothers. In short, we learn to explain good and bad events optimistically or pessimistically. However, Seligman argues that if a bad thing happens early in a child's life, and that bad thing is permanent (such as the death of a parent), then this event predisposes the child to pessimistic thinking. In such cases, '. . . all setbacks are soon catastrophised into permanent and pervasive losses,' he writes.[20]

Seligman tends to take an individualistic focus when studying optimism but recognises that culture plays some part. He argues that the USA has traditionally had an optimistic culture because historically it was founded and developed by people who left Europe and Asia and emigrated to this new land:

> What kind of mentality does it take to feel
> oppressed by caste and class, to leave family and
> possessions behind, and to journey in the hope of
> a better life? Optimism. These men and women
> had it in abundance and they became a nation of
> optimists.[21]

If the USA is the land of migrants and optimism then is Scotland the land of emigrees and pessimism? As we saw in earlier chapters this is indeed what history tells us. In his latest book *To the Ends of the Earth: Scotland's Global Diaspora*, Professor Tom Devine once again sets out the massive scale of migration from Scotland and makes clear that those who migrated were often the most skilled, leaving 'their native land in search of more opportunity, "independence" and through an ambition to "get on". . .'[22] So it is very likely that emigration siphoned off many Scots who were the most optimistic thus intensifying pessimism within Scottish culture.

But there are other pessimism-inducing factors at work in Scottish culture. As Neal Ascherson writes in *Stone Voices*: 'The key to understanding Scottish modern history is to grasp the sheer force, violence and immensity of social change in the two centuries after about 1760.'[23] Such events help us to explain why parents and elders continued to teach their children to expect the worst long after we were living a precarious, hand-to-mouth existence. What's more, it is all too easy to look at Scottish history and see how such rapid, and potentially traumatic events would have set many Scottish children up for pessimism in a similar way to the bereaved child who learns to 'catastrophise'. If we put these two factors together (being taught to expect the worst and to experience lasting losses) then we can see how pessimism would have been induced by the following:

- **Scarcity**: The Scots have a long history of learning and philosophy but there is a general consensus that life was always pretty tough for Scots. The climate and the terrain meant that Scotland was never a place of easy living and life expectancy was low. To survive we needed to 'ca canny' and maintain our guard.

- **The Act of Union**: Even if you think the Union has largely been beneficial for Scotland, losing sovereignty, and becoming incorporated into another country's political system, is one of the worst events to befall a nation. Scots MPs who signed the act did so mainly as a result of the terrible economic crisis triggered by the Darien disaster in the closing years of the seventeenth century.

- **Industrialisation**: Scotland was one of the first countries in Europe to industrialise and went through this process in a very short period of time. For many this meant being uprooted from their rural way of life.

- **Clearances/assault on Highland culture**: Historians show how Scottish Gaeldom was transformed from a tribal to a capitalist society in less than fifty years. Many were cleared off the land. Those who stayed were forced to speak English and to disown aspects of their traditional culture.[24]

- **Emigration**: As we have already seen, Scotland exported millions of her most able people. This must have had a negative personal effect on those left behind. Given the distance, cost and poor transportation, many Scots bade farewell to relatives destined for the New World believing that they would never see them again. For many the pain would have been unbearable.

- **Economic insecurity/restructuring/ deindustrialisation**: Many Scots jobs were in traditional heavy industries which were vulnerable to world wide recessions. The Great Depression of the 1920s and 30s hit Scotland hard. In more recent times hundreds of thousands of Scots were paid off as traditional industries such as coal mining, shipbuilding and steel collapsed. Even those jobs which were supposed to replace them were also lost. 'Bathgate no more' in the words of the famous Proclaimers' song.

- **War**: Scotland lost 200,000 men in the First and Second World Wars. In the First war 26.4 per cent of Scots who enlisted lost their lives. The equivalent figure for England was 11.8 per cent. Only the Serbs and Turks lost more men – mainly from disease. So many Scots died because they made such brave, hardy soldiers that they were often in the front line.

So even leaving aside the Scottish belief system and way of religion, we can see from this list that the trauma and insecurity many citizens historically endured would have affected the culture, predisposing the Scots to pessimistic attitudes.

Does It Matter If We Are Pessimistic?

More than a hundred studies have shown that whether people think optimistically or pessimistically affects various life outcomes.[25] Sports enthusiasts of all kinds are intuitively aware that the 'mental' part of performance can be just as important as the physical. Some of this is about optimism as it boosts sporting performance, both at team and individual levels. Research into baseball and basketball teams in the USA reveals that teams have their own explanatory styles and that this has a major impact when players are under pressure in the last few minutes of a game, or how they cope with defeat, thereby determining future performance, regardless of the quality of the team. Teams which are optimistic in the face of defeat are more likely to be successful in their next game; those which explain setbacks negatively perform more poorly. Research into swimmers reveals that the same trend holds for individual athletes. Quite simply, when under pressure optimistic sportsmen and women try harder – and are more likely to win.

What should be of even more interest to us in Scotland is the relationship between optimism/pessimism and health. Research indicates that as much as seven to ten years of life expectancy may be at stake in whether a person is an optimist or a pessimist. This is more significant for life expectancy than whether someone smokes a pack of cigarettes every day. The mechanism is not entirely known but there are two main explanations. The first is that negative emotions release stress hormones which undermine well-being. The second is that pessimism can encourage people to lose heart and give up. This is understandable: if you think the outcome is bound to be bad then why bother doing anything such as taking exercise or giving up smoking?[26]

In 2006 I helped to organise a large training style event on positive psychology in Glasgow with Professor Martin Seligman as the keynote speaker. A Scottish journalist was instructed to write a feature about it and phoned me up for a few quotes. Unable to keep the cynicism out of his voice he asked: 'And what has this got to do with the man coughing his guts out in Shettleston?'

I think I said 'everything' and if I did I was wrong. 'It's a contributory factor' was a more accurate answer. Men in the area have the lowest life expectancy in the developed world: of course, this is partly about poverty, unemployment and inequality. But it can't only be about this as other areas in Europe have worse figures yet better life expectancy for this group. Excess smoking and drinking also play a part but aren't themselves the cause as men in other cultures smoke more with less damaging consequences.[27] As there is a well-documented link between pessimism and ill-health, I am convinced that the prevailing culture and personal psychology must play *some* part. I am not alone. Scotland's Chief Medical Officer, Sir Harry Burns, argues that many of Scotland's health inequalities are driven by feelings of hopelessness, pessimism's close cousin.[28]

Winning and Losing Streaks

One of the first people to get in touch with me about my book when it was published in 2003 did so to say that while I had hardly mentioned football, everything I wrote particularly applied to Scottish football – the criticism and blame, the obsession with failure and 'getting it wrong', the Utopian dreaming, the lack of confidence. . . If he reads this second edition I'm sure he'll be aware of the particular relevance of this section on pessimism as it affects team performance.

Rosabeth Moss Kanter is Professor of Business at Harvard. In her book *Confidence: Leadership and the Psychology of Turnarounds* she draws on her research with teams as well as employing some of the positive psychology ideas we've already encountered.[29] Moss Kanter's focus is team performances. She argues that winning and losing don't tend to happen as single events and are usually part of winning or losing streaks. There are four main reasons why winning 'begets winning' and creates 'upward spirals' of success and confidence. First, since winning feels good it generates positive emotions which are not only contagious but also boost energy and morale. This then encourages people to put in more effort and hard work therefore reinforcing the likelihood of success.

Secondly, the positive emotion produced through winning cements relationships. When people are in a positive frame of mind they are more likely to be generous, supportive and tolerant of one another. This then reinforces team-work and commitment. It also fosters an environment where people can openly talk about mistakes and learn from them. All these factors are likely to increase the chances of success.

This then leads to the third factor: in a positive, winning environment people are likely to invest trust and time in the system which has so far produced success. This often means more stable leadership and investment in procedures (such as training) which are also more likely to lead to success.

Finally, winning brings rewards from the outside. This might be enthusiastic fans, media attention and investors. Again all of this contributes to a positive atmosphere and builds confidence.

When organisations and teams are caught up in this winning psychology, losing from time to time is not fatal. The positive emotion which they have generated 'buffers' the negativity of the loss and allows them to cope with failure with equanimity.

Moss Kanter is equally illuminating on the psychology and culture which sustains 'losing streaks' arguing that losing a few times in a row amplifies negative emotion and feelings of power-lessness. She argues that when things start to go wrong in this way 'people fall back on almost primitive self-protective behaviour'. People who fail get cut off from those positive emotions which sustain energy and relationships and create 'upward spirals'. Conversely, the negative chain reaction feeds negativity and therefore sustains the losing streak.

Moss Kanter argues that as losing sets in it triggers an

'emotional and behavioural chain reaction'. This involves amongst other things blame, criticism, lack of respect, isolation, inward focus, rifts, loss of teamwork, prejudice, rivalry, envy, loss of aspiration and motivation, fear of failure and paralysis. Indeed she argues that this passivity is one of the most 'damaging' aspects of losing streaks. The ensuing pessimism becomes a self-fulfilling prophesy and saps people's creativity and energy. Since moods are contagious a negative environment has a tendency to envelop people. Negativity depletes and drains people of energy thus undermining performance and setting people up for further failure.

Positive emotions are an important part of winning as they help sustain an upward trajectory but in Scotland as soon as things go well and positive emotion mounts, we take fright and caw the feet from it. So it's hardly surprising that while we may win from time to time we find it difficult to get on a winning streak.

The Effect of this Negativity

As players will tell you the pessimistic atmosphere in Scotland often has a big impact on them. The rugby player Gregor Townsend took part in a Centre event and recounted that when things went wrong on the pitch all the dire predictions and negativity pre-match would start ringing in players' ears. Good managers can coach their team to become not just more skilled, but also more resilient. But it is much more difficult if the fans and prevailing culture are working against their optimism – not nurturing it.

The problem with pessimists' logic is that it becomes

irrefutable. If you think you're not going to win you won't. As we saw earlier, optimists are less affected by stress – if they miss a shot or don't perform well they don't collapse under pressure. They keep believing they can turn things round.

I am certainly not of the view that self-belief is everything. As the Centre for Confidence and Well-being has been influenced by the work of Professor Carol Dweck we are very keen to promote the idea that success is not just about the quality of self-belief but skills, hard-work and effort. Critical feedback is a vitally important part of learning. I witnessed some primary school pupils give a presentation on confidence recently and winced as they read quotes from sports stars and celebrities (mainly American) about how you always, always have to believe in yourself no matter what others say. Unfortunately this is the mentality of the Pop Idol competitor whose performance is abysmal but he or she will not accept any negative feedback and often, egged on by family, turns and berates the judges.

Optimism has an important part to play in life but like all things it can be overdone. People who are overly optimistic can take unacceptable risks or become foolhardy, cavalier or just plain foolish.

Whenever the costs of failure is high it pays to be pessimistic. This means that we should at least consider that the worst might happen if we are doing anything where we risk lives, or our relationships, jobs or finances. In 2008 Scotland would have benefited if our banks had been in the hands of more pessimistic bankers. But in other areas of life most notably sport, and education, it pays to be optimistic as the cost of failure is not high.

More importantly to sustain optimism we do not need to be unrealistic; often all that is required is to focus on the most positive facts or to give ourselves the benefit of the doubt. Prior to our 2007 World Cup home match against Italy we simply needed to remember some key facts: Scotland had won all its recent qualifiers at Hampden – even against France. Italy had never won at Hampden. Yes Scotland had lost the last game against Georgia but with a weakened team. In the game against Italy we were fielding our best players.

Of course optimism is not enough on its own to win a match – skill, flair, luck all matter. The team may lose. If they do this is the point at which we should adjust our thinking. Even then what we need to do is put a positive spin on the facts. When Scottish teams lose we need to keep the result in perspective. Our worth as a nation is not based on the performance on a football or rugby field.

One thing that intrigues me is the polarised reaction to this book and the work I've done at the Centre for Confidence and Well-being. I am simultaneously a 'Californian style happiness guru' and overly critical and pessimistic about Scotland.[30] This suggests that I am exactly where I want to be – taking a balanced perspective.

I am too much of a sceptical Scot to be an uncritical follower of the positive psychology movement and this is why I have written various critiques on some of the underlying assumptions.[31] Nonetheless some of the research underpinning positive psychology is helpful allowing us to see why Scotland's love affair with negativity is a problem for us. We may be used to criticism, put-downs and cynicism but we are human beings and we need love, affection, respect, appreciation, kindness, encouragement, gratitude, optimism and most importantly hope. In a famous speech Martin Luther King reminded us: 'If you lose hope, somehow you lose the vitality that keeps life moving, you lose that courage to be, that quality that helps you go on in spite of it all.'[32]

The Wee Book of Calvin is promoted and treated by many readers as little more than a humorous attack on bland 'transatlantic psychobabble'. But it is much more than this. Its author, Bill Duncan, is a sensitive and insightful man who recognises what he calls 'the tragedy of Scottish identity'.[33] He is fully aware that the philosophy of life which he outlines in Scottish 'haiku' and autobiographical essays are part of the reasons why Scots are driven to drink and violence; how this view of life leads to emotional repression and by destroying relationships our chances of finding warmth and affection. There is real poignancy in the item in his Calvinist self-test which reads:

> You have lost someone who loved you but who
> was unable to suffer your inability to return love
> and you are aware of the space that this has placed
> in your life forever and your heart knows that you
> could not behave in a different way if you could
> relive this chance of happiness.[34]

Duncan recognises that the philosophy he outlines was once needed in a hard, cold land; that these views were once about survival. And yet he still wants to cling on to it. As a creature of the culture he parodies, Duncan has no choice but to polarise: either we are true to the life-denying, negative philosophy which he sets out or we completely compromise our identity as Scots and sell-out to American self-help values.

But does it have to be one or the other? Surely there's another way we can take which allows us to be more life-affirming Scots – turning a deaf ear to the sea-mew's shriek whilst rejecting any bland offering of 'chicken soup for the soul'?

Notes

1 Quoted in Angela Cran and James Robertson *Dictionary of Scottish Quotations* (Mainstream: Edinburgh, 1996), p.298

2 George Davie *The Democratic Intellect: Scotland and her Universities in the 19th Century* (Edinburgh University Press: Edinburgh, 1961), p.317

3 Bill Duncan *The Wee Book of Calvin: Air-Kissing in the North East* (Penguin: London, 2004)

4 Bill Duncan *Wee book of Calvin*

5 See http://www.chickensoup.com/

6 Mihaly Csikszentmihalyi *Flow: The Psychology of Optimal Experience* (Harper and Row: New York, 1992)

7 See Martin E.P. Seligman *Authentic Happiness* (Simon & Schuster: New York, 2002)

8 See M. Losada, M.&E. Heaphy 'The role of positivity and connectivity in the performance of business teams: A nonlinear dynamics model', *American Behavioral Scientist* (47(6) 2004), 740–765

9 Martin E.P. Seligman and Mihaly Csikszentmihalyi 'An introduction to positive psychology' in *American Psychologist* January, 2000.

10 Barbara L. Fredrickson 'The role of positive emotions in positive psychology: The broaden-and-build theory of positive emotions' *American Psychologist* (Vol. 56 (3), March 2001), 218-226

11 Barbara L. Fredrickson *Positivity* (Crown: New York, 2009)

12 See, for example, Robert A. Emmons and Michael E. McCullough *The Psychology of Gratitude* (Oxford University Press: New York, 2004)

13 See Tim Kasser *The High Price of Materialism* (MIT Press: Cambridge, 2002)

14 Mihaly Csikszentmihalyi *Flow: The Psychology of Optimal Experience*

15 *The Collected Poems of Alexander Scott* David S. Robb (ed.) (Mercat Press: Edinburgh, 1994), p.149

16 See, for example, S.C. Schieier in Snyder, C.R. & Lopez, J.S. (eds) *Handbook of Positive Psychology* (Oxford University Press: Oxford, 2005), pp.231-243

17 Martin E.P. Seligman*The Optimistic Child* (Harper Perennial: New York, 1996), p.52

18 See Carol Craig *Creating Confidence: A Handbook for Professionals Working with Young People* (Centre for Confidence and Well-being: Glasgow, 2007)

19 'Wellhouse futures: Grounds for Optimism' retrieved from http://www.localpeopleleading.co.uk/on-the-ground/back briefings/607/

20 Martin E.P. Seligman *The Optimistic Child* p.110

21 Martin E.P. Seligman *The Optimistic Child* p.50

22 T.M. Devine *To the Ends of the Earth: Scotland's Global Diaspora* (Allen Lane: London, 2011), p.105

23 Neal Ascherson *Stone Voices* (Granta: London, 2002), p.80

24 See T.M. Devine *The Scottish Nation 1700 -2007* (Penguin: London, 2006)

25 See Martin E.P. Seligman *Learned Optimism* (Pocket Books: New York, 1998)

26 For a summary of the latest research see Martin E.P. Seligman *Flourish* (Nicholas Brealey: London, 2011)

27 See Phil Hanlon et al, *Let Glasgow Flourish A comprehensive report on health and its determinants in Glasgow and West Central Scotland* (Glasgow Centre for Population Health, 2006)

28 'Harry Burns: "Properly functioning families are the key to making Scotland healthier" ', *The Scotsman* 20th December, 2009

29 Rosabeth Moss Kanter *Confidence: Leadership and the Psychology of Turnarounds* (Crown: New York, 2004)

30 T.M. Devine *The Scottish Nation*, p.642

31 For Carol Craig's and the Centre for Confidence and Well-being's views on Martin Seligman's book *Flourish* go to http://www.centreforconfidence.co.uk/ information.php?p=cGlkPTQwMQ==

32 Martin Luther King Jnr *The Trumpet of Conscience* (Harper & Row: New York, 1968)

33 Quote from Scottish Book Trust's website: http://www.scottishbooktrust.com/contacts/bill-duncan

34 Bill Duncan *The Wee Book of Calvin*

15. Facing the Future

I started to write this book in 2001 and in the following ten years the world changed dramatically. One of my main concerns back then was Scotland's low business birth rate, poor productivity and a prevailing climate in organisations which militated against Scotland competing well in an increasingly global world. My other concern was that Scotland had mounting social challenges, such as health inequality, which we were not adequately addressing. I also thought that many Scots were operating well below their capacity as individuals and I longed for Scotland to have a more dynamic culture.

Even within a year of the book's original publication in 2003 my thinking had changed dramatically and so had my concerns for Scotland. The well-being literature I was now studying shows that continually expanding a country's economy (Gross Domestic Product) does not improve happiness in the way that economists originally supposed. If countries are poor then boosting GDP results in substantial gains in subjective well-being but once people have a roof over their heads, food on their tables and some economic security then more money does not automatically translate into more happiness. This is partly why happiness levels in the UK have not improved since the 1950s despite growing affluence.[1] What's more, there is mounting evidence that the pursuit of economic growth is damaging in a variety of different ways.

First, consumer capitalism, the driver of a great deal of recent economic growth, is underpinned by materialist values which undermine well-being and a sense of confidence. The more we pursue money and what it can buy – status, fame, popularity and focus a great deal of attention on our appearance – the worse our well-being is likely to be. Individualistic values divert us from what is really important for human flourishing particularly relationships and a sense of meaning and purpose – serving a goal bigger than ourselves.[2] As we have seen in the banking crisis, MPs' expenses and phone hacking, materialist values such as these encourage greed and selfishness and lead to a decline in standards and principles.

Second, as economies like the UK's have grown in past decades they have become much more unequal, not less.[3] The rich have become much wealthier but the 'trickle down' to poorer segments of society has not led to the expected benefits. Of course, those at the bottom of the pile have more 'stuff' than ever before and, by third world standards, seem well-off. But this does not detract from the fact that they feel socially excluded and shamed by being short of money in a society obsessed by wealth and power.[4]

This leads to the third negative aspect of our economy. In a consumerist culture we are continually exhorted to desire new things and feel dissatisfied with our current lot. Indeed it is through consumption that we are encouraged to find satisfaction. Our whole economic system is based on growth – just maintaining current levels of wealth is not acceptable.

This inevitably leads to the fourth negative aspect of the continual quest for economic growth. Consumer capitalism is environmentally destructive. This is not simply about manufacturing processes and pollution or the overuse of carbon: it is also about the continual squandering and gobbling up of resources, the mounting waste and the loss of 'biodiversity'.[5] Quite simply, we cannot continue to grow economies indefinitely in a finite world yet rarely do we acknowledge this uncomfortable truth.

In short, we are living with an economic system which promotes socially destructive values, leads to pronounced inequality, does not improve individual and collective flourishing and which destroys the planet. If this is not enough of a challenge, as we have seen since 2008, it all means that the global economic system is unstable and unsustainable.

All of this is as relevant to Scotland as it is for any other country in the world. Indeed it is possible to argue that some of what has been outlined above, in terms of social inequality and the dominance of values which undermine well-being, is even more pertinent in Scotland given our particular problem with drink and drugs[6] and our poor record on child well-being.

Some would argue that if Scotland opts for political independence then we shall be able to chart our own course. Leaving aside all the difficulties such a detachment would present we need to rethink and renew whole aspects of our culture and life styles not just our constitution. Quite simply we need radical new ideas and practices. It is interesting to note that Gerry Hassan, one of Scotland's most prolific commentators, and an ardent supporter of devolution, has become increasingly frustrated not just by Scotland's track record on new thinking and policies but also by the prevailing complacency:

Scotland likes to see itself as a radical nation. An

egalitarian country. A country of socialism and more latterly social democratic and progressive values. A nation which never voted for the Tories in large numbers in recent decades, didn't like Mrs Thatcher and didn't buy into Thatcherism. A political community which has stood for timeless Scottish values of caring for the vulnerable, compassion and not buying into the certainties of the last few decades which have obsessed Westminster and Washington.[7]

However as he rightly points out, given our track record on inequality, poverty and social exclusion, there's little evidence that these supposedly 'radical' ideas translate into anything tangible. Indeed he argues that Scotland is 'a social democracy for the institutional classes, for the vested interests and for the middle classes.' In his view Scotland is still 'a managed society of the great and the good' – cautious, inward-looking and unwilling to make waves. He also argues that as far as these professional classes are concerned, 'the cupboard is bare policy and ideas wise'.

However, as Gerry Hassan himself is aware, we should not expect politicians to stock the shelves. Party politics is much less about ideas and values than it once was. We now have politics as consumerism. Politicians used to set out their ideas for a better society. Now they use focus groups and marketing strategies to appeal to the electorate as consumers. 'Vote for us and we'll help you realise your aspirations for yourself and your family' is their mantra. Voters are lured with sweeteners such as free bus passes or prescriptions or commitments to reduce or stabilise local or national taxation. However, the problem is that people's personal aspirations vie with one another and many are dissatisfied with what the system gives them, thus further eroding people's faith in politics and politicians.[8]

Short-term thinking is not conducive to the type of bold thinking and practices that are now needed to envision and step towards a different future. So if we can't rely on politicians to come up with bold new ideas we need to start doing it for ourselves. The good news is that it is already happening. There are all sorts of initiatives I can point to in Scotland where people manage to think creatively about the future or are taking action themselves to improve their communities. For example, Phil Hanlon, Professor of Public Health at the University of Glasgow, has created an informative and inspirational website called 'Afternow' which sets out the problems of our age and the type of actions required to start inching towards a different future.[9] This is no glib self-help website but a weighty intellectual effort of international renown. There are various innovative networks emerging throughout Scotland and a number of social enterprises and community environmental projects in places as diverse as Govan, Renton, Comrie, Ullapool and Fintry.

But we need even more innovative thinkers and activists – lots more of them. And we need them not just in one area of life but across the four quadrants, outlined in Chapter 1. In short, we need people to encourage us to contemplate and bring about inner, psychological and spiritual changes; renew our cultural values; change our personal and collective behaviour; and reconstruct, or at least radically alter, prevailing socio-economic structures and systems.

We also need to hear diverse voices and views – those who use services not just those who provide them; new Scots; young people; pensioners; gay men and lesbians; the poor and excluded. . . Scotland can't afford to ignore the views of half the population and particularly needs to hear women's voices.

In the next few years any discussion in Scotland will be undertaken against the backdrop of constitutional change particularly a referendum on independence. This could revitalise debate in Scotland, injecting a sense of optimism and self-belief into the culture. Given the importance of autonomy and control in people's lives it could galvanise and inspire and lead to a growing sense of national purpose. But equally it could have a negative effect by channeling a huge amount of intellectual energy into the constitutional question thus leaving less time to focus on some of the momentous challenges outlined above.

The constitutional question could also lead to a widening of the rift in Scottish life. Given our history and culture, such polarisation could easily lead to the tiresome situation where those on either side of the independence divide will portray their opponents not simply as people who hold contrary views on what is best for Scotland and the Scots but as worthless, self-serving sinners who act in bad faith.

What Scotland needs in the next few years as we contemplate the changes which confront us is an atmosphere encouraging debate as well as individual and collective confidence. As mentioned earlier, the artist and novelist Alasdair Gray once wrote that 'the curse of Scotland' is 'the wee hard men who hammer Scotland down to the same dull level as themselves'. We can't take away their hammers or stop them thundering on about what's right and proper but we can either stop paying them attention to them or begin to challenge their right to fashion Scotland in their own image.

We can do this if we rebel against some cherished Scottish values. Instead of knowing our place and fearing drawing attention to ourselves we must stick our heads above the parapet. Instead of apologising for wanting to break out of restrictive Scottish beliefs and practices, we must start valuing our opinions and making our voices heard. Instead of toeing the line and playing safe, we need to start taking more risks and learning from mistakes. Of course, we should continue to honour some fundamental Scottish principles and basic beliefs but we should not feel obliged to cling to them so tightly .

Societies which promote well-being and flourishing encourage a strong sense of belonging and allegiance to the group while simultaneously allowing people to express themselves as individuals.[10] I believe that Scots would benefit greatly if we could continue to focus on community and the collective while encouraging more individuality and self-expression.

Notes

1 For a summary of this literature see Richard Layard *Happiness: Lessons from a new science* (Penguin: London, 2005)

2 See Tim Kasser *The High Price of Materialism* (MIT Press: Cambridge, 2002)

3 Danny Dorling *Injustice: Why social inequality persists* (The Policy Press: London, 2010)

4 See Richard Wilkinson and Kate Pickett *The Spirit Level: Why more equal societies almost always do better* (Allan Lane: London, 2009)

5 For an outline of these arguments see Tim Jackson *Prosperity Without Growth: Economics for a Finite Planet* (Earthscan: London, 2009)

6 See 'Melting the Iceberg on Scotland's Drug and Alcohol Problem: Report of the Independent Enquiry (October, 2010)

7 Gerry Hassan 'Why is the cupboard bare?' in *Scottish Review* (online) No 376, 9th March, 2011

8 See Peter Oborne *The Triumph of the Political Class* (Simon & Schuster: London, 2007)

9 http://www.afternow.co.uk/

10 See Bruce K. Alexander *The Globalisation of Addiction: a study in the poverty of the spirit* (OUP: Oxford, 2008)

ACKNOWLEDGEMENTS

I could not have written the first edition of this book without the support, encouragement and insights of various people. I would particularly like to thank the following individuals for giving me comments on specific chapters or providing me with information: Andrew Bolger, Derek Brown, Robert Crawford, Douglas Gifford, Anne Johnstone, Annette Kuhn, Mike Russell, Nigel Smith, Linda Kinney, Gerry Rice, Frank Martin, and Beatrice Wickens. I am particularly indebted to Jim Greig for his insightful comments on the sections of the book dealing with the impact of religion on Scottish culture.

Gerry Hassan, in his former capacity as Director of Big Thinking, played an important part in the publication of the original book and I am indebted to him for his support. Thanks are also due to Kirsty Wark, not just for reading and commenting on the manuscript but also writing the foreword. I am also grateful to Alexander Scott's widow, Cath Scott for giving me permission to quote some of his short poems.

There are three people without whose help, support and encouragement this book would never have been written: my friends Jean Barr and Stewart McIntosh and my sister Marianne Craig. I will ever feel indebted for their patience, understanding and insights.

Alf Young, my partner for more than thirty years, played an

important part in the writing of this book. Apart from commenting on drafts, his newspaper columns on Scottish politics and the Scottish economy have been an important influence on me over the decades and have shaped my thinking on a number of issues.

The publication of this second edition has also relied on input and feedback from Jonathan Levie, Kaliani Lyle and Satwat Rahman. I would also like to acknowledge the support of the Centre for Confidence and Well-being's board of directors – Martin Stepek, Charlie Miller, Kate Dunlop, Phil Hanlon and Hazel Black and, particularly, the Centre's Chair, Fred Shedden, for his dedicated reading of various proofs.

I am delighted that this edition is much more attractive than the first. This is due in part to the use of Michael Scott's painting 'Under the Tarpaulin' on the cover. The image is used courtesy of the artist's estate and thanks are due to Mick's widow Gill Scott for her help. Derek Rodger of Argyll Publishing has been a pleasure to work with and has helped me to streamline the argument making the new edition a much more readable book.

Finally, I must add that I alone am responsible for the ideas contained in this book and for any, inevitable, mistakes and errors of judgement.

Carol Craig
September 2011

Index